M000114094

THUNDER
IN THE
HARBOR

Fort Sumter in the Civil War

Richard W. Hatcher, III

SB

Savas Beatie
California

First edition, first printing

ISBN-13: 978-1-61121-593-9 (hardcover)
ISBN-13: 978-1-61121-594-6 (ebook)

Names: Hatcher, Richard W. III, author.
Title: Thunder in the harbor : Fort Sumter and the Civil War / by Richard W Hatcher III.
Other titles: Fort Sumter and the Civil War
Description: El Dorado Hills, CA : Savas Beatie, 2023. | Includes bibliographical references and index. | Summary: "Both sides understood the military significance of Fort Sumter and the busy seaport, which played host to one of the longest and most complicated and fascinating campaigns of the entire Civil War. In April 1863, a powerful combined operation set its sights on the fort, Charleston, and its outer defenses. The result was 22-month land and sea siege, the longest of the Civil War. The widespread effort included ironclad attacks, land assaults, raiding parties, and siege operations. The defiant fort, Charleston, and its meandering defensive line were evacuated in February 1865"-- Provided by publisher.
Identifiers: LCCN 2023037987 | ISBN 9781611215939 (hardcover) | ISBN 9781611215946 (ebook)
Subjects: LCSH: Fort Sumter (Charleston, S.C.)--Siege, 1861. | Fort Sumter (Charleston, S.C.)--History. | Charleston (S.C.)--History--Civil War, 1861-1865. | United States--History--Civil War, 1861-1865--Causes.
Classification: LCC E471.1 .H383 2023 | DDC 973.7/3309757915--dc23/eng/20230905
LC record available at https://lccn.loc.gov/2023037987

Printed and bound in the United Kingdom

SB

Savas Beatie
989 Governor Drive, Suite 102
El Dorado Hills, CA 95762
916-941-6896 / sales@savasbeatie.com / www.savasbeatie.com

All of our titles are available at special discount rates for bulk purchases in the United States. Contact us for information.

This book honors all those who served at Fort Sumter, both military and civilian. Of special note are the following:

Private Daniel Hough, Co. E, 1st U. S. Artillery, the first soldier killed in the war, April 14, 1861;

Private Edward Galway, same company, mortally wounded April 14, died April 15;

Private John Doran, Co. H, 1st U.S. Artillery (my wife's third great uncle);

Private Edward Hatcher, Co. K, 1st South Carolina Artillery Regulars (a distant relative), wounded August 19, 1863, died November 19, 1863.

TABLE OF CONTENTS

LIST OF MAPS

Photos have been placed throughout the text for the convenience of the reader.

LIST OF ABBREVIATIONS

Adm.   Admiral
B&L   Battles and Leaders of the Civil War
CA   Coastal Artillery
CAC   Coastal Artillery Corps
CCC   Civilian Conservation Corps
CSR   Confederate State Records
CSS   Confederate States Ship
Dept.   Department
FMMR   Fort Moultrie Military Reservation
FOSU   Fort Sumter and Fort Moultrie National Historical Park Research File
GAR   Grand Army of the Republic
HDCP   Harbor Defense Command Post
HECP   Harbor Entrance Control Post
LOC   Library of Congress
NA   National Archives
NCO   Non-commissioned Officer
OAG   Office of the Adjutant General
OR   Official Records of the Union and Confederate Armies
ORN   Official Records of the Union and Confederate Navies
Pdr.   pounder
RG   Record Group
ROTC   Reserve Officer Training Corps
SHC   Southern Historical Collection
USMA   United States Military Academy
USS   United States Ship

Acknowledgments

$\mathcal{I}$ am indebted to numerous people and institutions who provided support and assistance in the preparation and writing of this book. Foremost among them are my wife Mary and daughter Ashton. Mary read the manuscript many times over, and her questions and suggestions aided in polishing the narrative. Her wealth of patience and insights were invaluable. Ashton's tireless work with each one of the illustrations adds a significant visual dimension to the book. Thank you both.

I am also grateful for the support and assistance of Fort Sumter Fort Moultrie National Historical Park staff, most especially Park Ranger Gary Alexander and Volunteer Russell Horres, who were ever receptive and responsive to my requests. I experienced the same degree of help from Assistant Director John Tucker (ret.) and Processing Archivist Karen Stokes at the South Carolina Historical Society; Patrick McCawley, Deputy Director of Archives and Records Management, South Carolina Department of Archives and History; and Grahame Long, Director of Museums, Historic Charleston Foundation. Hearty thanks also to the staffs at the following locales: City of Charleston, South Carolina: New York State Library Manuscripts and Special Collections; the Collections of the New-York Historical Society; the South Caroliniana Library; University of North Carolina at Chapel Hill, Louis Round Wilson Special Collections Library; and Duke University Libraries, the David M. Rubenstein Rare Book & Manuscript Library.

Many other people provided generous support as well: Beth Ward for her genealogical expertise and assistance, Garry Adelman and Bob Zeller of the Center for Civil War Photography, Peter Barrett, Adm. Percival Drayton historian, Olivia

Black, Volunteer Program Coordinator Antietam National Battlefield, and Keith Brady who kindly provided a photograph of Fort Sumter from his collection, Thanks also to the fine military historians: Jack Melton, publisher Historical Publications LLC, Ron Field, Prof. Kyle Sinisi, of the Citadel, Col. Darrell Combs, USMC Ret., and Col. Mark Johnson USA, Ret., and Francis Marion National Forest Heritage Resources Manager Robert Morgan (ret.) You all have my deep and abiding respect and gratitude.

It would be a grievous oversight if I failed to thank the staff at Savas Beatie for taking this book from rough manuscript to finished product: Tom Schott for his editing expertise and deep well of patience; Veronica Kane for her keen eye in designing the layout; Elise Hess who painstakingly assembled the people, places and things associated with Sumter's story into a comprehensive index; and Ian Hughes whose artistic choices for the book's cover invite readers into the history of the fort. Finally, I deeply appreciate Ted Savas's commitment to publishing historical works and for recognizing the importance of Fort Sumter's story and bringing it to press. Thank you all.

Introduction

Three ships carrying sea-worn British colonists approached a wide harbor in April 1670. They navigated between two barrier islands, passed a shoal at the harbor's mouth, and continued beyond the confluence of two large rivers, sailing up the left waterway. The vessels continued upriver several miles of what they named the Ashley River before stopping along the shore. They declared the new land the Colony of Carolina, in honor of King Charles II, and established the settlement of Charles Town on Albemarle Point. It soon became apparent that the peninsula between the Ashley and the other river, the Cooper, was more suited to settlement, and by 1680 the new colony took root on the Cooper River side of the peninsula. The new location provided what the other site did not: cooling sea breezes, a deeper ship channel, and crucially, an unobstructed view of ships entering the harbor.

Within just twenty years, Charles Town was walled and well-fortified in anticipation of attack. Spanish, French, native peoples, and pirates posed an ever-present danger, and for that reason, the colonists constructed a fort beyond the city. In addition to conflicts with the locals and the presence of pirates, wars in Europe also threatened to involve the small settlement. Spanish colonial expansion in Florida and specifically Queen Anne's War (The War of Spanish Succession, 1702-13) pointed to the need for a more effective defense, and thus Fort Johnson on James Island was completed by 1709. This fortification, about halfway between the city and the harbor's mouth, presented a significant obstacle to enemy ships entering the harbor. By 1712, the enormous colony had been divided into North and South Carolina.

Foreign and regional conflicts, including King George's War (The War of Jenkin's Ear/War of the Austrian Succession, 1740-48) and the French and Indian War (The Seven Years' War, 1756-63) threatened Charles Town's security. City leaders proposed a stronger defense in the 1750s and called for the construction of a line of earthworks across the peninsula and the erection of a new bastion on the Cooper River. The works were largely vacated within ten years. After another decade Charles Town had abandoned its walled city plan entirely.

A sustained period of peace between 1762 and 1775 encouraged tremendous growth in the area. New streets, businesses, and houses were constructed over the sites of former fortifications, and by the mid-1700s an enslaved African-based economy built on rice and indigo replaced the earlier economy reliant on the export of deer skins, timber, and naval stores. Charles Town rose to prominence as the fourth most populous city in the 13 colonies with the highest per capita income. The city, which had swelled to 12,000 souls, welcomed more shipping trade than the larger cities of New York, Boston, or Philadelphia.

The outbreak of the American Revolution in 1775 forced city leaders to address Charles Town's lapses in fortification maintenance and construction. Militias enlisted new members, new units organized, and work on the city's defenses began in earnest. Old defenses were repaired and new works were constructed. Chief among these was a fort on Sullivan's Island. Begun in February 1776, the site was chosen for its strategic location on the primary shipping channel. Southward, the Main Channel paralleled the shorelines of Folly and Morris islands and turned into the harbor within a few hundred yards off Sullivan's.

The fort, though incomplete and unnamed, mounted 31 cannon when a fleet of nine Royal Navy warships with more than 260 guns attempted to sail past Sullivan's Island into the harbor on June 28, 1776. The ensuing battle lasted nearly 10 hours. At the opposite end of the island, Patriot forces defeated British attempts to cross from Long Island (Isle of Palms). The resounding American victory on Sullivan's Island, a week before the issuing of the Declaration of Independence, was one of the first in what would be a long and bloody war. The fort was soon completed and named after Col. William Moultrie, the island's commander and the hero of the battle. Charles Town remained under Patriot control until 1780, when a six-week siege by the British forced its surrender on May 12.

After the Revolution, the city was renamed Charleston. Its defenses once again suffered neglect, this time in the afterglow of postwar peace. Yet another war between England and France in 1793 underscored the need for coastal fortifications, and the nascent American government selected Charleston as one of 21 sites for a "Second System" of fortifications. Ultimately, four installations were constructed. Fort Johnson on James Island, which had been destroyed during the Revolution, was rebuilt; an imposing installation named Fort Mechanic was erected near the tip of Charleston's peninsula, along with another fortification, Fort Pinckney, on Shute's Folly across from it. Engineers completed a new Fort Moultrie on the site of the first fort on Sullivan's Island.

The Quasi-War between the U.S. and France (1798-1800) refocused interest in seacoast fortifications. When an 1804 hurricane left Forts Moultrie, Johnson, and Pinckney in ruins, Congress appropriated funds to reconstruct the defenses. The third (and final) Fort Moultrie was completed in 1809—the only fortification at the mouth of Charleston Harbor. A new Fort Johnson was finished that same year. By 1811, the new brick fortification on Shute's Folly was completed and named Castle Pinckney.

The War of 1812 was a stark indicator of the insecurity of the American coastline. British troops landed with little opposition, marched on Washington, and burned the White House and other government buildings. After the war, Congress appropriated money for the construction of additional defenses, known as "Third System" fortifications on the nation's shores. Once again they recognized Charleston Harbor's economic and military significance and approved a new defensive work there.

The result was a masonry fort that became the political flashpoint that would trigger the onset of civil war 45 years later.[1]

---

1 Walter Edgar, ed., *The South Carolina Encyclopedia* (Columbia, SC, 2006), 146-149; Jim Stokeley, *Fort Moultrie, Constant Defender* (Washington, D.C., 1985), 1-41.

Chapter 1

On a Shallow Shoal in Charleston Harbor

1829–1860

On January 4, 1829, from Charleston, South Carolina, U.S. Army Corps of Engineers Lt. Henry Brewerton informed the commander of the Corps, Col. Charles Gratiot in Washington, D.C., of his arrival. Brewerton, the first engineer appointed for the project that would become Fort Sumter, established his headquarters at Fort Johnson, on James Island just over a mile west of the construction site. He served as "the superintending engineer of the construction of the defenses of Charleston harbor" until 1832. Brewerton was born in 1801 in New York City and was orphaned at an early age. He nevertheless secured an appointment to the United States Military Academy; in 1813, three months short of his twelfth birthday, he became a cadet. Despite his youth, Brewerton did well at West Point but was furloughed from February-September 1815 until he turned 14, the official minimum age for admittance. At 17, Brewerton graduated fifth in the class of 1819 and was assigned to the Corps of Engineers.

Six years before his arrival in Charleston, the U.S. Topographical Engineers surveyed the harbor and selected the construction site. At the Engineers' headquarters in Washington, plans for the fort had been prepared, and in 1827 Secretary of War John C. Calhoun approved the construction of a "pentagonal, three-tiered, masonry fort with truncated angles that was to be built on the shallow shoal extending from James Island." The site stood in the mouth of Charleston Harbor across the shipping channel about a mile west of Fort Moultrie on Sullivan's Island. In 1829 the fort's plans were approved and $25,000 was appropriated for its construction.

The 28-year-old Brewerton faced a tremendous task. He placed a buoy on the site and drove stakes into the shoal forming an outline to mark where to place the mole for the five-sided fort. As most stone quarries were located in New England, he placed ads in about two dozen of the region's newspapers for 30,000 tons of irregular stone weighing from 50 to 500 pounds or more each. A New York firm submitted the low bid at an average of $2.45 per ton.[1]

Due to the shallow water at the construction site, when the ships arrived laden with their heavy cargos, the stone was offloaded at Fort Johnson. From there lighters were used to transport and place the stone on site. Problems with the supplier, however, resulted in only 1,000 tons being delivered by the middle of 1830. These challenges persisted and in 1831 only 7,000 additional tons were brought to the site. The contract was rescinded and purchases were made on the open market. During the following two years 38,500 tons were added to the construction site. The mole now resembled a five-sided donut; the artificial island had broken the surface.

In 1832, Brewerton was transferred and Capt. W. A. Eliason assumed the supervision of the fort's construction. On April 18, 1833, the adjutant general's office issued Order No. 33, naming the nine forts then being built. One of those was the "new work now constructing in the Harbor of Charleston–South Carolina." It was named Fort Sumter in honor of Thomas Sumter. Born in Virginia, by 1764 Sumter had moved to South Carolina and during the Revolutionary War had risen to the rank of brigadier general in the state militia. Nicknamed "Gamecock" for his daring and tenacious fighting, after the war he served in the state's general assembly and the U.S. House and Senate. When he died in 1832, two months short of his 98th birthday, Sumter was the last surviving general officer from the American Revolution.[2]

Lieutenant T. S. Brown replaced Eliason in 1834. That fall Brown faced a situation that halted work on the project until 1841. With $220,000 already expended and 46,500 tons of stone in place as of November 3, 1834, Charlestonian William Laval notified the lieutenant that he had "taken out, under the seal of the state, a grant of all those shoals opposite and below Fort Johnson." The grant totaled 870 acres, including the fort's construction site. With this notification all work was halted. Laval's claim was vague concerning its boundaries, however, and

---

1 National Archives, Record Group 217, 1817-1850, 1829 Files, hereafter cited as NA/RG. Heath L. Pemberton, Jr., "Fort Sumter: Chorological Construction History With Architectural Detail," *Fort Sumter Historical Structure Reports*, 1829-1899, Sept. 1959, 1-4, hereafter cited as Pemberton, "Chorological Construction History."

2 1817-1850, 1830-1850 Files, NA/RG 217; Walter Edgar, *The South Carolina Encyclopedia* (Columbia, SC, 2006), 940-941.

Brig. Gen. Thomas Sumter

New York Public Library, hereafter NYPL

the shoal generally fell under 8 feet of water at low tide. Its legality would be determined by the state of South Carolina, and not until December 1837 was Laval's claim invalidated. In December 1840 a joint resolution of the legislature recommended that the governor cede the site and additional acreage to the Federal government, and the next year Gov. John P. Richardson ceded 125 acres to the United States. That year work on the fort was resumed under the direction of Capt. Alexander H. Bowman.

By 1845 the foundation was completed, with approximately 70,000 tons of material in place. Courses of cut stone blocks were placed on the foundation on top of which the brick would be laid. Including the esplanade and wharf a total of 109,000 tons of stone and granite had been placed at the site. At high tide the foundation stood 5 feet above the surface. The project now entered a new phase, with the construction of masonry scarp walls, casemates, two barracks buildings, the officers' quarters, five cisterns, four powder magazines, two hot shot furnaces, and 135 gun emplacements. Also, the mole was filled with sand and shells. Once filled the artificial island was about two and a half acres, with one acre comprising the parade ground.

Over the next 15 years the imposing brick fort rose from the stone and granite foundation. The five scarp (exterior) walls were seven feet thick and composed of a brick shell with the interior filled with rammed concrete. The first- and second-tier support piers, though not as thick, were constructed in the same manner. The gorge wall extended 321 feet in length. On its exterior the esplanade was 25 ½ feet wide and 290 feet long. From the center of the esplanade the wharf extended over 140 feet. But storms and strong tides had caused about 45 feet of the end to become unusable. The sally port, the fort's principal entrance, rested in the center of the gorge.

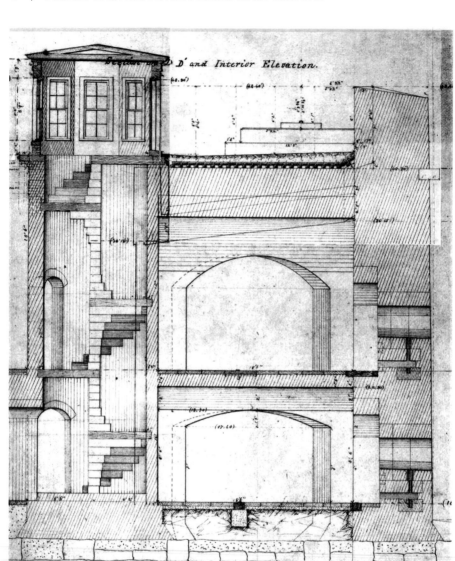

1846 construction drawing of a stair tower, three-gun tiers, and scarp (exterior) wall.
National Archives and Records Administration, hereafter NARA

At the gorge's angles, the left and right flank walls ran for 171 feet then joined the 192-foot-long left and right face walls that met at the salient angle. The five walls rose to a height of just over 48 feet above the foundation. The flank and face walls were built to mount three tiers of gun emplacements. The first and second were composed of casemates and the third, the barbette tier.

Beneath the center of the floors of the face and flank walls and the sally port were cisterns. Rainwater collected from the terreplein through a drainage and gutter system and drained into each wall's cistern. A similar system collected rainwater for iron tanks in the officers' quarters and enlisted barracks. The overflow from the tanks was conducted to the cisterns. The flank and face cisterns each held 5,200 gallons and the one at the gorge approximately 4,200 gallons.

An examination of extant construction documents from 1843-48 and 1857 reveals that most of the bricks for the project were made by skilled slave labor at brick kilns on plantations along the Cooper and Ashley rivers near Charleston. According to these records almost four million bricks were purchased. The grey or brown bricks (9 x 4½ x 2¼ inches) cost $8-9 per thousand.

The number of workers and their skills varied. Among the civilian employees the supervising engineer hired were crews to operate lighters and barges transporting building materials and workers, masons and carpenters (white, slave, and free), stone cutters, blacksmiths, clerks, overseers, and cooks. The largest number were laborers, crews of which ranged from a dozen or so to 70 at any one time. While most of the workers were white, some were African American, both slave and free.

Fort Sumter was built to mount 135 guns with a garrison of 650 officers and men. The first- and second-tiers held 41 casemates each and the barbette tier held 53 gun emplacements. The three-story officers' quarters was located in the center 290 feet of the gorge wall's interior. The sally port was on the first floor at the building's center. To its right were the apartments for 50 officers and their families. The area to the left of the sally port housed the ordnance, commissary, quartermaster, and medical operations. At each end of the building sat two powder magazines, one on the first-tier and one on the second. Of note, the windows along the first two tiers of the gorge were narrow and served as loopholes for firing muskets to help repel an amphibious assault. As it was too shallow for warships to move into position to bombard this wall, only the third-tier was built to mount cannon.

The 128-foot-long enlisted barracks, three stories tall, were located along the center of the left and right flank walls. The first floor of each contained a kitchen and mess hall, while the two upper floors held living quarters for 300 non-commissioned officers and enlisted men. The tops of the roofs of all three buildings towered almost 10 feet above the parapet, and proved inviting targets on April 12-13, 1861.[3]

From 1841 to 1858 several Corps of Engineers officers were assigned to supervise Fort Sumter's construction, including Capts. Alexander H. Bowman, Jeremy F. Gilmer, and George W. Cullum. All were West Point graduates and career officers. Both Bowman and Cullum had long careers, and each served as the superintendent of their alma mater. Bowman had 40 years' service and rose to the rank of lieutenant colonel. Cullum served 41 years and attained the rank of brevet major general. Gilmer, a North Carolinian, resigned his commission in 1861 and served in the Confederate Corps of Engineers. He rose to the rank of major general and chief engineer of the Confederate Engineer Bureau in Richmond. From August 1863 to April 1864, he served as second in command of the Department of South Carolina, Georgia, and Florida, with headquarters in Charleston, before being ordered back to Richmond.

On April 28, 1858 Brevet Capt. John G. Foster relieved Captain Cullum and assumed the duties of the chief engineer in Charleston Harbor, plus Forts Macon and Caswell in North Carolina. A New Hampshire native, he stood fourth in the famous West Point class of 1846. His fellow graduates included George B. McClellan, Jesse L. Reno, Thomas J. Jackson, Samuel D. Sturgis, George Stoneman, George E. Pickett, and Cadmus M. Wilcox. Assigned to the Corps of Engineers, in 1847 Foster found himself attached to a company of "Sappers, Miners, and Pontoniers" in the Mexican War. The brevet second lieutenant would earn two brevet promotions, the first for "gallant and meritorious conduct" in the battles of Contreras and Churubusco, where he was promoted to brevet first lieutenant. His promotion to brevet captain came in the battle of Molino de Rey, where a musket ball tore into his lower left leg, breaking both bones. The war was now over for the young officer, who went to the family home in Nashua to recover. He returned to duty in 1848 with a permanent limp. For the next 10 years Foster performed duties at various locations, including service as the principal assistant professor of engineering at West Point.[4]

Foster arrived in Charleston in late April 1858 but was neither at Sumter nor in the city itself when a heart-breaking chapter in the fort's history occurred. On August 21, the USS *Dolphin* seized an illegal slave ship, the *Echo*, bound for Cuba, where the "human cargo" was to be sold. It had departed Angola with 450 men,

---

3 Pemberton, "Chorological Construction History," 5-18; 1830s-1850 Files, NA/RG 217.

4 George W. Cullum, *Biographical Register of the Officers and Graduates of the U. S. Military Academy* (Boston and New York, 1891), 2: 256-260, hereafter cited as Cullum, *Biographical Register; John C. Waugh, The Class of 1846, From West Point to Appomattox: Stonewall Jackson, George McClellan, and Their Brothers* (New York, 1994), *passim*.

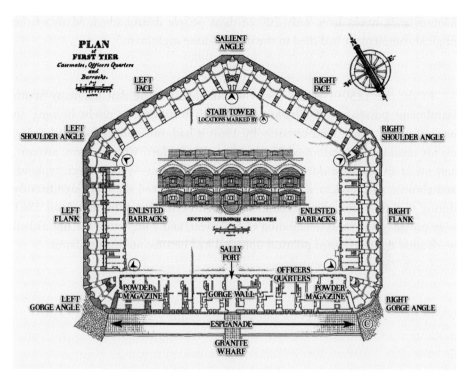

Identification of Ft. Sumter's first-tier walls, angles, and other features. Each arrow within a circle designates a stair tower location. *Author's Collection, hereinafter AC*

women, and children crammed below decks, and during the passage more than a quarter of them died from malnutrition or disease. A naval officer's report referred to the "cargo" as "poor wretches" who looked "half starved . . . some of them . . . mere skeletons." The *Echo*'s captain, arrested for violating the 1820 Federal law abolishing the trans-Atlantic slave trade, sailed on the *Dolphin* to Key West. An officer and a detachment from the U.S. ship were placed on board and with its crew sailed the ship to Charleston, arriving on August 27. Charleston's U.S. Marshal ordered the crew jailed and the Africans sent to Castle Pinckney. Shortly thereafter they were relocated to Fort Sumter. Thirty-five more people died during the quarantine at the two fortifications. At one point a boat captain sold 50 cent tickets to those Charlestonians who wished to visit the fort and gawk at the human misery on display there.

President James Buchanan ordered the USS *Niagara* to take the suffering Africans to Liberia, and on September 21 they were ferried to the *Niagara*. The ship sailed the next day with 271 former slaves aboard. When it arrived at

Monrovia six weeks later, only 200 of these people disembarked. Many of the original complement had died in the months-long nightmare.[5]

*   *   *

In the late 1850s Captain Foster was doubtless aware that for many South Carolinians possession of Charleston Harbor's fortifications might become an issue of states' rights. And certainly by 1860 it had, but politics had no bearing on his mission. He performed his duties within budget, with workers, artisans, and materials available during three seasons of the year—yellow fever, typhoid, and cholera, so prevalent in the summer months, slowed the work significantly during that time. But the six months between November 1860 and April 1861 were probably the most demanding of his career, and completing the unfinished work amid unprecedented political upheaval had become an urgent matter.

5 Nathaniel Cheairs Hughes, Jr., and Gordon D. Whitney, *Jefferson Davis In Blue* (Baton Rouge, 2002), 30-31; "Slaver in the Bay" and "Arrival of a Slaver," *Charleston Courier*, Aug. 28, 1858, and "U.S. District Court-The Slaver Case," Sept. 7, 1858; Anonymous, "The Echo," Fort Sumter and Fort Moultrie National Historical Park, July 22, 2020, Fort Sumter and Fort Moultrie National Historical Park Research File, hereafter cited as FOSU Research File.

Chapter 2

A Tempting Prize

November–December 1860

Even before Abraham Lincoln's election in 1860, secessionist talk in South Carolina had intensified. On November 5, the General Assembly convened in Columbia to select presidential electors and remained in session awaiting the results of the national election. Upon receiving news of Lincoln's victory, it authorized an election to select delegates to a convention to decide whether South Carolina would remain in the Union. Lincoln's victory heightened tensions throughout the state; in Charleston, the U.S. district judge and attorney both resigned their positions.

Stationed at Fort Moultrie, 1st Lt. James T. Talbot described the local atmosphere in mid-November. "I went to Charleston yesterday for the first time since the secession excitement commenced and spoke with several persons representing the different shades of political opinion. I find every man, woman and child unanimously in favor of [the] secession of South Carolina."[1]

Charlestonians not only talked about secession, but publicly demonstrated as well. On November 10, members of the "East Bay Artillery" repeatedly fired a cannon celebrating word from Columbia that the legislature had called for a secession convention. The gun was soon nicknamed "Old Secession" and fired regularly at events supporting the state's desire to leave the Union. Large canvas "secession banners," often illustrated with a snake coiled around a palmetto tree, hung from buildings or across city streets. The serpent image harkened back to the

---

1 Theodore Talbot to Adelaide Talbot, Nov. 16, 1860, Theodore Talbot Papers, LC, transcription FOSU Research file. Hereafter cited as "Talbot to mother."

Lt. Theodore Talbot

Library of Congress, hereinafter LOC

Revolutionary era's "Don't Tread On Me" flag designed by South Carolina patriot Christopher Gadsden. Other flags commonly used one or more stars to represent South Carolina and other states of the Deep South, coupled with a pro-secession word or phrase. On December 17 the citizens raised one of these flags on the "secession pole" at the Charleston Hotel. In the harbor, numerous vessels flew some version of a secession banner rather than a U.S. flag.[2]

Several days later, Talbot noted the arrival of the new commander at Fort Moultrie. "Major Anderson arrived here yesterday. I had never seen him before. . . . He is a man about 50 years of grave and polite demeanor and said to be an excellent officer."[3]

Robert Anderson was indeed "an excellent officer." Including four years at West Point, the 55-year-old Kentuckian had served almost 39 years in the Army. He was assigned to the 3rd U.S. Artillery after graduation and worked as a private secretary to his brother, Richard C. Anderson, Jr., the U.S. Minister to Gran Colombia. He then served as an artillery instructor at Fort Monroe's artillery school and at West Point. A veteran of the Black Hawk and Seminole wars, Anderson served as a staff officer for three years, including service as an aide for General Winfield Scott. In the Mexican War, Anderson fought from the siege of Vera Cruz through the battle of Molino del Rey, where he earned a promotion to brevet major after suffering a serious wound. From 1848-60, he performed garrison duty and sat on various

2 Articles from the *Charleston Courier*: "Hang Out Your Banners," Nov. 12, 1860; "The Banners Flying" and "An Honored Gun," Nov. 17, 1860; "Inauguration of a Secession Pole," Nov. 19, 1860; and "The Courier Flag," Jan. 7, 1861.

3 Theodore Talbot to Mary Louisa Talbot, Nov. 20, 1860, Talbot Papers, FOSU Research File, hereafter cited as "Talbot to sister."

Maj. Robert Anderson

LOC

military boards. Anderson also translated a French artillery manual for the U.S. Artillery.

Promoted to major in 1857, Anderson was assigned to the 1st U.S. Artillery. While serving on a commission to examine the "Organization, System of Discipline, and Course of Instruction" at West Point, he received orders on November 15, 1860 to report to Fort Moultrie, relieve its commander Bvt. Col. John L. Gardner, and assume command. His extreme competence and numerous qualifications, coupled with his service there in the 1840s, played a role in his selection to such a politically sensitive post. Two other factors influenced the decision. The British had captured Lt. Col. Richard C. Anderson, his father, in 1780 at the fall of Charleston. Also, it was known that his politics tended to be pro-southern: both his and his wife's families owned slaves.[4]

Anderson arrived at Fort Moultrie on November 19. There he found 56 mounted guns and a garrison of 75 officers and men, including eight members of the regimental band, two sick soldiers, and seven "confined privates." Brevet Colonel Gardner's lack of discipline and indifference to security had allowed citizens to enter without challenge and wandering cattle grazed on the parapet. The major quickly returned order and discipline to the post.

On November 23 he submitted his first report to the Army's adjutant general, Samuel Cooper. It included an inspection of the harbor's forts with the Corps of Engineers' Capt. John G. Foster, who was thoroughly familiar with them. The report also stated that Moultrie and its undersized garrison were not conducive to mounting an effective defense against a land attack. Several sand dunes about 400

---

4 Cullum, *Biographical Register*, 2:347-352. On March 26, 1842, Anderson, then 36, married 20-year-old Eliza B. Clinch, the eldest child of Bvt. Brig. Gen. Duncan L. Clinch of Georgia, who could not attend the wedding. General Scott gave the bride away. Robert Anderson FOSU Research File.

Ft. Moultrie, *Frank Leslie's Illustrated Newspaper*, Jan. 5, 1861. *Fort Sumter Fort Moultrie National Historical Park, hereinafter FOSU*

yards from the fort's eastern wall provided cover for an approaching force. Two dunes that were higher than the fort's walls and roofs of nearby houses provided excellent positions for sharpshooters. At Fort Sumter, Foster estimated that in about 17 days the guns for the "lower tier of casemates will be mounted." The fort's four magazines were "in excellent condition" with nearly 40,000 pounds of cannon powder and a "full supply of ammunition for one tier of guns." Plus, it was ready to comfortably accommodate one company, and "indeed, for the temporary reception of its proper garrison." Most importantly, Anderson appraised Fort Sumter as "the key to the entrance to this harbor, its guns command this work [Fort Moultrie], and could soon drive out its occupants. It should be garrisoned immediately."[5]

5 *The War of the Rebellion: A Compilation of the Official Records of the Union and Confederate Armies*, 128 vols. (Washington, D.C., 1880-1901), Series 1, vol. 1, pages 74-76. Hereafter cited as *OR* 1:90-91. All references are to Series 1 unless otherwise noted; *Fort Sumter Letter Book . . . [,] July 27, 1854-April 9, 1861*, 262-263, transcription FOSU Research File, original in Charleston, SC Museum collections.

While Anderson and Foster reviewed Charleston's defenses, political unrest in the state escalated. On December 6, South Carolinians selected delegates to the state's convention to consider the issue of secession. The convention assembled in Columbia on December 17, but an outbreak of smallpox necessitated its relocation to Charleston, where it reconvened the next day. The legislature, governor, and others joined the delegates.

The legislature convened in Hibernian Hall on Meeting Street. On the same block, newly elected Gov. Francis Pickens occupied a suite in the Mills House Hotel, which was just a block away from his City Hall office at Broad and Meeting streets. The convention delegates assembled at St. Andrew's Hall, two blocks east on Broad Street, at noon on December 20, 1860. In a closed session all 169 delegates voted unanimously for secession; within eight minutes the issue had been settled and the convention adjourned at 1:15 p.m. An enormous cheer erupted from the great crowd packing the street in front of the hall and beyond. Numerous spontaneous celebrations broke out across the city. Shops and businesses closed, cannon roared, and houses displayed secession flags, while in drinking establishments, men repeatedly toasted the new republic. From the windows of the *Charleston Mercury*, broadsides proclaiming "THE UNION IS DISSOLVED!" fluttered from the windows.

At 6:30 p.m. the delegates reconvened and formed a column on Broad Street to march around the corner to Institute Hall on Meeting Street. In that hall, which was the largest public meeting space in Charleston, 3,000 secessionists cheered the delegates as they took their seats. Governor Pickens, members of the general assembly, former governors, and invited guests—including Virginian Edmund Ruffin, the decidedly pro-slavery, longtime radical godfather of the secession movement—attended the historic event. In alphabetical order, each delegate rose when called, walked to the stage, and signed the ordinance. Two hours later, when the last delegate had affixed his signature to the document, South Carolina left the Union and declared itself an independent republic.

In the streets outside, the cheers and huzzahs of unqualified joy echoed those that had erupted in the hall. Blazing bonfires, noisy fireworks, and pealing church bells added to the commotion. The cannon fire of earlier in the day resumed and militia units marched, their bands playing the "Marseillaise" and other martial tunes. Citizens wearing secession cockades walked behind bands and paused at the homes of prominent citizens to hear impromptu speeches. The celebrations continued throughout the next day. Three days after the convention, fireworks were still going off, and Mayor Charles MacBeth, concerned about the threat of fire, issued a proclamation forbidding such activities within city limits. Citizens ignored the rules until either the supply of fireworks or the people themselves were exhausted.[6]

Telegraph lines immediately flashed the news across South Carolina and the nation. Communities throughout the state and the South reacted much like Charleston, with speeches, parades, and the booming of cannon. Militia organizations, their ranks swelled with new recruits, paraded, and new units were organized. Many Northerners, meanwhile, viewed South Carolina's secession as both illegal and a threat to the Union as a whole.

President Buchanan was attending a wedding reception in Washington on the night of December 20 when he heard a commotion in the hall. Sarah Pryor, wife of Congressman Roger Pryor of Virginia, saw South Carolina Congressman Lawrence Keitt jumping for joy with a piece of paper in his hand. She asked Keitt if he was crazy and he responded, "Oh! South Carolina has seceded! Here is the telegram. I feel like a boy let out of school." Mrs. Pryor went to the president and whispered the news to him. Momentarily stunned, Buchanan left the reception without saying a word. Both of South Carolina's senators had already resigned and returned home after Lincoln's election, and before the end of December the rest of the state's congressional delegation would do the same.[7]

*   *   *

Francis Pickens had been in office only four days when his state seceded. Though he was still called "governor," he was arguably the president of the Republic of South Carolina. His most immediate concern was the status of the U.S. installations and forces within his jurisdiction, especially those in Charleston. He selected three commissioners to arrange the transfer of Federal property to the new republic. They arrived in Washington on December 26 and Buchanan arranged to meet with them as "private gentlemen," not in their official capacity. The president believed he had no authority to transfer property; he said Congress should decide the issue, and that he would pass the commissioners' proposal to that body. Before that happened, Anderson transferred his command from Fort Moultrie to Fort Sumter, and when word of this reached Washington on December 27, cracks already apparent in Buchanan's administration widened. On December 8, the first member of his cabinet had resigned, and over time others followed suit.

While Anderson's orders gave him command of Fort Moultrie, he had no authority over Captain Foster's engineer operations. And although the two officers

---

6 E. Milby Burton, *The Siege of Charleston, 1861-1865* (Columbia, SC, 1970), 7. Breaking the fireworks ordinance incurred a $10 fine for each offense.

7 Sara Agnes Rice [Mrs. Roger] Pryor, *Reminiscences Of Peace And War* (New York, 1904), 111-112.

did work together, Foster reported to and received his directives from the Corps of Engineers' headquarters in Washington. Anderson's communications to and from Washington went through the Army's adjutant general's office. The pace of work on Forts Sumter and Moultrie quickened. Foster ordered engineer Lt. George W. Snyder to reside at Sumter, and Anderson detailed Lt. Jefferson C. Davis, 1st U.S. Artillery, to assist him.

On December 3, Congress met but took no action on the status of the U.S. installations in Charleston Harbor. That same day, Lieutenant Davis arrived at Castle Pinckney with civilian engineer employees to ready the fortification in case the Federal government sent reinforcements. The obsolete 1809 fort, located on Shute's Folly in the mouth of the Cooper River, stood only a mile from Charleston and well within range of its artillery. Ordnance Sgt. James Skillen met them there. He had re-enlisted for his fifth five-year tour of duty in 1859 and lived at the fort with his daughter, Kate. Davis's assignment at Castle Pinckney was short-lived. Foster had requested another engineer officer to assist him, and Lt. Richard K. Meade, Jr. arrived on December 10. The next day Meade relieved Davis to return to his duties with Company E at Fort Moultrie.[8]

In a December 9 report to Adjutant General Cooper, received three days later, Anderson wrote: "Fort Sumter is a tempting prize, the value of which is well known to the Charlestonians, and once in their possession, with its ammunition and armament . . . and garrisoned properly, it would set our Navy at defiance, compel me to abandon this work, and give them the perfect command of this harbor." Three days after Anderson sent that document, assistant adjutant general Maj. Don Carlos Buell arrived at Fort Moultrie from Washington. His mission was to assess the overall situation and provide Anderson with verbal instructions from Secretary of War John B. Floyd. The commander was told to "hold possession" of the harbor's forts. Because his force was small, however, Anderson might only be able to hold one fortification. He was thus given the option to place his command in whichever installation he "may deem most proper to increase its power of resistance." If attacked he was to defend himself "to the last extremity." With that single command, Anderson's responsibilities had been expanded to include defense of all forts in Charleston Harbor.

When Buchanan learned of Buell's verbal communication, he forbade a defense to the "last extremity." Instead, he instructed Floyd to inform Anderson, "It is neither expected nor desired that you should expose your own life, or that of your men, in a hopeless conflict in defense of the forts . . . it will be your duty to yield to necessity and make the best terms in your power." These orders did not, however,

8 *Fort Sumter Letter Book*, 268, 274, 277; James Skillen File, FOSU Research File; *OR* 1:90-91.

remove Anderson's option to relocate his command to any other of the harbor's defenses. Anderson's December 9 and 18 reports, Buell's instructions on December 11, and the escalating tension and activity among the South Carolinians all suggest that Anderson was seriously considering moving his garrison to Fort Sumter as early as December 18.[9]

That same day South Carolinians began constructing earthen batteries along the harbor's shoreline at Mount Pleasant and near Breach Inlet, at the opposite end of Sullivan's Island from Fort Moultrie. While repairs and improvement of the fort's defenses continued, Capt. Abner Doubleday occasionally provided a show of firepower to the increasing number of civilians who roamed at all hours in the fort's vicinity. Sometimes, during drills with an 8-inch howitzer, the gun fired rounds of double canister—96 cast iron balls (48 per container)—weighing over 100 pounds. They slammed into the water in a shotgun-like pattern, creating an impressive and intimidating display for witnesses ashore and afloat. The harbor steamers *Nina* and *General Clinch* patrolled regularly between Forts Moultrie and Sumter; the latter ironically had been named in honor of Anderson's late father-in-law. These vessels were charged with preventing troops from moving to Sumter from Moultrie.[10]

On December 18, Anderson reiterated that "the sand hills and the houses surrounding the fort will afford safe shelter for sharpshooters, who may, with ordinary good luck, pick off the major part of my little band, if we stand to our guns, in a few hours." Concerned that an attack on the fort would put the enlisted men's wives and children in danger, Anderson began preparing to move them to safety to Fort Johnson on James Island. Although it had been abandoned since 1826, some of its still serviceable buildings could provide housing. On December 26, Anderson ordered Lt. Norman J. Hall, acting quartermaster, to procure several boats and sail for James Island. Once there he would not land but instead wait for two cannon reports and then sail to Fort Sumter. That afternoon the boats left Moultrie's dock loaded with the passengers and rations. The garrison would soon follow.

Anderson informed Capt. Foster of his plans and instructed him to ready boats for a move at dusk. Near sunset, Capt. Doubleday looked for Anderson to invite him to tea. Finding him on the fort's parapet with some officers, Doubleday learned of Anderson's plan and was allowed 20 minutes to ready his company.

9 *OR* 1:103.

10 *OR* 1:106, 129-131; W. A. Swanberg, *First Blood: The Story of Fort Sumter* (New York, 1957), *86;* Samuel Wylie Crawford, *The Genesis of Civil War: The Story of Sumter, 1860-61* (New York, 1887), 94, 97; Abner Doubleday, *Reminiscences of Forts Sumter and Moultrie in 1860-'61* (Charleston, SC, 1998, reprint of 1876 original), 40.

Brig. Gen. Abner Doubleday

LOC

After attending to his wife's safety, Doubleday formed Company E, ordered the men to the boats, and began rowing to Sumter.

Foster, assistant surgeon Samuel W. Crawford, Lt. Davis, and a small rear guard remained at Moultrie to man five guns and fire on any patrol boat attempting to interfere with the crossing. Doubleday and his men crossed successfully but were met at the dock by civilian workers, many wearing secession cockades, who moved out onto the wharf to protest the soldiers' arrival. Doubleday ordered his troops to fix bayonets and advance on the workers, who were placed under guard once inside the fort. Company E secured the installation. The boats returned to Sullivan's Island and ferried Company H under Capt. Truman Seymour to Sumter. Several other trips brought Anderson, Crawford, and a substantial amount of ordnance—including almost a thousand stands of grape and canister, fuses, friction primers, and other implements needed to fire Sumter's guns.

Foster, Davis, and the rear guard remained at Moultrie. Once alerted to the garrison's safe arrival at Sumter, they fired the signal for Hall to take the women and children there. They then spiked Moultrie's cannon on the side facing Sumter, set fire to the gun carriages, cut down the flagpole, and crossed to the fort at the mouth of the harbor.[11]

---

11 OR 1:2-4, 5, 108-109; Crawford, *Genesis of Civil War*, 102-112; Doubleday, *Reminiscences*, 59-67.

Chapter 3

Here We Are Impregnable

December 1860–April 1861

The transfer of men and materiel proceeded smoothly and without incident. Lieutenant Talbot, among the first of the garrison to arrive at Fort Sumter, recorded his impressions. He thought the operation had been skillfully executed, and the secrecy of it "secured its complete success." Major Anderson had pronounced Fort Moultrie indefensible, but in Sumter, which commanded the harbor, "we are impregnable." Anderson's move had rendered the South Carolinians' threats empty because "we actually command them." Although they would "undoubtedly distort our reasons for the move . . . we can afford to laugh at them having won." Moultrie, its guns spiked and vital equipment destroyed, had been rendered useless.[1]

By 8:00 p.m. on December 26, Anderson and his command, excepting Capt. Foster, Lt. Davis, and the rear guard, had settled in Fort Sumter. He reported to Adjutant General Samuel Cooper: "The step which I have taken was, in my opinion, necessary to prevent the effusion of blood." He also reported that he had ordered the spiking of Moultrie's guns, the destruction of "old" 32-pounder carriages, the felling of the flagpole, and the destruction of all ammunition that could not be moved to Sumter. His report did not arrive in Washington until December 29, but a wire revealing the news had reached the capital two days earlier. Secretary of War Floyd responded immediately, questioning the information. The news was "not believed" because Anderson did not have any orders authorizing the move into Sumter. Floyd wanted explanations. Later that day, Anderson verified

---

1 Talbot to mother, Dec. 26, 1860, Talbot Papers, FOSU Research File.

the movement. If Moultrie had been attacked, both his command and the harbor would have been lost, for if "attacked, the garrison would never have surrendered without a fight."

During the morning of December 27, several trips transferred hospital supplies as well as artillery, ammunition, and implements not taken the night before. Eventually, Foster, Davis, and the rear guard crossed the channel to join the rest of the garrison. Before leaving Moultrie, they burned the carriages of the guns facing Sumter, and their barrels collapsed onto the parapet.[2]

Talbot correctly predicted "a sensation" in the city. Clouds of smoke rising from Moultrie indicated something was amiss. The day after Christmas, Mayor MacBeth dispatched a fire engine to the installation, but as the vessel carrying it prepared to leave the dock, news of Anderson's action arrived. Word spread rapidly; excited citizens and assembled militia units soon clogged the streets. Governor Pickens ordered aide-de-camp Col. James J. Pettigrew and Maj. Ellison Capers to Fort Sumter to meet with Anderson. Pettigrew informed Anderson of an agreement between former governor William H. Gist and President Buchanan stating that no reinforcements would be sent to any U.S. installations in the harbor. Anderson acknowledged ordering the transfer and responded that he had not reinforced any of the fortifications; he had simply transferred the existing garrison from one fort under his command to another solely to prevent bloodshed. He admitted that the possibility of armed patrol boats landing hostile troops at will on Sullivan's Island near Fort Moultrie influenced his decision. "In this controversy between the North and the South," Anderson said at the meeting's end, "my sympathies are entirely with the South." When Pettigrew emphasized that Pickens wanted him to "courteously but peremptorily" return to Fort Moultrie, Anderson refused. "Then sir, my business is done," Pettigrew curtly replied, and he and Capers returned to Charleston.[3]

At that time Sumter stood about 90 percent complete. Although the walls towered above the harbor, the interior was yet unfinished. Both barracks buildings were incomplete; Anderson, his garrison, and the enlisted men's wives, sisters, and children occupied the nearly finished officers' quarters. The completed barbette and first-tier had four guns mounted on the parapet and 11 in the first-tier casemates, but the second-tier was far from ready. Not one of its 41 embrasures was finished. Some had been sealed off with dry-laid bricks; bricks laid with mortar closed some; still others were only partially closed. Gaping 8-foot square openings to the outside, inviting points of entry for an amphibious assault, characterized the

---

2 *OR* 1:2-3; Crawford, *Genesis of Civil War*, 105-108.

3 *OR* 1:3; Crawford, *Genesis of Civil War*, 108-111; Doubleday, *Reminiscences*, 79-80.

remaining embrasures. Brick walls 3 feet thick sealed these openings. Two feet of sand, boards, barrels, flagstone, or other construction material bolstered the brick from behind. One-inch-thick boards closed the flank embrasures.

The one-acre parade ground was crowded with six temporary wooden buildings serving as workshops or storehouses, along with stacks of flagstone, bricks, and lumber, and mounds of sand and seashells. While 15 of the fort's 81 guns on site were mounted, the remaining 66 pieces, with their chassis and carriages, lay on the parade ground. The heavy guns ranged from 24-pounders to 10-inch Columbiads, all with more than enough ammunition to mount a defense. Combined with what had been ferried from Moultrie, Fort Sumter held more than 5,400 solid shot and shell, more than 2,700 stands of grape and canister, and 3,100 friction tubes. Its four magazines contained over 39,000 pounds of cannon powder and 4,200 buck and ball cartridges. All it lacked was time to position the guns from the parade ground and a sufficient garrison to operate them.[4]

On the morning of December 27, Major Anderson directed the eight-man regimental band to the fort's third-tier; the rest of the garrison formed one side of a square on the parade ground near the flagpole. About 150 civilian engineer employees lined up on the other three sides. The women and children looked on, and at least two male "colored servants" were present. Anderson knelt next to the flagpole while Chaplain Matthias Harris invoked a prayer. Anderson then stood, the soldiers presented arms, and he raised the 20-by-36-foot, 33-star garrison flag he had taken, along with the storm flag, from Fort Moultrie. The band played "The Star-Spangled Banner" as the banner rose over the top of the fort, clearly visible 3 miles away in Charleston.

After the ceremony, the work of preparing the fort's defenses began in earnest. Pro-secessionist employees were dismissed immediately and sent to Charleston. Throughout the winter more workers left voluntarily, and by April only 43 remained. Those who stayed contributed greatly to the business of mounting guns, preparing cartridges, and securing embrasures. Each completed project bolstered Sumter's defenses.[5]

After Pettigrew and Capers reported Anderson's refusal to return to Fort Moultrie, Governor Pickens ordered Pettigrew to seize Castle Pinckney. With

---

4 Pemberton, "Fort Sumter: Chronological Construction History," 25-26, and Frank Barnes, "Fort Sumter: December 26, 1860," 1, 4-18, 23-24, both in *Fort Sumter: Historic Structure Reports*; "Inventory of Ordnance and Ordnance Stores at Fort Sumter, SC, Feb. 15, 1861," NA/RG 94, OAG.

5 Crawford, *Genesis of Civil War*, 112; Doubleday, *Reminiscences*, 71-72, 144-145, 153; Talbot to sister, March 3,1861, Talbot Papers; Maury Klein, *Days of Defiance: Sumter, Secession, and the Coming of the Civil War* (New York, 1997), 164; *OR* 1:18. By April 12, when the bombardment began, only one black servant remained.

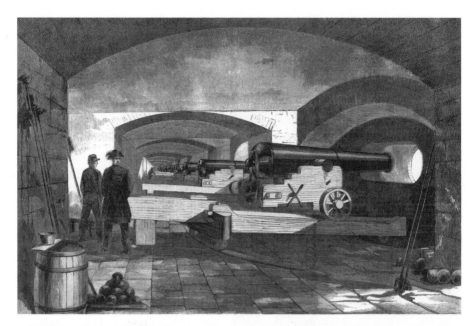

Ft. Sumter's right face first-tier guns bearing on Ft. Moultrie, *Harper's Weekly*, Jan. 26, 1861.
FOSU

---

elements of three infantry companies, Pettigrew arrived at the fortification aboard the *Nina* around 4:00 p.m. on December 27. Finding the gate and embrasures secured, he ordered the troops to deploy scaling ladders. Pettigrew located Lt. Meade upon the parapet and informed him of the governor's order to take charge of the fort. Not surprisingly, Meade refused to recognize Pickens's authority, but he could do nothing to stop the South Carolinians from seizing the fortification. In short order, the *Nina*'s "Palmetto Flag" flew over its ramparts; Castle Pinckney thus became the first U.S. military installation taken by troops from a seceded state.

Lieutenant Meade, Sgt. Skillen, the fort's keeper, and his daughter, Kate Skillen, were allowed to leave, and Meade rejoined Anderson's command at Fort Sumter. Meade served through the April bombardment. In May 1861, after his native state Virginia seceded, he resigned his commission and joined the Confederate Army.[6]

---

6 *OR* 1:3, 4, 109; Crawford, *Genesis of Civil War*, 113-116; Burton, *Siege of Charleston*, 13; Richard Kidder Meade, Jr., & Skillen Files, FOSU Research File. Lieutenant Meade, an 1857 West Point graduate, rose to the rank of major and served in the Army of Northern Virginia through the Seven Days Battles. On July 31,1862, he died of typhoid at his parents' home in Petersburg and was buried in the family plot at Blandford Church, just south of the city. Sergeant Skillen and Kate travelled north, and he was assigned to the U.S. Arsenal in Rome, New York. Kate Skillen later married Sgt. William A. Harn of Company E, 1st U.S. Artillery, who was stationed at Fort Sumter.

Lt. Richard K. Meade, Jr.

AC

The same day Castle Pinckney was seized, Pickens ordered Lt. Col. Wilmot DeSaussure to secure Fort Moultrie. Aboard the steamers *Nina* and *General Clinch*, DeSaussure and 200 men arrived after dark and entered the abandoned fort without incident; the "Palmetto Flag" was hoisted above its walls and was easily seen from Fort Sumter, just over a mile away. On the 30th, militia troops took possession of Charleston's U.S. Arsenal, commanded by Military Storekeeper Capt. F. C. Humphreys, without incident. During the lowering of the U.S. flag, Humphreys was permitted a 32-gun salute, one shot for each of the states still in the Union. When the militia raised a "Palmetto Flag" one gun was fired in South Carolina's honor. Humphreys, born in Massachusetts, resigned his commission in April, was commissioned a major in the Confederate Army, and performed the same duties as military storekeeper. A "Palmetto Flag" was also raised above the cupola of the U.S. Customs House and Post Office that operated in the Exchange Building at the intersection of East Bay and Broad streets, which had been the most visible sign of the Federal government's power in Charleston. All the U.S. employees there resigned, were sworn in as South Carolina officials, and continued performing their duties. The sole American flag still flying in the Charleston area was at Fort Sumter.[7]

On January 3, 1861, Abner Doubleday was surprised to see his wife, Mary, arrive at the fort; Capt. Foster's wife, Mary and her sister, who had obtained permission from Governor Pickens, were already there. That evening Capt. Seymour's wife, Louisa, who did not have a pass, was able to make it to the fort from Sullivan's Island. While they all wished to stay at Sumter, there was no way to make them comfortable, and Major Anderson thought it best for them to leave.

---

7 "The Treason Complete" and "A Coincidence," *Charleston Courier*, Dec. 31, 1860; Crawford, *Genesis of Civil War*, 116, 125; *OR* 1:5-9, 109.

The wives of Doubleday and Seymour left before midnight; Mrs. Foster and her sister departed the next day. Once back in Charleston they made their way north.

On January 6, Anderson's own wife, Eliza, arrived at Sumter. She had made the trip from New York accompanied by Peter Hart, a sergeant who had served in Anderson's company during the war with Mexico. After leaving the Army he became a police officer in New York. Mrs. Anderson located Hart, persuaded him to accompany her on the journey, and if possible, stay with her husband. Governor Pickens agreed to her request for passage to the fort for both with the stipulation that Hart serve as a civilian and not a soldier. Captain Foster employed him as a carpenter, although his actual job was to operate the fort's boat between Sumter and Fort Johnson. After a brief visit Mrs. Anderson returned to New York.[8]

As the new year dawned it became apparent to President Buchanan that Anderson's action was beyond reversing, and he decided to send both men and provisions to fortify and sustain the relocated Federal garrison. To avoid provoking an armed confrontation he employed the civilian steamer *Star of the West* for the job rather than a U.S. warship. Although intended to be a clandestine mission, it was anything but. Southern sympathizers in New York City telegraphed newspaper reports on the action to the governor. On December 31, Pickens had ordered a battery constructed on Morris Island. Citadel cadets then manned the so-called Fort Morris and its 24-pounder field howitzers. When the *Star of the West* left New York on January 5 laden with arms, munitions, provisions, and 200 newly enlisted U.S. Army recruits, South Carolinians knew the ship would reach Charleston about three days later.

Around midnight on January 8, the *Star of the West* arrived off the entrance to the harbor's Main Channel. The secessionists had extinguished the Morris Island lighthouse and the harbor's range lights, and with no harbor pilot aboard, the ship's captain had to wait for dawn to navigate the channel to Sumter. After 6:00 a.m. the U.S. flag was raised on the *Star of the West*, and it began moving toward the fort. The guard boat *General Clinch* steamed up the channel signaling the U.S. ship's presence to the troops at Forts Morris and Moultrie. The cadets manned their guns and fired a warning shot across the bow. Undeterred, the *Star* hoisted a larger U.S. flag and continued toward Sumter. At this point the Fort Morris battery opened on the vessel, striking it twice. Once Fort Moultrie opened fire, the *Star* reversed course and began its return trip to New York. Within Sumter, Major Anderson, unaware of the plans to resupply his garrison, watched as the events unfolded. He dispatched his men to the guns on the parapet, but because

8 *OR* 1:109; Doubleday, *Reminiscences*, 95-96, 98-100; Klein, *Days of Defiance*, 196; 1863 Anderson, Robert File A591, NA/RG 94.

Fort Morris was out of range and he was ignorant of exactly what was happening, his guns remained silent.

Anderson protested to Governor Pickens about firing on a ship under U.S. colors. If the governor could not provide a satisfactory response within "reasonable time," no vessel would be allowed to pass within the range of Fort Sumter's guns. The governor responded that turning back the supply ship was "perfectly justified" and added that it was apparent Anderson wasn't fully aware of the relationship between his government and South Carolina. To underscore his position, Pickens ordered four ships loaded with stone to be sunk at the Main Channel's entrance and then sent representatives to Anderson with a demand for the fort's surrender. It was rejected.

On January 9, Anderson sent Lt. Talbot to Washington to deliver copies of Pickens's correspondence on the incident and to provide an oral report of the overall situation. In the dispatch accompanying the documents Anderson wrote, "Lieutenant Talbot . . . [is] enabled to give you full information in reference to this and to all other matters." Talbot returned to Fort Sumter with a response from new Secretary of War Joseph Holt, which stated in part that South Carolina was still considered part of the Union, not a foreign power, and that Anderson not opening fire on January 9 was "fully approved by the President." No reinforcements would be sent, he continued, but Anderson should "report frequently [on his] condition."[9]

By mid-January, the tension had subsided and Pickens reestablished mail service, however indirect, to the fort. Postmaster Alfred Huger at the Exchange Building placed mail in a secured bag and sent it to Fort Johnson on James Island. From there all the official and personal mail, as well as newspapers and packages, proceeded to the U.S. garrison. In addition, the fort's commissary officer was allowed a weekly purchase of fresh meat and vegetables from Charleston using the same shuttle.[10]

While Anderson and Pickens sparred verbally, the legislature continued to meet in Hibernian Hall on Meeting Street, where it adopted the final design of a flag to represent the state's independence on January 28, 1861. The next day the *Charleston Mercury* described it as "consisting of a blue field, with a white palmetto tree in the middle upright. The white crescent in the upper flag staff corner remains as before, the horns pointing upward." The banner's design incorporated symbols of the Patriot victory on Sullivan's Island on June 28, 1776. Its color reflected the blue uniform coats of the 2nd South Carolina, which had defended the incomplete

9 *OR* 1:9-10, 134-137, 140; Crawford, *Genesis of Civil War*, 183-184, 192; Doubleday, *Reminiscences*, 103; Talbot to mother, Jan. 21, 1861.

10 *OR* 1:144-145; Talbot to mother, Jan. 21, 1861.

palmetto log fort, and the crescent had been the unit's emblem. The legislature added the upright palmetto tree in the center to symbolize the defense of the state. South Carolinians raised their new colors for the first time on January 30, 1861, above the cupola of the Exchange Building, proclaiming their commitment to a second American revolution and their defiance of the U.S. garrison flag waving above Fort Sumter.[11]

Within Sumter, Anderson had grown increasingly aware of the danger to the remaining women and children in the fort and made arrangements with Pickens for them to leave. On January 30, 20 women, 17 children, and five infants were taken to the Charleston Hotel. Four days later, they boarded the steamer *Marion* for their journey to New York. As the ship passed the fort, the garrison lined the parapet and fired a salute. Once the *Marion* reached New York, the women and children were housed at Fort Hamilton, where they awaited news of their husbands, brothers, and fathers.[12]

After their departure, Lt. Talbot proudly informed his mother of the men's morale amidst the Charleston tensions:

> When we reflect that the first fatal shot from our side may precipitate a bloody civil war we are willing to forget ourselves and allow them to accumulate all the odds against us that they may please to do, confident that should the occasion demand it, we can make a defence worthy of our just and honorable cause. Our men are in excellent spirits and since I have been in the Service I have never seen duty more faithfully and efficiently performed than by our little command.

Shortly after Talbot posted this letter, Charleston photographer George S. Cook visited the fort and took several photographs of the officers. On March 23, 1861, one of Cook's group shots appeared as an engraving on the front page of *Harper's Weekly*.[13]

Fueled by South Carolina's success, the secession movement swept quickly throughout the Deep South: Mississippi, Florida, Alabama, Georgia, and Louisiana seceded in January, followed by Texas on February 1. Delegates from the seceded states met in Montgomery, Alabama on February 8, 1861, and established the Confederate States of America, with former U.S. senator Jefferson F. Davis as its president. The fledgling government sent three commissioners to Washington to

---

11 Wylma A. Wates, *A Flag Worthy of Your State and People* (Columbia, SC, 1996), 11; "The State Flag," *Charleston Mercury*, Jan. 29, 1861; "The State Flag," *Charleston Courier*, Jan. 31, 1861.

12 *OR* 1:145, 151, 153, 161-162; Talbot to mother, Jan. 30, 1861.

13 Talbot to mother, Feb. 6 and 24, Mar. 18, 1861; Talbot to sister, Mar. 12, 1861, Talbot Papers, FOSU Research File.

negotiate the transfer of Federal property in Charleston and Pensacola, Florida, to the Confederate States. But like the commissioners Governor Pickens had sent, their mission failed. Both Fort Pickens at the mouth of Pensacola's harbor and Fort Sumter remained in Federal hands. The situation was no longer one to be negotiated by the states; it was a national problem to be resolved by the Confederate government.

On March 1, President Davis informed Governor Pickens that he had ordered Brig. Gen. P. G. T. Beauregard to Charleston to assume command. Beauregard, the Confederate Army's first commissioned brigadier general, arrived on March 3, and three days later issued General Orders No.1, which delineated the scope of his command, including "all the troops . . . on duty in and near Charleston Harbor" as well as all fortifications and operations in the area. On March 6, the seven-starred banner, the Confederacy's first national flag, replaced the South Carolina flag atop the Exchange Building, and the "Stars and Bars" soon became a common site on fortifications, public buildings, vessels, and other locations.

Beauregard, a Louisiana native, had entered West Point in 1834 at the age of 17, and in the two years between 1835 and 1837 had contact with 1st Lt. Robert Anderson, an artillery instructor at the academy. Beauregard, who grew up speaking French, served as an assistant French instructor his senior year and ranked second in his graduating class in 1838. He was commissioned a brevet second lieutenant in the Corps of Engineers and received numerous assignments before the Mexican War. As a first lieutenant during that war, he served from the battle of Tampico through the assault and capture of Mexico City. Wounded twice in battle, he received brevet promotions to major. After the war he returned to his engineer duties and was promoted to captain in 1853. In January 1861 he was appointed superintendent of the United States Military Academy (USMA) and assumed his post on the 23rd. Three days later Louisiana seceded and two days after that Beauregard was relieved of his post after less than a week. His claim for a reimbursement of $165 for mileage back to Louisiana went unpaid. The Creole officer's resignation letter of February 9 requested it take effect on or before June 1. Secretary of War Holt dated it February 20.

Beauregard quickly placed his two-plus decades' experience as an engineer officer to good use, improving existing fortifications and constructing new earthen batteries and forts. In early April, 42 heavy guns and mortars and a 12-pounder Blakely rifled cannon were placed on Morris, Sullivan, and James islands, and in Mount Pleasant. The gun emplacements sited onto Fort Sumter assured 360 degrees of coverage on their target. Anderson observed in a report to his superiors that Beauregard's command "insures . . . in a great measure the exercise of skill and sound

Brig. Gen. P. G. T. Beauregard

LOC

judgment in all operations of the South Carolinians in this harbor."[14]

On March 10, Lt. Talbot wrote his mother that the Southerners were "straining their energies to meet the impending storm." He noted the daily increase and improvement of the works around him. Nor were the Confederates idle. "A shot fired from one of their batteries the other morning struck our wharf. We thought the ball had opened and our batteries were immediately manned, but as they did not continue firing we came to the conclusion that it was accidental which it proved to be." The commander of the battery that had damaged Sumter's wharf personally sailed to the fort and extended his "profound apology."

Two days later Talbot wrote, "There seems to be no alternative for Mr. Lincoln now but to bring on a bloody Civil war against the United South or to withdraw us from Sumter and endeavor to keep the states not yet seceded in the Union. Heaven grant that his counsels may be wise and preserve that peace which he professes to desire."[15]

The day after Beauregard arrived in Charleston, Abraham Lincoln was sworn in as the 16th president of the United States. His inaugural address clearly stated that he regarded secession as illegal and would not relinquish any Federal installations or property in the seceded states. On March 13, Capt. Gustavus V. Fox met with the president and proposed a naval expedition to reinforce Fort Sumter. But instead of sending an expedition, Lincoln sent Fox to meet with Anderson. During their conference, the major said he did not think the plan to resupply Sumter would work and that by mid-April the military rations brought from Fort Moultrie in December, plus those at the fort for the engineer employees, would be exhausted.

14 T. Harry Williams, *P. G. T. Beauregard: Napoleon in Gray* (Baton Rouge, 1954), 1-50; Cullum, *Biographical Register*, 2: 697-698; *OR* 1: 191, 259-261, 266-267; "The Confederate Flag," *Charleston Courier*, Mar. 6, 1861.

15 Talbot to mother, Mar. 10, 1861, and Talbot to sister Mar. 12, 1861.

Upon receiving Fox's report, the president sent his friends Ward Lamon, a former law partner, and Stephen Hurlbut, a Charleston native and Illinois attorney, to Charleston. Pickens met with Lamon and informed him that to avoid war no attempt should be made to send reinforcements to Sumter and that the president must accept the secession of the Southern states. Lamon told the governor he believed the fort probably would be evacuated. Lamon then visited Fort Sumter and learned that the garrison's rations were perilously low. Hurlbut, meanwhile, visited relatives and friends in the city and reported to Lincoln that "the Separate Nationality is a fixed fact, that there is a unanimity of sentiment," and "there is no attachment to the Union" within the city.[16]

On April 3, an official dispatch arrived at Sumter stating that Talbot, whose tuberculosis restricted the nature of the duties he could perform, had been promoted to brevet captain and assigned to the adjutant general's department. Anderson wrote the adjutant general, Col. Lorenzo Thomas, that he had relieved Talbot of duty at Fort Sumter. Further, Anderson would "avail [himself] of this opportunity of stating that he has been zealous, intelligent, and active in the discharge of all his duties here, so far as his health permitted him to attempt their performance." Talbot once again made the trip to Washington to deliver dispatches and an oral report with an update on conditions inside Sumter.

In his last letter from Fort Sumter Talbot told his sister, "We thought that we should certainly receive some orders from Washington yesterday in relation to our departure from this post. If no orders are received in the meantime, I think it not unlikely that within a week Major Anderson will take the responsibility of making his own terms and withdrawing the Troops. We are as you know short of rations."[17]

On April 4, in his second meeting with Fox, Lincoln decided to send a naval relief expedition and to notify both Anderson and Pickens of the plan. The message to Anderson stated that the expedition would arrive before April 15, and if the U.S. flag were flying over the fort an attempt would be made to deliver provisions. If the "effort was resisted" the attempt to relieve the garrison would include reinforcements as well as provisions. He also told Anderson to exercise his judgment "to save yourself and command, [and if] a capitulation becomes a necessity, you are authorized to make it." State Department clerk Robert S. Chew, accompanied by Lt. Talbot, delivered Lincoln's notification to Pickens on April 8. The governor was informed that an attempt would be made to "supply Fort Sumter with provisions only," and if it weren't resisted "no effort to throw men, arms, or ammunition will be made, without further notice, or in case of an attack upon the

16 *OR* 1:197-198, 200, 209, 211, 218, 222, 230; Klein, *Days of Defiance*, 341-344.

17 *OR* 1:232; Talbot to sister, Apr. 2, 1861.

fort." Beauregard, called into the meeting, read the message and refused Talbot's request to return to Fort Sumter. The newly promoted officer thus returned to Washington with Chew.

The Confederate commander then wired Secretary of War Leroy P. Walker with the news. Walker's response was unequivocal: "Under no circumstances are you to allow provisions to be sent to Fort Sumter." In a later dispatch he ordered the mails to be stopped. Only the day before, Beauregard had stopped all provisions and mail going to the fort and was "calling out [the] balance of contingent troops." Officials at the Charleston post office seized two official letters, one from Anderson the other from Foster. Anderson's communiqué reported on the scarcity of rations, and based on Lamon's statement Beauregard believed that although the Federals would soon evacuate Sumter, an expedition was in en route. [18]

Within the fort, efforts to place the guns in position had been continuing steadily. On December 27, Capt. Foster had reported that "the remaining force was at once put to work mounting guns . . . and otherwise preparing to meet and repulse any attack." By April 12, they had successfully mounted 25 32- and 42-pounders in the first-tier casemates. On the barbette tier, 27 guns ranging from 24-pounders to 10-inch Columbiads were in position. Four 8-inch Columbiads had been positioned on the parade ground as mortars directed toward Cummings Point on Morris Island, and a 10-inch Columbiad was sited toward Charleston. Three 8-inch howitzers sat at the sally port, one inside the main gate and the other two mounted outside on either side of the entrance, aimed down the esplanade. A total of 60 guns had been mounted. Not all were immediately available, however; 11 were in the first-tier casemates with sealed or closed embrasures.

Six "Machicoulis" galleries, wooden, box-like structures, were constructed on the parapet, one at the center of each of the flank and face walls; on the gorge parapet three commanded the sally port. All extended 3 or 4 feet beyond the edge of the parapet, and each was prepped for firing muskets and equipped with a trap door to drop primitive, hand grenade-like shells on enemy troops. "Thunder barrels," each loaded with rock fragments and an explosive shell, were positioned to be dropped off the parapet and detonate near the base of exterior walls. Also on the parapet, piles of brick fragments and stones had been stacked to be thrown at an attacking force.

Outside the sally port's main gate stood a newly built stone and brick wall 3 feet, 6 inches thick and 6 feet high with an opening in the center to accommodate the muzzle of an 8-inch howitzer behind the wall. Against the exterior of the postern gates at each end of the gorge wall stood a 3-foot-thick brick wall.

18 *OR* 1:251-252, 291-293; Crawford, *Genesis of Civil War*, 383-386.

Magazine ventilators and windows were sealed except for some on the second floor left partially open to allow for musket fire. Foster also positioned two 50-pound powder charges covered with stones on the esplanade. These fougasses were at the base of the gorge wall on either side of the sally port halfway between the entrance and the end of the wall.

Holes cut between the first and second floor interior walls in the officers' quarters allowed "free communication through them . . . from one flank to the other." Two rooms were set up as a hospital, and another two as ordnance rooms. To protect these facilities from shell fragments, two "splinter-proof" traverses were built on the parade ground. Splinter-proofs also protected the Columbiads mounted on the parade ground and the guns on the parapet. The temporary buildings on the parade ground had been removed and most of the lumber used for fires. The flagstones for the second-tier floor were placed upright and flat against the barracks' first floor walls and at the open ends of the first-tier casemates on the two faces. Thirteen 32-pounders, the channel light lantern, and two construction shell-bins still littered the parade ground.[19]

On the afternoon of April 11, three members of Beauregard's staff—aide-de-camp James Chesnut, Jr., Lt. Col. A. R. Chisolm, and Capt. Stephen D. Lee—arrived at Fort Sumter to deliver a message demanding the fort's evacuation. They informed Anderson that he would be allowed to take his command's arms and property, as well as personal property, to any U.S. post he chose. Additionally, "The flag which you have upheld so long and with so much fortitude, under the most trying circumstances, may be saluted by you on taking it down." After meeting with his officers Anderson responded that "it is a demand with which I regret that my sense of honor, and of my obligations to my Government, prevents my compliance. Thank you for the fair, manly and courteous terms proposed, and for the high compliment paid me." Nothing was left to be said.

As Chesnut, Chisolm, and Lee prepared to leave, Anderson mentioned that if the Confederates "did not batter him to pieces" he would be out of food in a few days and evacuate the fort. The officers reported this information to Beauregard, who in turn telegraphed it to Secretary of War Walker. "Do not desire needlessly to bombard Fort Sumter," Walker responded that evening. "If Major Anderson will state the time at which . . . he will evacuate, and agree that in the meantime

---

19 H. L. Scott, *Military Dictionary: Comprising Technical Definitions; Information On Raising and Keeping Troops; Actual Service, Including Makeshift And Improved Material; And Law, Government, Regulation, And Administration Relating To Land Forces* (New York, 1864, reprint, Yuma, AZ, 1984), 317, 394; Barnes, "Fort Sumter: April 12, 1861," *Fort Sumter: Historic Structure Reports*, 1-8; OR 1:178. Fougasses are powder charges frequently placed in the ground in a pit or shaft over the which an enemy must pass during an attack.

Ft. Sumter's 33-star storm flag. *FOSU*

he will not use his guns against us unless ours should be employed against Fort Sumter, you are authorized thus to avoid effusion of blood. If this or its equivalent, be refused, reduce the fort as your judgment decides to be most practicable."[20]

That evening, Maj. P. F. Stevens watched Sumter's garrison flag from a traverse at the "Iron Battery" on Cummings Point. The banner "[s]uddenly . . . split in two distinct parts, dividing from the front edge to the back just along the lower extremity of the 'Union.'" Wondering aloud "if that is emblematical," the men with him observed that "it appeared ominous." The banner flew in that condition briefly before it was hauled down and replaced by the storm flag.[21]

Beauregard sent the three officers back to Fort Sumter at 11:00 p.m. With them was Roger Pryor, a pro-secession Virginian who had resigned his seat in the U.S. House of Representatives on March 3. When Pryor arrived in Charleston on April 10, Beauregard appointed him a volunteer aide-de-camp on his staff. Since Virginia had not yet seceded from the Union, Pryor remained in the boat while Chesnut, Chisolm, and Lee met a second time with Anderson at 12:45 a.m. on April 12. The major responded that he would leave the fort at noon on April 15 if he did not receive additional supplies or orders to stay. Anderson also reserved the right to use his guns when he deemed the situation proper. That evening the ships of the Federal relief expedition had been spotted off the harbor's entrance, and an attempt to reinforce Fort Sumter was expected at any moment. It was now 3:15 a.m. and the staff officers informed Anderson that his response was

20 *OR* 1:13, 59-60, 301.

21 Leslie D. Jensen, *The Fort Sumter Flags: A Study in Documentation and Authentication* (Harpers Ferry, WV, Mar. 1982), 84.

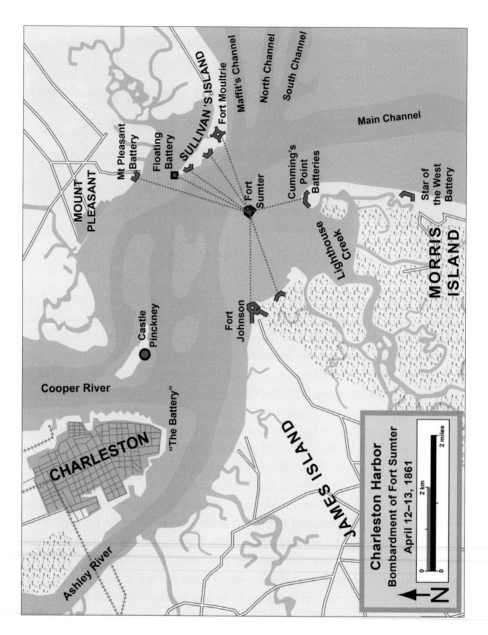

Charleston Harbor
Bombardment of Fort Sumter
April 12–13, 1861

unacceptable, and the Confederate guns would open fire in one hour. The officers left immediately for Fort Johnson, arriving at 4:00 a.m.[22]

In the predawn darkness of April 12, 1861, a 10-in. mortar shell fired from the battery located below Ft. Johnson, arced over the harbor and exploded above Ft. Sumter. It was joined by forty-two more Confederate cannon and mortars raining shot and shell on the Union fortification until the afternoon of the 13th, thirty-four hours later. Their distances to the fort varied from only 1,325 yds. (the Cummings Pt. batteries), to 1,800 yds. (Ft. Moultrie), 2,000 yds. (Ft. Johnson), and 4,000 yds. (the "Mount Pleasant Battery").

Chapter 4

Grand and Awful

April 12–15, 1861

At 3:00 a.m. on April 12, even as Anderson rejected Beauregard's final evacuation demand, the first ships of Lincoln's relief expedition appeared off the harbor's entrance. The passenger steamer *Baltic* and the revenue cutter *Harriet Lane* had sailed through heavy weather and arrived safely, but two of the expedition's three tugboats, one of which had sprung a leak, had turned back. The mission's principal vessels, the U.S. warships *Pawnee*, *Powhatan*, and *Pocahontas*, followed. The *Pawnee* arrived at 7:00 a.m. and awaited the *Powhatan*, the expedition's most powerful ship, but it had been ordered at the last minute to Pensacola to support the U.S. garrison at Fort Pickens. This information had not been shared with the other ships of the relief effort. The *Pocahontas* did not arrive until 2:00 p.m. the next day.[1]

Beauregard's men soon reached Fort Johnson after leaving Sumter, which loomed in silhouette against the faint blush of the predawn sky. Once there, they located the artillery commander on James Island, Capt. George S. James of Company C, South Carolina Artillery Battalion, then made their way to the East Battery under Lt. Henry S. Farley. His battery stood 2,300 yards (1 ⅓ miles) from Sumter and mounted two 10-inch seacoast mortars. Captain James offered Roger Pryor the honor of firing the first shot, but he declined, saying that he "could not fire the first gun of the war." The staff officers then left for Charleston. James consulted his watch, counted down the minutes, and at 4:30 a.m. gave the command to

---

1 OR 1:11; *Official Records of the Union and Confederate Navies in the War of the Rebellion*, 30 vols. (Washington, D.C., 1894-1920), Series I, Vol. 4:250-254, hereafter cited *ORN*. All references are to Series I unless otherwise noted.

Lt. George S. James, 4th US Arty, c1856. After SC's secession he resigned his commission and was appointed captain of Co. C, SC Artillery Battn. On Sept. 14, 1862, Lt. Col. James commanding the 3rd SC Inf. Battn. was killed at Fox's Gap, South Mountain, MD. *FOSU*

fire. Lieutenant Farley pulled the lanyard of Gun No.1 and the fiery concussion thrust a 98-pound shell upward into the pale early morning light. About 20 seconds later it burst in the air over Fort Sumter. The first shot in the War for Southern Independence had been fired. A shell from a 10-inch mortar in the nearby West Battery followed.[2]

At Cummings Point on Morris Island, approximately three-quarters of a mile south of Fort Sumter, the 10-inch mortars in the Trapier and Point batteries opened fire at 4:48 a.m. Colonel DeSaussure, who commanded the island's artillery, reported: "Shortly after 5 a.m., when the early dawn enabled the guns to be properly worked, the fire commenced from the three 8-inch Columbiads in the Iron Battery and the two 42-pounders in the Point Battery."

"Private" Edmund Ruffin was on duty at the Iron Battery's Gun No. 1. Ruffin, a witness to the signing of South Carolina's Ordinance of Secession, had traveled to Tallahassee and witnessed Florida's secession also. He went back to Charleston and soon returned home to Virginia. Frustrated that the Old Dominion had not yet left the Union, he vehemently expressed his dissatisfaction in a February 27 diary entry. "I will be out of Virginia before Lincoln's inauguration, & so will avoid being . . . under his government even for an hour." He vowed to "become a citizen of the . . . Confederate States, & will not again reside in" Virginia until she also seceded.

Ruffin reached Charleston on March 1, three days before Lincoln's inauguration, and received a warm welcome. Southerners held Ruffin in high regard as an agricultural innovator; he had developed a method for restoring

2 OR 1:60; Robert Lebby, "The First Shot on Sumter," *South Carolina Historical and Genealogical Magazine* (July 1911), 141-145.

thousands of nutritionally depleted acres to productivity. As one of the South's most vocal proponents of secession, Governor Pickens issued Ruffin a pass for free access to any of the harbor's fortifications. Since he believed U.S. forces might land on Morris Island as part of an attempt to relieve Fort Sumter, the 67-year-old Ruffin was determined to serve as a soldier there. On April 8, the Citadel's superintendent loaned him a musket and accoutrements, and he arrived on the island the next day. Several units invited him to join them, and he accepted Capt. George B. Cuthbert's offer to fall in with the Palmetto Guard. Stationed in the Point and Iron batteries, the infantry company served as cannoneers. Ruffin said Cuthbert had notified him that, on the night of April 11-12,

> his company [had] requested . . . me to discharge the first cannon to be fired, which was their 64 lb. Columbiad, loaded with shell. By order of Gen. Beauregard, made known the afternoon of the 11th, the attack was to be commenced by the first shot at the fort being fired by the Palmetto Guard, & from the Iron Battery. . . . Of course I was highly gratified by the compliment, & delighted to perform the service—which I did. The shell struck the fort, at the north-east angle of the parapet.[3]

Across the harbor's mouth at Fort Moultrie, Lt. Col. Roswell S. Ripley commanded all the artillery on Sullivan's Island, the Floating Battery anchored at the island's western tip, and the mortar battery near the harbor's shoreline in Mount Pleasant. He had trained a total of 20 cannon and six mortars on Fort Sumter. Ripley reported that after the shot from the East Battery, "The commands went quickly and quietly to their posts, and very soon every battery bearing upon the fort had commenced."

Inside Moultrie that morning was 1st Sgt. John O'Grady, once a private in Company H, 1st U.S. Artillery, who had been arrested there in August 1860 for the murder of fellow Irishman James Keogh on Sullivan's Island. Although the charge apparently had been dismissed, the state's attorney general seated a grand jury in January 1861 that indicted O'Grady for murder. That same day he enlisted in Company B, South Carolina Artillery Battalion at Moultrie; U.S. Army records of February 4, 1861 listed him as a deserter. O'Grady wasn't the first member of the U.S. artillery to transfer his allegiance. John Holland and Charles P. Grundshig, both privates in Company E, 2nd U.S. Artillery at the U.S. Arsenal in Augusta, Georgia, deserted in January 1861, and enlisted in Company C, South Carolina

---

3 *OR* 1:43-47; William Kauffman Scarborough, ed., *The Diary of Edmund Ruffin*, 3 vols. (Baton Rouge, 1976), 1:557, 559, 561, 581-585, 588.

Artillery Battalion in Hamburg. All three soldiers witnessed and presumably participated in the attack on their former comrades inside Fort Sumter.[4]

The opening rounds escalated into a bombardment that swelled into a steady circle of continuous fire directed at the fort. Assistant Surgeon Francis L. Parker, who was on Morris Island, recalled: "And now shell answers shell and batteries from the various points send back to each other their warlike sounds until the whole circle plays on Sumter, lighting up momentarily their guns' outlines, scarcely visible in the morning light." Inside the beleaguered fort, Sgt. James Chester wrote, "shot and shell went screaming over Sumter as if an army of devils were swooping around it."[5]

Charlestonians crowded every housetop, piazza, wharf, and open space in The Battery (White Point Garden) to view the bombardment. They watched as hot shot—solid iron cannonballs heated in furnaces until red hot—streaked through the air to land inside Fort Sumter and tracked shells with burning fuses arcing toward the works, some bursting in air before reaching their target. The concussion of the heavy guns reverberated 3 miles across the water into the city.

On April 16, Richmond's *Daily Dispatch* included excerpts from the *Charleston Mercury*'s account of the bombardment. "The Battery, the wharves and shipping in the harbor, and every steeple and cupola in the city, were crowded with anxious spectators of the great drama," the paper reported. "Never had such crowds of ladies without attendants visited our throughfares." Emma Holmes noted in her diary that as she looked through a telescope at The Battery, she "saw the shots as they struck the fort and the masonry crumbling." Many feared for husbands, fathers, and sons in harm's way. Another spectator, Clara Victoria Dargan, expressed the anxiety all felt. "In the faint morning light with red sun struggling to rise through the heavy bad coloured clouds [came] the flash and report of mortars and cannon with now and then a huge shell bursting just above the fort. . . . It was grand. It was awful." Assistant Surgeon Parker continued in this vein:

There stands the bold defiant fort, as quiet as death. No light is seen, not a sign of life appears, not even a sentinel can be distinguished, but high above her floats her proud banner, the Stars and Stripes, the flag which for 75 years has never quailed

4 *OR* 1:39-43; Mark Johnson, "Emory Upton's Twenty-Six: Desertion and Divided Loyalties of U.S. Army Soldiers, 1860-1861," *Journal of Military History*, no. 3 (2017), 14-16. Records detailing the indictment's outcome have not been found.

5 F. L. Parker, "The Battle of Fort Sumter As Seen From Morris Island," 33, in Lawrence S. Roland and Stephen G. Hoffius, eds., *The Civil War in South Carolina: Selections From The South Carolina Historical Magazine* (Charleston, SC, 2011); James Chester, "Inside Sumter in '61," in Robert Underwood Johnson & Clarence Clough Buel, *Battles and Leaders of the Civil War*, 4 vols. (New York, 1887-88), 1:66, hereafter cited as *B&L*.

before an enemy or fallen in disgrace. . . . The question is asked on all sides, what is Anderson doing? Why doesn't he return fire? Admiration burst from all sides as the flag still waves defiantly aloft, seemingly careless of damage or of the shot and shell whistling around her.[6]

Sixty cannons were mounted inside Fort Sumter: 26 in the first-tier casemates, 26 on the barbette, five on the parade ground, as well as two outside and one inside the sally port. Despite the ferocity of the attack, Anderson had determined to await sufficient light for his gun crews to site their targets before returning fire.

That morning the garrison consumed a meager ration of pork, water, and some farina that Crawford had found in the hospital. Anderson then divided his command into three reliefs, each to work the guns in two-hour shifts. "Of the forty-three workmen constituting the Engineer force," Foster reported, "nearly all volunteered to serve as cannoneers, or to carry shot and cartridge to the guns." Because the pieces on the parapet and parade ground were exposed to enemy fire, the major allowed only the 32- and 42-pounders in the first-tier casemates to fire.[7]

Captain Doubleday's Company E comprised the first relief. Doubleday personally led a detachment to the right gorge angle casemates facing the three Confederate batteries on Cummings Point, and at 7:00 a.m. aimed the first shot in defense of the Union. The 32-pounder solid ball struck but ricocheted off the Iron Battery's sloping wall. Soon Lt. Jefferson C. Davis and Dr. Crawford, commanding the company's two other details, joined the action by firing on the Sullivan's Island fortifications. After Company E completed its two-hour shift Captain Seymour and Company H took over. When confronted by a shortage of breech sights, Seymour resorted to using the blade of a table knife to estimate the elevation in aiming the guns. Parker continued his observation of the fort's response to the shelling: "Major Anderson is not asleep. Sumter has opened. Her cannonballs strike . . . and ricochet far out into the marsh and creek. Shot succeeds shot; now she answers Moultrie and is paying her regards to the floating battery. Our men

6 John F. Marszalek, ed., *The Diary of Miss Emma Holmes, 1861-1866* (Baton Rouge, 1994), 29; Elizabeth Wittenmyer Lewis, *Queen of the Confederacy: The Innocent Deceits of Lucy Holcombe Pickens* (Denton, TX, 2002), 139.

7 *OR* 1:225; Crawford, *Genesis of Civil War*, 426. Foster's diagram, dated March 27, 1861, shows 27 guns mounted in the first tier, and nine at closed embrasures. This included two 32-pounders and two 42-pounders in the right face, and one of the latter at an enclosed embrasure. Foster's report (*OR* 1:19), however, stated that this tier held a total of 21 guns, as did the casemate. But a count of the guns in this report adds up to 23 in the first tier, with three 42-pounders mounted in the right face. The discrepancy indicates that in the roughly two weeks preceding the bombardment, guns were still being moved and mounted.

are being made acquainted with the sound of balls—they are falling all about us. The action is general."[8]

When the Federals opened fire, they drew from a supply of 700 cartridges. Army regulations specified that the bags were to be made entirely of wool, but a shortage of that material dictated that they use every available substitute, including surplus company "clothing . . . coarse paper and extra hospital sheets." With only six needles in the fort, the rate of fire exceeded the men's ability to sew new cartridge bags. By mid-day just six guns continued to fire—two toward Morris Island, and four toward Fort Moultrie and the batteries along the western end of Sullivan's Island. Foster reported that the effect of the fire was "not very good." Inefficient for long range fire, they inflicted little damage. From Fort Moultrie Lt. Col. Ripley reported, "the enemy's shot had told with great effect upon the quarters . . . continually perforating them and breaking them up; but . . . no material damage was done." Only one or two rounds were fired at Fort Johnson, and none at Castle Pinckney or Charleston. Most of the fire concentrated on the Iron Battery at Cummings Point. Firing continued until dark and sewing cartridge bags went on until midnight, when Anderson ordered it stopped.[9]

The Confederates' accuracy improved as the morning progressed. Parker wrote at 10:00 a.m., "Now we have got the range. . . . Our shells fall and burst upon the parapet, others fall within . . . the point and iron batteries are telling on Sumter . . . clouds of brick and mortar rise from her impenetrable walls." Within the fort and despite Confederate fire, a few members of the garrison ventured onto the parapet and fired one or two of the guns. Upon firing the third round from a 10-inch Columbiad at the right gorge angle, the gun and its carriage recoiled off the chassis. The combined weight of more than eight tons slammed into the 8-inch seacoast howitzer next to it and knocked it and its 4-ton carriage off the chassis. On the right flank parapet fire from Moultrie dismounted an 8-inch Columbiad and cracked the barrel of another. Confederate rounds damaged only three guns despite heavy fire from the surrounding batteries.

Throughout the day, the barracks caught fire three times (all extinguished) from exploding shells or hot shot. Confederate rounds also caused considerable damage to the roof and third floor of both buildings. Rounds fired from the west end of Sullivan's Island shrieked over the parapet, "completely riddling the offices' quarters, even down to the first floor." Foster reported "well directed and . . . well

---

8 Doubleday, *Reminiscences*, 145-146; Crawford, *Genesis of Civil War*, 429-430; *OR* 1:18-19; 1863, Anderson, Robert File A591, NA/RG 94; Parker, "Battle of Fort Sumter," *The Civil War in South Carolina*, 33-34.

9 *OR* 1:18-21, 40, 212.

sustained" shelling from 10-inch mortars. Half of the rounds "came within or exploded above the parapet of the fort . . . and only ten buried themselves in the . . . parade without exploding." Solid shot repeatedly struck the fort's exterior. Foster's evening inspection, however, revealed that "the work was not damaged to any considerable extent." The deepest penetrations he found were only 11 inches from an 8-inch Columbiad solid shot and a solid cast iron bolt from the rifled 12-pounder Blakely gun, both located at Cummings Point. As night fell, the Confederates continued firing a round every 10 to 15 minutes even as storms approached.[10]

At the mouth of the harbor, Capt. Gustavus Fox on the *Baltic* reported a constant blowing gale. Hence with only the *Pawnee*'s guns to support the relief mission, Federal forces made no attempt to land provisions or troops at Sumter. They could only watch as Confederate artillery pounded the fort. By the time the *Pocahontas* arrived the next afternoon, it was too late.

Foster reported early on the morning of April 13 that "[t]he last of the rice was cooked" and served with pork, "the only other article of food left." After breakfast, the garrison reopened a brisk fire, which continued "as long as the . . . supply of cartridges lasted." At daylight the Confederate guns resumed firing, rapidly and with increasing accuracy. Several solid rounds from the Blakely struck an embrasure at the right gorge angle. One threw stone fragments into the casemate and wounded four soldiers, and a shell fragment severely wounded a civilian employee.[11]

By 9:00 a.m. plumes of smoke started rising from the roof of the officers' quarters. Hot shot from Fort Moultrie's guns had found their mark, and flames began threatening one of Sumter's magazines. Little water was available to fight the fire as the three cisterns in the quarters had been destroyed the previous day. With exploding shells raining onto the parade ground, Anderson ordered as much powder as possible be removed before flames forced the magazine to be closed. Soldiers relocated 50 barrels into casemates before the fire and heat forced them to close the magazine doors and pack dirt against them.

The Confederates increased their rate of fire upon seeing the roof in flames; the blaze soon engulfed the entire building. A strong south wind blew sparks and flames onto the barracks buildings and by noon all were engulfed. "The heat and smoke inside was awful," Pvt. John Thompson wrote. "The only way to breathe was to lay flat on the ground and keep our faces covered with a wet handkerchief." Anderson ordered the entire garrison into the left and right face first-tier casemates. He ordered five barrels to be draped with wet blankets, the remaining to be pushed outside through

10 Parker, "Battle of Fort Sumter," in *The Civil War in South Carolina*, 34; *OR* 1:20-21, 24.

11 *OR* 1:11, 21-22.

the embrasures. When the flames inevitably reached the "magazines of grenades . . . arranged in the stair towers and implement rooms of the gorge, they exploded, completely destroying the stair at the west gorge angle, and nearly . . . the other." Under these conditions, and with a diminishing number of cartridges, Sumter's rate of fire fell to only one round every 10 minutes.[12]

On the 12th rounds had struck the flag staff several times and when a shell fragment cut the lanyard, the colors got entangled on the pole. After two more hits on the morning of the 13th, the staff fell to the parade ground. Lieutenant Norman J. Hall dashed out immediately and recovered the 10-by-20-foot storm flag (it had replaced the garrison flag, which had ripped during a storm two days earlier). Lieutenant Snyder and engineer employees Peter Hart and Edward Davis attached it to a spar and secured it onto the parapet in the middle of the right face opposite Fort Moultrie.

From Morris Island, former U.S. senator from Texas Louis T. Wigfall, a volunteer aide on General Beauregard's staff, witnessed the storm flag falling, and, completely on his own authority, approached Sumter under a flag of truce. Wigfall, with a white handkerchief attached to the end of his sword, arrived at an embrasure, met an astonished soldier, and requested a conference with the commander. Upon hearing the news, Anderson and Lt. Snyder made their way through the burning sally port and onto the esplanade to meet the ex-senator. But Wigfall had entered the fort through the embrasure and missed Anderson altogether. Taken to a group of officers, he stated that he had come from Beauregard to arrange raising a white flag to suspend hostilities since the flag was down and the buildings were burning. The officers pointed to the U.S. flag flying from the parapet and told him that only Anderson could authorize a white flag. Further, Confederate batteries should be the ones to cease firing. Wigfall pointed out the silent Cummings Point guns and offered his handkerchief to signal the guns on Sullivan's Island to cease also. The Federal officers refused to take it but permitted him to wave it from an embrasure. A corporal offered to relieve Wigfall after a short time, but when a round struck near the opening, the soldier jumped back exclaiming that "he would not hold [Wigfall's flag], for it was not respected."

Anderson then joined the group and Wigfall, hoping to secure plans for an evacuation, repeated what he told the other officers. When queried about the terms offered, Wigfall stated, "Any terms that you may desire—your own terms— the precise nature of which General Beauregard will arrange with you." Anderson replied he would accept the terms Beauregard offered on April 11th—that the

12 Ron Chepesiuk and John Thompson, "Eye Witness to Fort Sumter: The Letters of Private John Thompson," *The South Carolina Historical Magazine*, 55; James Chester, "Inside Sumter in '61." *B&L*, 1:66.

soldiers would evacuate with their arms and all private and company property, fire a salute as the U.S. flag was lowered, and board a vessel to carry them to any northern port he selected. Anderson ordered that a hospital sheet be displayed from the parapet and that the U.S. colors be lowered. Wigfall returned to Morris Island, and the rate of Confederate fire began to diminish. By 3:00 p.m., all the remaining guns had fallen silent.

When Beauregard learned that Sumter's flag was down, he dispatched official members of his staff, Capt. Stephen D. Lee and volunteer aides Roger Pryor and William Porcher Miles, to speak with Anderson. Shortly after they set out, Beauregard learned of the white flag and sent two more staff members, Maj. D. R. Jones and volunteer aide Charles Alston, Jr., to the fort. The officers and aides met with Anderson and only then learned of Wigfall's premature overtures, but the consternation over Wigfall's unauthorized meeting was soon resolved. The parties agreed to the April 11 terms and began making arrangements for the surrender and evacuation of Sumter the next day.[13]

Almost immediately after the raising of the white flag and the lowering of the U.S. national banner, the city of Charleston and the fortifications in the harbor erupted in jubilation. Holmes recorded, with no small amount of hyperbole, "As soon as the surrender was announced," pealing bells and artillery salutes honored "one of the most brilliant & bloodless victories in the records of the world." In addition to the din of church bells and cannon, fireworks exploded and bonfires burned long into the night as thousands marched triumphantly through the streets.

During the bombardment, Confederate guns fired approximately 3,000 solid shot and shells at Fort Sumter; Foster reported that 600 had struck its scarp walls. Doubleday estimated that 1,800 had been fired into the fort. "[T]he upper story was pretty well knocked to pieces . . . while the parapet had been choked with 'heaps of rubbish.'" The men were exhausted from their rotating service on the guns, fighting fires, meager rations, and a lack of sleep. On Sunday morning, April 14, Anderson and his command prepared to leave the fort. A hundred-gun salute would accompany the final lowering of the U.S. colors, and Company E received the honor of firing it. Smoldering buildings and wind conditions, however, worried everyone. "[S]parks were floating around everywhere," Doubleday noted, "and there was no safe place to deposit the ammunition." Even the makeshift shelters between the guns that had been constructed of oak timbers and iron plates didn't guarantee safety from the blowing sparks.

---

13 *OR* 1:23-24; Crawford, *Genesis of Civil War*, 439-440, 446-447; Doubleday, *Reminiscences*, 162-163; Chester, "Inside Sumter in '61," 73; Ron Field, *1st South Carolina Artillery (Calhoun's/Rhett's)* (Gloucestershire, UK, 1999), 4.

Right gorge angle damaged by guns at Cummings Point on Morris Island. *LOC*

The salute began at 2:00 p.m., but while gunners loaded the 47th blank round, it discharged prematurely, and at least one spark landed among a nearby stack of shielded cartridges. The "powder exploded, tearing the strong sheets of iron . . . into fragments, and scattering them abroad like feathers . . . one of our brave fellows was dead —quite dead—rent almost in two."

That "brave fellow" was Pvt. Daniel Hough, serving his third five-year enlistment in the 1st U.S. Artillery. The Irish native was the first soldier to lose his life in the war. The salute stopped; a coffin was constructed, and Hough was buried in Fort Sumter's parade ground. Captain Lee reported a burial with military honors, with members of Capt. J. H. Hallonquist's Company B, South Carolina Artillery Battalion presenting arms as his body was lowered into the ground. Three members of the Palmetto Guard "placed a neat and appropriate head-piece over the grave." Dr. Crawford reported that five more men were wounded in the accident. Private Edward Galway was mortally wounded, died in Charleston on the 14th, and was buried in St. Lawrence Cemetery. Three other soldiers suffered slight wounds and left with the rest of the garrison on the *Baltic*. The fourth, severely wounded, was taken to the city. He was allowed passage north six weeks later upon his recovery.

Guns on the right flank barbette fired the surrender salute. One discharged prematurely resulting in Pvt. Daniel Hough's death, mortally wounding Pvt. Edward Galway, and wounding four others. *NYHS*

The *Charleston Daily Courier* reported news of the accident on April 16 as part of a larger article entitled, "ADDITIONAL INCIDENTS [OF] THE GLORIOUS AFFAIR OF FORT SUMTER." It also provided a human-interest element regarding the arrival of Lt. Jefferson C. Davis's sister, Matilda Anne, at the fort. She was accompanied by the Bonetheaus of Charleston, with whom she had stayed while her brother was serving under Anderson's command:

> Mr. and Mrs. H. B. Bonetheau enjoyed the honor of being the first civilians to enter . . . Fort Sumter. On Sunday morning they accompanied Miss Davis, who has for some time been a guest in their family, to the battered fortress. They were courteously received by Lt. Davis, brother of the young lady, under their charge, and conducted over the fortifications. Miss Davis was then conducted to the Isabel, and Mr. and Mrs. Bonetheau, through the politeness of the young Lieutenant, were allowed to witness the simple and beautiful ceremony observed in saluting the flags. They were also eye-witnesses of the sad accident which sent one brave man into eternity instantly. From whose effects another has died, and several are still suffering.[14]

14 Marszalek, *Holmes Diary*, 29; *OR* 1:24, 56, 66; "The Two Men of Major Anderson's Command," *Charleston Mercury*, April 15, 1861; Doubleday, *Reminiscences*, 166, 171; *ORN* 4:255; A. Fletcher, *Within Fort Sumter; or, A View of Major Anderson's Garrison Family For One Hundred And Ten Days*

Five U.S. soldiers and one civilian in the fort's garrison were wounded during the 36-hour bombardment, and only four Confederates were reported to have suffered slight wounds. The only death to occur was that of Lt. James H. Powe's "handsome bay horse." Stabled "some distance in the rear of Fort Moultrie," the horse "fell, shot through from side to side" by a solid round from Fort Sumter.

Following Private Hough's hasty funeral, the salute resumed and concluded on the fiftieth round. After lowering the 33-star U.S. flag, the command formed on the parade ground; the sergeants hoisted the flag, still nailed to the spar, to their shoulders and prepared to march out of the fort. Major Anderson carried the garrison flag with the soldiers behind him and the civilian workers at the rear. As the procession marched toward the sally port, the band played "Yankee Doodle," but it struck up "Hail Columbia" in Anderson's honor as he exited the works. The garrison boarded the *Isabel* after 4:00 p.m., but because of the delay caused by the accidents and Hough's burial, the ship waited until the morning the next day, April 15, to set sail.

Once Anderson and his command boarded the *Isabel*, Gov. Pickens, Gen. Beauregard, and other military officers, politicians, and dignitaries entered Sumter and raised the first national Confederate flag and South Carolina's state banner. Cheers erupted and salutes exploded from cannon in the surrounding fortifications. Spectators, some of whom paid as much as 50 cents for places on the boats moored near the fort, added their cheers to those within. Beauregard reported to Secretary of War Walker that "before sunset the flag of the Confederate States floated over the ramparts of Sumter." On the *Isabel*, it was impossible not to hear the unmistakable sounds of salutes, cheers, and celebrations that erupted from nearly every point in and around the harbor.

On the morning of April 15, the *Isabel* made its way out to the Federal relief expedition. Anderson and his men then transferred to the *Baltic* for their journey north. The North's first heroes of the war arrived in New York on April 19.[15]

(New York, 1861), 64-65; Crawford, *Genesis of Civil War*, 470; William Marvel, "The First to Fall: The Brief and Bitter Life of Daniel Hough," unpublished, n.d., 1-11, FOSU Research File; "A Lady in the Fort," *Charleston Courier*, Apr. 16, 1861; Stephen D. Lee, "Civil War Journal of Colonel Stephen D. Lee," typed transcript, Stephen D. Lee Papers, 1784-1929, FOSU Research File.

15 James Harrington Powe, *Reminiscences & Sketches of Confederate Times By One Who Lived Through Them*, Harriet Powe Lynch, ed. (Columbia, SC, 1909), 11; *OR* 1:24, 33, 42; Doubleday, *Reminiscences*, 172-173; Scarborough, *Diary of Edmund Ruffin*, 1:598-600.

An Armed Fortress of the Confederate States

April 1861–December 1862

President Lincoln's first action after Fort Sumter's surrender was to issue a proclamation on April 15 calling for 75,000 men from various state militias for 90 days' service to augment the national army and subdue the rebellion. The proclamation also called on Congress to convene in two and a half months for a special session on July 4. By the end of May Virginia, North Carolina, Tennessee, and Arkansas, after earnest internal debate, had joined the Confederacy.

The same day Major Anderson surrendered, General Beauregard appointed Lt. Col. Roswell S. Ripley as Fort Sumter's commanding officer. The Ohio native was an 1843 West Point graduate and a Mexican War veteran. While serving at Fort Moultrie in 1852, he married wealthy Charleston widow Alicia Middleton Sparks and resigned from the Army the following year. After briefly working in the newspaper business, Ripley found his niche as an arms dealer, most notably brokering the sale of Sharps breechloading carbines to the British in 1855. On December 27, 1860, Governor Pickens appointed him a major in the state militia. Ripley accepted a lieutenant colonel's commission as commander of the South Carolina Artillery Battalion on January 27, 1861. Since the Palmetto Guard had returned to Morris Island, his small garrison at Sumter was comprised of only Company B from the battalion.

In addition to commanding the fort's garrison, Ripley also had to repair the damage sustained over the two days of the bombardment. The destruction was evident at every turn. Captain Francis D. Lee of the engineers estimated the cost of repairs at $350,000. Engineers began removing the rubble and debris and repairing

Brig. Gen. Roswell S. Ripley, Ft. Sumter's first CS commanding officer. *LOC*

and/or rebuilding the wreckage. They recovered enough lead from the burned buildings that at least 45 pigs (approximately 60 pounds each) were sent to the Charleston Arsenal, as was damaged sheet copper. Many of the Charleston businesses employed by the U.S. Corps of Engineers during the fort's construction worked on the restoration project. Shortly after Ripley assumed command, he placed a Dante quote over the sallyport: *Lasciate ogni speranza, voi ch' entrate*—"Abandon all hope, ye who enter." Ripley left the fort before summer's end, and in August was promoted to brigadier general in the Confederate Army as commander of the Department of South Carolina and the state's coastal defenses.[1]

Although the victory at Fort Sumter catapulted P. G. T. Beauregard into the national spotlight as the Confederacy's first military hero, he retained his duties as commander of Charleston's defenses. Anticipating that U.S. forces might soon attempt to retake the fort, he ordered the redirection of the harbor's other guns to cover its entrance. He also surveyed the coast from Port Royal to Charleston to locate sites for new defensive works. In mid-May he wrote President Jefferson Davis that his preparations were almost complete. On May 28, the "Hero of Fort Sumter" was ordered to Richmond, the Confederacy's new capital, and Col. Richard H. Anderson replaced him.[2]

Work to return Fort Sumter to fighting trim continued over the following months. Major John Johnson's account, *The Defense of Charleston Harbor*, detailed the vast progress accomplished before he took over as Sumter's engineer on June

1 Jennifer Madeline Zoebelein, "Charleston's Forgotten General: Roswell Sabine Ripley," M.A. thesis, The College of Charleston and The Citadel, April 2008, 11-23; Compiled Service Records of Confederate General and Staff Offices, Roswell R. Ripley File, NA/RG 109; *OR* 1:28; Lee, *Civil War Journal*, 7; "Interior view of Fort Sumter, Charleston, S.C.," caption, Stereo View No. 30, University of South Carolina Digital Collections.

2 T. Harry Williams, *P. G. T. Beauregard: Napoleon in Gray* (Baton Rouge, 1954), 65; 1st Infantry Regiment, Richard H. Anderson File, NA/RG, 109, CSR, SC. Commissioned a brigadier general on July 19, 1861, Anderson was ordered to Pensacola the following month. Ripley then assumed department command.

10 in. Columbiad mounted as a mortar on the parade ground, behind it a hot shot furnace and the burned right flank barracks. *New York Historical Society*

21, 1863. The second-tier embrasures were converted to narrow loopholes, while the salient's three casemates were completed and guns mounted. On the rampart's "eastern angle" a brick and concrete traverse protected the barbette guns from ship enfilade fire. Stone, about 15 feet high, reinforced the magazines on the fort's exterior. To help defend the wharf a brick caponniére [sic], mounting "two casemate-howitzers," was constructed near the sally port. Both hot shot furnaces were restored, and the barracks and quarters were rebuilt, but at a reduced height. New additions included: a telegraph line that ran to James Island then to headquarters in Charleston, a gas works, bakery, forge, fire engine, "shoe-factory" and "a machine" to convert salt water into fresh.[3]

The Federals made no attempt to retake the fort in the summer of 1861, and from June 8 to July 15 Sumter transferred over 500 stands of grape, canister, and spherical shot, plus 3,700 pounds of powder and artillery implements, to other Charleston fortifications. By the end of September, the fort's armaments totaled 72

3 John Johnson, *The Defense of Charleston Harbor, Including Fort Sumter And The Adjacent Islands, 1863-1865* (reprint, Freeport, NY, 1970), 18-20; Barnes, "Fort Sumter: April 7, 1863," *Fort Sumter Historic Structure Reports*, 1950, 3-4.

CS civilian workers eating a meal on the parade ground, 1861. *Keith Brady Collection*

cannons, ranging from 24-pounders to 10-inch Columbiads, six 10-inch seacoast mortars, almost 44,000 pounds of powder, 18 "Harpers Ferry muskets," and 6,000 buck and ball cartridges.[4]

In late summer, Company B's Captain Hallonquist transferred, and Capt. Alfred M. Rhett assumed command of the company and fort. Fresh companies also arrived: Company C in July, followed by Company F in October. By November Fort Sumter housed the entire battalion, six companies totaling 560 men, and its

4 "Abstract of Ordnance & Ordnance Stores issue to Sundry posts during the 2nd Quarter 1861 from Fort Sumter S.C.," & "Return of Ordnance and Ordnance Stores received, issued and remaining on hand at Fort Sumter So. Ca. Commanded by Brig. Genl. R. S. Ripley during the quarter ending the 30, September, 1861," Ripley File, NA/RG 109, CSR.

Maj. Thomas Wagner

SCL

headquarters. Lieutenant Colonel William R. Calhoun commanded both the battalion and the fort, with Maj. Thomas W. Wagner second in command. In December 1861, the unit was expanded to 10 companies, and it was designated the 1st South Carolina Artillery Regiment Regulars in March 1862. Promotions followed: Calhoun rose to colonel, Wagner to lieutenant colonel, and Rhett to major. Six companies served at the fort while the remaining four defended other harbor fortifications.[5]

* * *

Only one U.S. ship, the USS *Niagara*, patrolled the waters outside Charleston Harbor pursuant to Lincoln's institution of a blockade of the coastlines of the seceded states. Though it had been a presence off the bar since May 11, with four channels to cover, the *Niagara* had little impact on restricting blockade runners entering and exiting the harbor. Though it continued to grow, the blockade operated with only limited effect into the summer. This would change once the U.S. Navy implemented operations, one of which specifically targeted South Carolina.

On November 6, 1861, an expedition of 15 U.S. warships mounting 148 cannon, under Flag Officer Samuel F. Du Pont, appeared off Port Royal Sound, South Carolina, an excellent harbor between Savannah and Charleston. The Federals intended to seize it and establish a base of operations against the Confederacy's southeast coast. An additional three dozen transports carrying more than 12,000 troops under Brig. Gen. Thomas W. Sherman accompanied the warships. The Navy attacked on November 7, and the fleet's firepower quickly overwhelmed the two sand and log forts mounting 43 guns at the sound's entrance. The Confederates abandoned the forts and retreated inland.

5 Field, *1st South Carolina Artillery*, 5-7.

Gen. R. E. Lee, commander Dept. of South Carolina and Florida, Nov. 1861-March 1862. *LOC*

Port Royal became the base for the U.S. Navy's South Atlantic Blockading Squadron, and Sherman's forces moved into Beaufort and onto Hilton Head Island and other points in the area. The general established the operations center for the U.S. Army's Department of the South on Hilton Head. Du Pont, whom Congress thanked for his role in the victory, was promoted to rear admiral in 1862. In Richmond, just two days before the battle, Gen. Robert E. Lee had been appointed commander of the new Department of South Carolina and Georgia.

Lee arrived in Charleston on November 6, 1861, learned of Du Pont's fleet, and promptly set out for Beaufort, though he did not arrive until after the battle. News of the defeat sent waves of panic rippling through Charleston and residents feared the Federals would advance immediately on the city. Many fled to the interior or sent valuables to safer locations. The Federals, however, were busy securing their bases and did not move up the coast.[6]

A month later, on the night of December 11, a non-military disaster struck the city. Fire broke out at the H. P. Russell & Co. sash and blind factory at Hassell and East Bay streets, not far from the Cooper River. A brisk wind picked up and quickly increased to gale force, driving flames, sparks, and cinders southwest across the city. Fire companies were sorely outmatched, and the supply of water was inadequate to the fire's size. With numerous fire units' members serving in the army, the firemen's rolls were depleted, and even though soldiers assisted in battling the blaze, it burned across the peninsula throughout the night. Grand and simple houses, businesses, churches, and every other building in its path, including Institute Hall, were consumed as the flames roared toward the Ashley River. The fire burned itself out the next day as the wind died, leaving a black smear across the peninsula. Five hundred forty acres of the city had gone up in smoke.[7]

6 Burton, *Siege of Charleston*, 69-76, 84; *OR* 6:309, 326.

7 Burton, *Siege of Charleston*, 80-84.

The Cooper River docks, untouched by the flames, continued to berth the blockade runners that slipped past the U.S. Navy vessels offshore. To create an impediment to entering the harbor, the Union scuttled 16 defunct whaling ships loaded with granite at the mouth of the Main Channel on December 19-20. This was referred to as the "Stone Fleet," and a month later 14 more hulls were sunk in Maffit's Channel off Sullivan's Island. Both efforts failed. Strong tides and fast currents quickly broke up and dispersed the wrecks, and the granite sank into the fine silt bottom.[8]

Lee determined that he was unable to defend every navigable inlet along South Carolina's 180-mile-plus coastline. Troops and heavy artillery were in short supply; he commanded just 13,100 men, many in incomplete defenses. He reported to Secretary of War Judah P. Benjamin that either the U.S. Navy or Army could easily defeat isolated coastal defenses. On February 18, 1862, Benjamin ordered him to "[w]ithdraw all forces from the islands . . . to the mainland [and] save artillery and munitions of war." Lee in turn wrote Ripley that he favored abandoning "all exposed points as far as possible within reach of the enemy's fleet . . . and taking interior positions where we can meet on more equal terms."[9]

Lee then established his headquarters on the Charleston and Savannah rail line at Coosawhatchie, about halfway between the two cities. Easy access to the telegraph allowed him to call for reinforcements should Federal forces attempt to cut rail lines. The previous December, he had divided the South Carolina coast into five military districts. The Second, headquartered in Charleston, included the city and Fort Sumter with General Ripley in command. On March 2, 1862, as Lee firmed his organizational and defensive plans, he received a telegram from Davis stating that he wished to see him, "with the least delay." The general left Charleston the next day, met with Davis, and on March 17 became the president's military advisor. When Gen. Joseph E. Johnston was wounded at the battle of Fair Oaks on June 1, Davis appointed Lee commander of the Army of Northern Virginia. In Charleston, Maj. Gen. John C. Pemberton, who had been Lee's second in command, rose to department commander and set up headquarters in the city on April 27.[10]

Federal forces had made no attempt against Charleston since Sumter's surrender over a year earlier, and day-to-day life within the fort had settled into a routine of stolid predictability. Soldiers drilled, guards walked the parapet, and officers issued orders and communicated with superiors. The garrison spent leisure

8 *OR* 6:43-44; *ORN* 12:421-424, 510-515.

9 *OR* 6:326, 390, 394.

10 Ibid., 6:312, 344-345, 400, 402.

time writing letters, playing cards, or fishing; everybody was eager to see some action. Lieutenant William Grimball of Company E told his mother on March 8: "At the Fort we are living in a perfect gale not of excitement, but of wind. . . . Now and then however there is excitement about an attack, which soon subsides, as we look sea ward and see day after day the same monotonous & apparently . . . motionless hulks far off on the horizon."[11]

Two incidents interrupted the monotony of fort life that spring. The first was when Pvt. Toristorio Jimpliss of Company H drowned on April 20. Six days later Company A's Pvt. William McGarity deserted only two months into his enlistment. Three days after he disappeared, the *Charleston Mercury* posted notice of a $30 reward for his arrest and delivery to the fort. McGarity was apprehended October 1 and returned to duty. Records indicate no punishment, but they do show that his pay and enlistment bounty were due at least through February 1863. Two years later and still in service, McGarity was captured March 12, 1865, at Fayetteville, North Carolina. On June 16, 1865, after swearing the oath of allegiance at Hart's Island in New York Harbor, he was released.[12]

*　*　*

General Pemberton followed Judah Benjamin's instructions to withdraw troops from the coastal defenses and ordered the removal of guns and equipment on Cole's Island in the mouth of the Stono River, as well as from Fort Pickens further upriver on Battery Island. The Stono marked the western edge of James Island, and the Ashley River and Charleston Harbor at its northern tip separated it from the city. Incomplete defenses across the middle of the island were only a few miles from Charleston. With Cole's and Battery islands abandoned, U.S. forces could move unopposed onto James Island, and if Fort Johnson on the opposite side of the island fell, its guns could be turned on the city.

An unexpected and greatly improbable consequence occurred on the night of May 12. One of the civilian vessels the Confederates hired to transfer materiel from these installations was the *Planter*, which mounted two guns. After loading four guns and other materiel from Coles Island, the ship docked at a city wharf. The white crew then disembarked, leaving the slave crew on board. Robert Smalls,

---

11 William Grimball to Mother, March 8, 1862, Grimball Family Papers, SHC, Transcript, FOSU Research File. All subsequent citations of the letters of William and Arthur Grimball are from the Grimball Family Papers, FOSU Research File, unless otherwise noted.

12 1st Artillery, NA/RG 109, CSR, SC. McGarity's records that state he was captured "Feb. 12, 1865" at Fayetteville. Federal troops occupied Fayetteville after the Confederates evacuated on March 10-11, 1865. It appears then that the "Feb. 12" entry was erroneous, and he was captured on March 12, 1865. OR 47/2, 791.

the pilot, seized the opportunity to execute an escape plan he and fellow crew members had devised. Under Small's direction, the ship left the dock about 3:00 a.m., picked up family members at another wharf, and steamed out into the harbor. The familiar vessel moved easily past Castle Pinckney, Fort Ripley, and Fort Sumter into the open ocean. As planned, the crew surrendered the *Planter* to a blockading ship, and continued to Port Royal. There Smalls reported to Rear Admiral Du Pont that the Confederates had withdrawn from the mouth of the Stono River and Battery Island. Du Pont dispatched ships to confirm the report.[13]

The *Planter* incident was only one of a number of events in April and May that gave Pemberton headaches. In 1861, Confederate troops from several seceded states had been called to Virginia to defend against a Union invasion. A year later, steady demands for more units to defend Richmond and other threatened locations continued to reach Pemberton's desk. Orders called for him to send four infantry regiments to Corinth, Mississippi, in the aftermath of the bloody battle at Shiloh, followed by a directive for Brig. Gen. Maxcy Gregg's Brigade to leave for Virginia to help defend Richmond against the Union's Army of the Potomac, which was advancing up the peninsula east of Richmond.

As multiple units left Pemberton's command, U.S. forces moved from Port Royal and established batteries, including two with rifled guns, below Fort Pulaski. On April 10-11, 1862, after a 30-hour bombardment, the fort and garrison surrendered. The Federals did not advance on Savannah, a hundred miles from Charleston, but the city was effectively blockaded by the Union troops in Pulaski and U.S. ships patrolling the area waters. If the Confederate government had not recognized the threat posed by the Federals in South Carolina and Georgia before, it certainly did now.

President Davis issued a proclamation on May 1, 1862 that suspended the writ of habeas corpus and established martial law on South Carolina's coast from the Santee River to the South Edisto River. The same day, Governor Pickens's declaration of martial law broadened the scope by proclaiming martial law in and over Charleston, 10 miles beyond the city limits, and its adjacent islands. Pemberton was charged with enforcing these strictures and was further authorized to "impress labor of all kinds for public works and defense" from the Santee to the Savannah rivers, as though martial law had been established there as well.[14]

*   *   *

---

13 Burton, *The Siege of Charleston*, 94-97.

14 *OR* 6:470, 481-482, 489, 491-492.

Robert Smalls and the *Planter, Harper's Weekly,* June 14, 1862. *FOSU*

The war had already lasted longer than anticipated, and both North and South recruited, organized, and equipped burgeoning numbers of men and materiel for their armies and navies. While the overall number of troops fluctuated in the Department of South Carolina and Georgia throughout 1862, the Second Military District, which included Charleston and Fort Sumter, continued to maintain a large number of troops and artillery. The critical nature of the Charleston area was reflected in the fact that of all the reallocations of troops to other parts of the South, the number of companies in Fort Sumter's garrison never fell below five and was frequently higher until the summer of 1863. The establishment of martial law eased Pemberton's struggle to defend such a large geographic area with diminishing numbers of troops. But he had other problems. The governor grew increasingly chafed about his decisions. Pickens and other political leaders circulated a rumor that Pemberton might order Charleston's evacuation. This news reached Davis and spawned General Lee's blunt and emphatic communication to Pemberton on May 29, 1862: Savannah and Charleston must be defended "to the last extremity," especially the latter, whose loss "would cut us off almost entirely from communication with the rest of the world, and close the only channel through which we can expect to get supplies from abroad." Both cities required "the most perfect state of defense . . . even if that meant fighting . . . street by street and house by house." [15]

On May 20, Pemberton received a jarring letter from James Chesnut, head of the state's Department of the Military. Chesnut reported that "several worthy and distinguished . . . Charlestonians" had informed him that "disaffection prevails in a large portion" of Sumter's garrison, "extending to . . . threats of mutiny and refusal to fire against the enemy." Pemberton acknowledged his awareness of the issue and noted that he had directed General Ripley to investigate "the reliability of similar reports current in this city." He further speculated "that there are disaffected individuals among the rank and file of Fort Sumter as in most corps in Confederate service," but he did not think it widespread. He was certain that the fort's officers had "confidence in the courage, patriotism, and discipline of the men."

Three weeks later on June 12, Colonel Calhoun, Sumter's commander, alerted Pemberton to "reports of ill will" in the garrison. His officers were "aware of the rumors and the seditious language by one or two of the men, but still [had] confidence in the loyalty, courage, and fidelity of their commands." And if it were decided to "make any change in the garrison" he requested that his regiment "be sent into the field" with as many companies as possible. Ultimately, the unit continued to serve in the defenses of Charleston, and the loyalty issue faded away. [16]

Pemberton also had problems with Ripley, the Second District commander. Dissatisfied and "not in harmony with those above and below him," Ripley had requested a transfer. On May 24, he received orders to accompany two regiments to Richmond, and Brig. Gen. Hugh W. Mercer was ordered to bring two Georgia regiments to Charleston and take command of the district. [17]

15 Ibid., 486, 498, 523-524, 529, 736.

16 *OR* 6:508, 517-518, 562-563.

17 Ibid., 503-504, 519, 521.

Unrest among the senior staff in Charleston scarcely affected the monotony and routine of the men's lives in the fort. Musket practice and regular drills and live firing of various pieces of the fort's artillery kept the men focused. [18]

After more than a year, Charlestonians had become accustomed to the presence of the headquarters of both the Department of South Carolina and Georgia and the Second District there. The military moved throughout the city and rented office space and warehouses for its ordnance, commissary, medical, and quartermaster operations. It also set up military hospitals. With martial law in effect, the provost marshal operated two offices, one military and the other civilian. Colonel Johnson Hagood of the 1st South Carolina Infantry served as provost marshal, and among other duties he enforced prohibition of "distillation of spirituous liquors" and the closure of distilleries. The sale of "spirituous liquors" also was prohibited, and establishments that did so faced closure. A court martial would determine the punishment to be meted out to anyone violating this prohibition.

The offices also issued passes to military and civilians alike. Many residents, young single women included, used these passes through spring and early summer to visit dozens of camps both in and outside the city. Patriotic ladies of Charleston, like other southern women, supported the cause by forming societies to raise money, sew for the troops, and care for those in hospitals. Organizations such as the Soldiers' Relief Association, the Ladies Auxiliary Christian Association, and the Ladies' Clothing Association sprang up in Charleston even before the firing on Sumter a year earlier. Their goal was to provide soldiers what the army didn't. When the South Carolina Executive Council appropriated $300,000 in February of 1862 to build a gunboat to be named the CSS *Chicora*, Miss Sue L. Gelzer wrote the *Charleston Daily Courier* suggesting that the city's women follow the example of those in New Orleans, who had raised money to construct a gunboat. South Carolina ladies responded by sponsoring numerous activities to generate funds. Between April 30 and May 3, "Johnson's New Orleans Minstrels Burlesque Opera Troupe and Brass Band" performed four concerts at Hibernian Hall. The hall also hosted a "Ladies Fair" in May. General admission was 25 cents and raffle tickets for donated items sold for a dollar each. By the end of the campaign, the ladies had raised $25,000 toward the $200,000 needed for the boat's construction. The Confederate Navy had originally planned to christen it the *Charleston*, but the ladies suggested that the name be changed to the *Palmetto State*. The contract for building the warship went to Marsh and Sons shipyard at the foot of Market Street on the Cooper River. About six weeks later the Eason Shipyard, just a few blocks

18 "Voucher No. 10," Ripley File, NA/RG, 109, CSR, SC.

away, began construction on the *Chicora* (launched in August); the CSS *Palmetto State* followed in September.[19]

*   *   *

On June 2, 1862, nearly three weeks after Robert Smalls reported the troop withdrawals from the Stono, Maj. Gen. David Hunter, who had replaced Thomas Sherman as the Department of the South's commander, launched an expedition against Charleston. By the 9th two small divisions under the command of Brig. Gens. Isaac Stevens and Horatio Wright were encamped along the banks of the Stono on James, Battery, and Sol Legare islands. Hunter had about 7,000 men, plus Du Pont's warships, only 8 miles as the crow flies from Charleston.

Nearby Confederates immediately reported the Union incursion. Pemberton, who had about 4,400 troops on James Island, began devising plans to drive the Federals away from Charleston. Skirmishing occurred on June 3 and 10, and an 8-inch Columbiad in the "Tower Battery," the closest Confederate fortification, fired at the Federal camps.

On June 12 Hunter departed James Island and returned to Hilton Head, leaving Brig. Gen. Henry Benham in command with orders to avoid a general engagement and only provide security to the camps. Benham considered harassing fire from the Tower Battery as a threat and immediately ordered Stevens and Wright to prepare an attack on it for dawn on June 16. Thus unfolded the battle of Secessionville, a resounding defeat for the Union troops. The Federals sustained 700 casualties out of 4,500 troops engaged, while the Confederates lost around 150 out of about 2,000. Word of the victory spread quickly to Charleston. Sorrow tempered the general elation, though, because many of the casualties were Charleston's sons. Federals troops withdrew and returned to Hilton Head and by July 7, none remained. Whatever excitement Fort Sumter's garrison felt during the battle on James Island dissipated quickly and monotonous life returned inside the fort and out. At the end of August, Grimball lamented the dull duty and routine to his sister Elizabeth. "[G]arrison life presents almost nothing which would interest an outsider," he told her. "The same number of roll calls & drills, the same amount [of] action and inaction . . . each day [repeated] every other." [20]

---

19 Articles from the *Charleston Courier*: "Soldiers Relief Association" and "The Gunboat to be built and equipped by the patriotic Women of South Carolina" (Mar. 3, 1862), "Johnson's New Orleans Minstrels" (Apr. 30, 1862), and "The Ladies of Charleston" (May 1, 1862); Burton, *The Siege of Charleston*, 125-126.

20 Patrick Brennan, *Secessionville: Assault on Charleston* (Campbell, CA, 1996) 33, 62-63, 75-86, 119, 121-123, 125-137, 277-278, 291; *OR* 14:529.

On the other hand, he described in uncharacteristic detail an event that shattered the monotony. Corporal George H. Berger of Company E had been convicted of "attempting to desert to the fleet and . . . of trying to seduce others of his comrades to join him." As the regiment's junior officer, Grimball had the disagreeable duty of commanding the firing squad of thirteen privates and a corporal. "[S]o much practicing of funeral dirges and funeral marching by the band and men" would have surprised a visitor. He was drilling the squad in one corner of the parade ground "as if we were preparing for a show, and not for a reality." Berger's execution was conducted on the beach about a mile from Fort Moultrie. The troops were drawn up in a hollow square of three sides, and in the center of the open side was fixed a post to which the would-be deserter was tied. It was over in a matter of minutes. Grimball confessed he did not want to witness such a sight very often.[21]

*   *   *

Governor Pickens's disdain for John Pemberton had slowly increased and despite the victory at Secessionville, he used political intrigue to arrange the general's removal as departmental commander. On September 17, 1862, Pemberton was ordered to Richmond, promoted to lieutenant general, and given command of the Department of Mississippi and Eastern Louisiana. A new Department of South Carolina and Georgia commander and familiar face returned to Charleston when P. G. T. Beauregard arrived in the city on September 24. Three days later the general's command was expanded to include East Florida, and in October it was designated the Department of South Carolina, Georgia, and Florida. Beauregard quickly issued a statement in which he underscored the importance of Charleston and Savannah. His duties, he wrote, might require defending two of the "most important cities in the Confederate States" against the concerted Federal efforts. He would "rely upon the ardent patriotism, the intelligence, and unconquerable spirit of his officers and men" to succeed. To do this, however, "it is essential that all shall yield implicit obedience to any orders emanating from superior authority."[22]

Beauregard inspected his command in early October. At Fort Sumter he found a garrison of about 350 men and 84 cannon: 67 smoothbores, 17 rifled and banded guns (previously smoothbore), and seven 10-inch mortars. Within the fort, the men yearned for action through the tiresome routine of drill and general duties. Lieutenant Grimball told his mother, who had moved to Spartanburg from the coast: "We are living down here as usual, informed every week that, there will

21 William Grimball to Sister, Aug. 29, 1862.

22 *OR* 14:613, 601, 608–609, 630.

be [an] attack within the next ten days, which . . . period has hither to passed in the same unbroken quiet of the past. Should this attack ever come it will be a tremendous affair plainly, I should think, to be heard in Spartanburg, and one historical from its greatness."

On October 22, he noted: "The cry of wolf has been so often echoed that it is hard to believe it now other than an imaginative wolf a quiet gentle little animal that intends no harm and won[']t hurt us." In a letter to his sister Elizabeth, he reported that everything at Fort Sumter was as "usual [with] work & preparation increasing daily." He entertained no doubts about the fort's formidable defenses. "[W]e can blow any thing wooden out of the water," and even ironclads "will be hammered right me[r]rily" and "tested to their utmost." On the last day of October, the routine was broken by a little pomp and a bit of fun. "We had a grand Review of the whole garrison here last Thursday by Gen. Ripley in person," Grimball wrote. "Mrs. Ripley and himself brought down a large number of Ladies. . . . After the parade, there was a Blockade luncheon, and two guns were fired of[f] by two different Ladies, and then the whole tribe left, expressing themselves so, oh, so pleased with Fort Sumter and its occupants." Several weeks later on December 3, he noted:

> We had quite an alarm some nights ago. Colonel [Lawrence M.] Keitt [20th SC Infantry] gave a dinner on Sullivans Island, at which the big bugs got pretty mellow so after it they amused themselves about one o'clock at night with firing all around the harbor on the Island[.] I understand there was great excitement in the city men & women in their respective shirts & shifts, all expecting the Yankees & rushing to the wharves.[23]

*   *   *

The first genuine challenge Beauregard faced had simmered for more than a year before coming to a boil and attracting the notice of the War Department in Richmond. It had consequences for both the officers involved and the fort's command structure. During the April 1861 bombardment, an incident occurred between two of Ripley's officers at Fort Moultrie, Capt. (now Col.) William R. Calhoun and Lt. (now Maj.) Alfred M. Rhett. Ripley had ordered Calhoun, a member of his staff, to redirect the fire of some of Rhett's guns. Instead of passing the order to the lieutenant, Calhoun redirected the guns himself. Rhett was offended that Calhoun had ignored the chain of command. Their relationship

---

23 *OR* 14:619-621; Grimball to Mother, Oct. 6 and 22, 1862, Grimball to Sister, Dec. 3, 1862, and to unknown, letter fragment circa Oct. 31, 1862.

deteriorated from there. In the early summer of 1862, they clashed over the unit's recent recruiting efforts and the quality of men enlisted.

In July Calhoun became ill, and while he was on furlough Rhett was promoted to lieutenant colonel. A month later, Calhoun submitted his resignation citing continuing poor health, but before that, on August 7, Rhett in conversation with other officers questioned Calhoun's—whom he referred to as a "damned puppy"— ability to command despite his West Point training. Upon hearing this, Calhoun challenged Rhett to a duel. Although banned in South Carolina since 1812, dueling between gentlemen persisted. At 5:00 p.m. on September 5, outside the city limits, Calhoun missed his target, but Rhett's shot delivered a mortal wound and Calhoun died a few hours later. Following a civilian inquest, Rhett was arrested and bound over for trial.

The incident stirred wide discussion in Charleston. Emma Holmes's diary notes that the feud was bitter but said the parties would have settled the affair after the war had it not been for words between Rhett and Captain Arnoldus Vanderhorst about Calhoun's character. Rhett and Vanderhorst had also dueled but inflicted no damage on each other, perhaps because:

> He [Rhett] had no personal issue with V[anderhorst] with whose family he is connected by his sister's marriage, but all his insolence and arrogance have been directed against Calhoun. . . . The first duel, however, brought on the second, which terminated so fatally. . . . Col. Calhoun [had] known, as well as many others, for some time past, that Rhett [had] been practicing constantly with a pistol for the express purpose of killing him.

Holmes also stated that the incident polarized elite families in the city, and family connections among these played a large role in assigning blame. She added on September 6, "The Rhetts have been hitherto hated enough, now the name is almost execrated—the public are unanimous against him. Duelling [sic] is expressly against the rules of war & the penalty very severe, and it is universally hoped that he will be arrested, court-martialed and broken of his commission."

On February 12, 1863, a Charleston grand jury returned a "no bill" of indictment against Rhett on the charge of murder, and he ultimately walked free of civilian charges. In Rhett's absence, Maj. Joseph A. Yates assumed command of the regiment and the fort. Unhappy with this turn of events, Rhett requested a military investigation, and though the official court of inquiry pronounced the duel fair and within the rules of the (outlawed) civilian code of honor, it recommended that proceedings be initiated against Rhett for violating the 25th Article of War, which forbade duels. General Beauregard settled the matter, declaring in General

Order No. 19, dated January 30, 1863, that the charges had been dropped. Rhett's military records indicate he was appointed colonel of the 1st South Carolina Artillery on December 11, 1862, with the promotion backdated to September 5, 1862, the day he killed his commanding officer.[24]

Many of the men of the Fort Sumter garrison, had likely formed opinions about the incident and the character of their officers, but by the middle of December, the thoughts the men at the fort had turned toward the approach of Christmas and plans were made to lighten the mood within the fort.

Grimball wrote his brother Harry, a Citadel cadet, on December 15: "We had as you heard quite a ball at the Fort. There were I suppose over a hundred guests . . . too many by far for the small space we had to entertain them in." At 2:00 p.m. a ten-gun salute was fired in honor of the arrival of Gen. Beauregard, his staff, and a "large number of ladies." Then the garrison passed by Beauregard and his staff in review. "The men did well," and everyone "was loud in their praises of the regiment, which of course pleased the officers highly."

Adjourning to the "dancing rooms" [the officers' upper gallery], the regimental band commenced to play, and the ball began. "Fancy dancing was most in vogue . . . [and] Mrs. Sam Ferguson . . . must be considered the belle of the evening. At one time, her hair tumbled down. She did not mend it, but went galloping around with her locks streaming behind her. . . . I tried the fancy dances & got on tolerably well . . ." About 8:00 p.m. "the supper room was opened which was festooned with flags," and everyone "made a rush for something to eat and I am afraid many were disappointed, for not expecting so many people the Committee had only prepared a moderate supper, which was very soon gobbled up. . ." At 9:00 p.m. everyone left and the fort and, everything "assumed the quiet and dignity suitable to an armed fortress of the Confederate states."[25]

---

24 Field, *1st South Carolina Artillery*, 7-8; Marszalek, *Holmes Diary*, 196.

25 William to brother (Harry), Dec. 15, 1862. Grimball Family Papers, FOSU Research File.

Chapter 6

Worthy of Its High Reputation

January–April 1863

To the surprise of some of its officers, controversial Col. Alfred Rhett assumed command of Fort Sumter in late January 1863. On January 12, Lt. Grimball wrote: "The public feeling so expressive immediately . . . after his duel with Col. Calhoun seems to have died out . . . [which Rhett] shrewdly waited for . . . before pushing himself in to the position vacated by the death of his antagonist."[1]

Several days later, Lt. Col. Alfred Roman of Beauregard's staff inspected the fort and was effusively pleased that the "eyes of the Confederacy were" fixed upon this "bulwark of our eastern defenses," which was "worthy of its high reputation." Hardly anyone visited the fortification, officially or otherwise, without pronouncing it "a model of order and good management, the best school of discipline and military bearing and held by the first and most efficient garrison of the South." The gallant Rhett and his "able and gentlemanly officers," with their proverbial "zeal, endurance and regularity of service," knew well what the country expected of them, and the troops presented a splendid appearance. "I doubt whether any corps in the old United States Army ever looked as well." The weather had prevented infantry and artillery practice, but as a previous witness to these drills, Roman gushed that "no corps in our Army, except perhaps the Fort Moultrie regiment, would compare with any advantage to the Fort Sumter garrison." He continued: "The regularity and mechanical precision of their manual of arms is remarkable; their five hundred muskets, their thousand hands, move as if one musket only and

1 Grimball to Mother, Jan. 12, 1863.

one pair of hands were put in motion. In that respect and in many others regarding important details of the service the seven companies of the First South Carolina Artillery now at Fort Sumter have no rivals."

Roman reported a six-month supply of provisions at Sumter, with beef issued daily. In a missive to his mother, Grimball noted that the officers' mess consisted chiefly of beef and pea soup and cost him $30 a month; there was no bread or butter. "It is only the strictest attention to my money matters which enable me to make both ends meet," he wrote. He also observed that the men's morale was high, but everyone nevertheless appreciated a break from military routine. Grimball continued: "It has been very gay among the officers of the troops stationed around the harbor lately. Capt[.] [Henry S.] Farley of our Regiment had a pleasant party at Castle Pinckney about a week ago, and three days ago, there was one at Fort Pemberton. . . . On Wednesday there is to be a ball in Charleston given by twenty young men . . . who each subscribed fifty Dollars. . . . I am invited specially but am uncertain whether I will be allowed to go."

In the last two days of January 1863, the Sumter garrison helped defend against one of two threats against the city of Charleston. Nine months earlier, the Confederates had evacuated the Stono River defenses below Fort Pemberton and placed obstructions in the river off the fort and Battery Island. These proved no deterrent to U.S. warships patrolling the river, which stayed out of range of Pemberton's guns. One of the vessels, the USS *Isaac Smith*, boldly moved up and down the Stono, shelling C.S. positions and any troops who showed themselves. Confederates on James and Johns Islands monitored the *Smith*'s movements and devised an attack plan. Lieutenant Colonel Yates, second in command of the 1st South Carolina Artillery and Fort Sumter, was selected to execute it.

Yates departed the fort with Companies D and I on January 28. Joined by several artillery, infantry, and cavalry units, the contingent took up concealed positions on the two islands. Two days later, around 4:30 p.m., the *Isaac Smith* steamed upriver past masked batteries and concealed sharpshooters. After anchoring, the ship immediately drew fire from both banks, returned fire, and retreated downriver. With her "steam and chimney" disabled from three artillery rounds, the warship surrendered with casualties of 25 killed or wounded. The Confederates lost one mortally wounded cannoneer.

The Confederates towed the *Smith* up the Stono and into Wappoo Cut to the Ashley River, and then to Charleston, where Yates and his command received a hero's welcome. In March, while on detached service in Georgetown, South Carolina, a member of Beauregard's staff presented the sword of the *Isaac Smith*'s commander to Yates on the general's behalf. The Southerners renamed the repaired warship the CSS *Stono*. Later that year it was refitted as a blockade runner, and its

Col. Alfred M. Rhett, 1st SC Artillery Regiment Regulars. *University of South Carolina Libraries*

8-inch guns and 30-pounder Parrott Rifle joined the harbor's defenses. On its first venture out, the ship ran aground near Fort Moultrie, and the Confederates eventually burned it.[2]

The same night as the action on the Stono, the CSS *Chicora* and CSS *Palmetto State* steamed toward the mouth of the harbor about 11:00 p.m., hoping to disrupt the blockade at the harbor's entrance. With deep drafts and weak engines, neither vessel was seaworthy, and both had trouble operating in the strong outgoing tidal current. They anchored close to Fort Sumter and awaited the flood tide before moving against the nine enemy warships near the entrance.

Around 5:00 a.m. on January 31, the pale, bluish-gray gunboats, coated in grease to help deflect artillery rounds, sailed into the heavy haze and surprised the Federals. The *Palmetto State* rammed a vessel and sent a round into its boiler. Though the warship surrendered, it escaped and limped back to Port Royal. The *Chicora* fired into a ship that disappeared into the haze, and then shelled another, temporarily disabling it and killing 20 crew members and wounding many more. The captain struck his colors to signal surrender but also escaped; *Chicora*'s engines couldn't power a pursuit. The Confederate gunboats engaged four more Union ships with stronger engines that easily outdistanced them. At 7:30 a.m., Flag Officer D. C. Ingraham on the *Palmetto State* ordered his vessels to disengage, "leaving the partially crippled and fleeing enemy fleet about seven miles clear of the bar." As they returned, Fort Sumter and other fortifications fired salutes in their honor. When news of the victory reached the city, it stirred excitement "almost equal to the day of the Battle of Fort Sumter."

Beauregard and Ingraham immediately proclaimed the blockade broken. The HMS *Petrel*, in the harbor at the time, carried Charleston's British consul 5 miles beyond the U.S. blockade's usual position. Even using spy glasses, the consul

2 *OR* 14:199-204, 756, 802-804; Grimball to Mother, Jan. 12, 1863; "A Sword of Honor," *Charleston Courier*, Mar. 14, 1863.

spotted no other ship. General Ripley, who escorted the French and Spanish consuls out of Charleston, reported the same. The British ship's captain and the diplomats consulted, and while no official announcement was issued, they agreed that the blockade "was legally raised as claimed by the proclamation." International law prohibited its reestablishment for 30 days, allowing blockade runners free passage into and out of the harbor. Union Admiral Du Pont disagreed, declaring the blockade had not been broken, and by the end of the day, U.S. warships began to reappear.[3]

Throughout the war, activity within the city and harbor defenses exemplified ongoing adaptations to current conditions. Military engineers, officers, soldiers, civilian mechanics, and laborers worked ceaselessly to improve existing fortifications, construct new ones, reposition armaments, and position obstructions in the channels. Engineering work on harbor obstructions commenced in 1862. Crews also placed a boom of heavy timbers, weighted and coupled with iron, at the harbor's mouth between Sumter and Moultrie. Strong tidal currents and storms, however, twice broke apart the obstruction and destroyed whole sections of it. In 1863 crews devised a stronger barrier stretching between the forts using some of the surviving sections, a rope obstruction, and beer barrels as floats. Along the barrier, 15-foot sections of paired ropes floated freely to foul propellers and rudders. The obstruction on the Sumter end had a 300-yard opening in it. The Confederates maintained this obstruction and the one inside the harbor until the city's evacuation in February 1865. The obstructions would play an important role in defending the city against Union ironclads.[4]

Confident of an eventual naval attack, Beauregard had 150 heavy guns and mortars mounted in the harbor's defenses. At Sumter and on Morris and Sullivan's Islands, 77 of these were trained on the Main Channel. The channel's navigational lights had long been extinguished and its buoys removed. Aiming markers, which the fortifications along the channel used to range their guns, replaced them. The guns close to the water, like those in Fort Sumter's first-tier casemates, could employ ricochet fire to skip cannonballs across the water and strike targeted ships

---

3 *OR* 14:204-209; Burton, *Siege of Charleston*, 129.

4 Burton, *Siege of Charleston*, 132, 268-269; Johnson, *Defense of Charleston Harbor*, 29-30. Starting about 700 yards in front of Fort Ripley, crews drove a 2,000-yard-long double row of pine pilings running north into the bottom. A three-quarter mile opening off Fort Johnson served as the Main Channel. The Southerners painstakingly maintained the line, constantly repairing logs that continually decayed or broke off during storms. It proved an effective impediment until Charleston's evacuation.

at or near waterline. The gun crews, knowing that ships entering the harbor were confined to the channel, confidently awaited the inevitable assault.[5]

*   *   *

The arrival of the USS *New Ironsides* in Port Royal on January 18 heralded a notable change in naval strategy against Charleston. The 4,120-ton "broadside ironclad" frigate was 230 feet long, and its 11-inch-thick oak sides increased to 16 inches at the waterline. Two layers of iron plates 7 inches thick covered the oak amidships for 170 feet on both the port and starboard sides. Three inches of oak overlaid by an inch of iron plating comprised the deck. The *New Ironsides* mounted two 8-inch Parrotts, one each fore and aft on the deck, and on the gun deck below seven 11-inch smoothbore Dahlgrens were arrayed on both sides. The latter gun's heaviest round was a 166-pound solid cast iron ball. The warship thus was capable of delivering a 1,162-pound broadside, the most powerful in the U.S. Navy.[6]

In August 1861, Gustavus Fox, who had led the failed Fort Sumter relief expedition the previous April, had taken office as assistant secretary of the Navy. Both Secretary of the Navy Gideon Welles and President Lincoln shared Fox's longstanding desire to take Charleston with naval forces. For Fox and Welles, seizing the cradle of secession using ironclads would earn the Navy laurels and help justify the extreme expense of building these new warships. They considered seizing Charleston a moral imperative as well as one weighted with political and symbolic significance. Though unconvinced of the ironclads' ability to overwhelm Charleston's formidable defenses, Du Pont began planning the attack because his superiors wanted the birthplace of treason captured.

In 1863, Welles ordered seven of the Navy's 10 new *Passaic*-class monitors to Port Royal to join the *New Ironsides*. Based upon the design of the USS *Monitor*, these vessels were larger, more heavily armed, and more thickly armored. To test the new monitors' capabilities against fortifications, Du Pont ordered the USS *Montauk* and several smaller wooden warships to engage Fort McAllister. The earthen fort's eight guns guarded the Ogeechee River below Savannah. On January 27 and February 1, the monitor and fort engaged for four hours, inflicting only minor damage on each other.

Du Pont thus questioned the advantage of using the monitors against Charleston. After the second engagement at McAllister, he asked a friend, "[I]f one ironclad cannot take eight guns, how are five to take 147 in Charleston harbor?" His concerns seemed genuine when the USS *Passaic*, USS *Patapsco*,

5 *OR* 14:605-606.

6 *ORN* 13:518; William Roberts, *USS* New Ironsides *In The Civil War* (Annapolis, MD, 1999), 11, 14.

and USS *Nahant* engaged the fort, with neither side sustaining any real damage. Beyond his doubts about their effectiveness, Du Pont also worried about their general seaworthiness.[7]

Before the end of March, the *New Ironsides*, seven monitors, and the ironclad USS *Keokuk*, carrying a total of 32 heavy guns, would be anchored in Port Royal sound. Five monitors, the *Catskill*, *Montauk*, *Weehawken*, *Nahant*, and *Nantucket*, each mounted a 15- and 11-inch Dahlgrens in their turrets. The 15-inch Dahlgrens fired the heaviest round, a 440-lb solid shot. The *Patapsco* and *Passaic* each carried an 11-inch Dahlgren and an 8-inch Parrott rifle. The ironclad *Keokuk* had an 11-inch Dahlgren in each of its two fixed turrets. The *New Ironsides* carried the remaining 16 guns.[8]

Welles and Fox wanted nothing less than for the squadron to reduce Fort Sumter and capture Charleston. Du Pont, however, favored a joint operation with the Army. Brigadier General Truman Seymour of Hunter's command had been a captain in Fort Sumter in April 1861 and harbored a burning desire to recapture the fort. After Sumter's surrender, Seymour served in the Army of the Potomac and transferred to the Department of the South in November 1862. Eagerly compiling information on Charleston's defenses, he proposed that the Army take Morris Island and station rifled artillery at Cummings Point. He believed that these guns, along with the Navy's, would enable the squadron to fight its way into the harbor and take the city.

The War Department ordered Maj. Gen. John G. Foster, another former member of the April 1861 Sumter garrison, to support the operation, and he brought 10,000 men with him from North Carolina. Like Seymour, Foster longed to see the U.S. flag flying again over the fort. Expanding on Seymour's plan, he proposed a combined operation of the warships and land-based rifled artillery. After the guns mounted in breaching batteries on Morris and Sullivan's Islands reduced Fort Sumter, the ships could move in and capture Charleston. Hunter rejected the plan and told Foster the Navy would proceed alone. Disgusted, Foster returned to North Carolina without his troops.[9]

On the afternoon of April 5, the fleet, which included five wooden warships, arrived off the Main Channel's entrance to Charleston Harbor. Admiral Du Pont planned an attack for the next day, but haze obscured the view, so he delayed it until

---

7 Gideon Welles, *The Diary of Gideon Welles, Secretary of the Navy Under Lincoln and Johnson*, 3 vols. (Boston, 1911), 1:236-237; Stephen R. Wise, *Gate of Hell: The Campaign for Charleston Harbor, 1863* (Columbia, SC, 1994), 25-26.

8 *ORN* 13:27.

9 Wise, *Gate of Hell*, 26-27.

the 7th. To prepare the ships for the engagement, crews spread tallow an inch thick on the ironclad frigate, monitors, and ironclad's exteriors, and stacked sandbags on decks to deflect rounds and absorb shock. They also overlaid the deck of Du Pont's flagship, *New Ironsides*, with untanned hides covered by sandbags. Between decks, sandbag barricades stacked 3 feet deep added protection against raking fire. All told, 6,000 sandbags shielded the ship.

The rear admiral's battle plan focused solely on Sumter and made no reference to Charleston. He ordered the squadron to ignore Morris and Sullivan's Islands' fortifications and position themselves 600-800 yards off Fort Sumter's right face, "firing low and aiming at the center embrasure." His instructions prescribed that "[a]fter the reduction of Fort Sumter . . . the next point of attack [would probably] be the batteries on Morris Island." By his order the five wooden warships would participate in this phase of the attack.

It is unclear why Du Pont settled on this plan; possibly he hoped for support from Hunter. But if he successfully seized Fort Sumter and Morris Island, he could join forces with the Army and move on Charleston. Hunter had accompanied the Navy flotilla on Army transports with 10,000 troops and some siege guns but planned no significant participation in the attack and wanted to be in position to occupy Charleston if the naval assault forced the city's surrender. Although he landed a brigade on Folly Island and mounted two masked guns trained on Morris Island across Light House Inlet, they remained silent throughout the engagement.[10]

Favorable conditions—clear weather, high tide, and calm water—prevailed at noon on April 7, when the nine ships weighed anchor and, compelled by the narrow channel, began moving single file toward Sumter. Du Pont had taken the tides into consideration while planning the attack and timed his movement to coincide with an outgoing tide, thereby ensuring that any disabled ship would drift away from the harbor rather than risk being pushed by the incoming tide and captured. The USS *Weehawken* led the way, followed by the USS *Passaic*, USS *Montauk*, USS *Patapsco*, USS *New Ironsides*, USS *Catskill*, USS *Nantucket*, USS *Nahant*, and USS *Keokuk*. A wooden torpedo raft designed to sweep for mines between Sumter and Moultrie was attached to the *Weehawken*'s bow, allowing crew members to hook and draw mines onto the raft's deck and disarm them. Though potentially useful, the unwieldy raft didn't attach securely to the ship and was actually more of a detriment to the monitor's operation than it was protection against torpedoes. At some point during the battle, the crew jettisoned the bothersome raft and it drifted onto Morris Island.[11]

10 Wise, *Gate of Hell*, 28-29; Roberts, USS New Ironsides, 47, 51; *ORN* 14:8-9, 26.

11 *ORN* 14:3-112.

The Confederate forts and batteries received word in ample time to prepare for the impending engagement. On April 11, the *Mercury* revealed that "just as the officers [at Sumter] had seated themselves for dinner," the fort's commandant learned of the fleet's advance. Signal Corps Pvt. Arthur Grimball, who served with his brother William, informed their brother Berkley on April 14: "[W]e were at dinner and the news came from the Ramparts that the fleet were edgeing [sic] in." After determining that the warships were about 4 miles below Morris Island, Rhett wired Beauregard that "the Turrets are coming," whereupon he and his officers returned to the mess to complete their meal.

Colonel Rhett's official report states that at 2:30 p.m. "the long roll was beaten and every disposition made for action." The officers and men, uniformed as if on dress parade, assumed their positions with cheers. About 25 minutes later as the band played "the national air" from the parapet, the defenders hoisted the state flag and regimental colors at opposite ends of the gorge. The first national flag flew on the main staff at the salient angle. According to Grimball, "[W]e fired a salute of thirteen Guns[,] dressed the fort in flags, the band playing Dixie." This may have been the only formal opening of a combat action in the entire war.[12]

With Morris Island to its left, the squadron steamed up the channel. Once past Battery Wagner and the Cummings Point Battery, Fort Sumter loomed less than a mile away. But the guns of both sides remained silent. At 2:50 p.m., Fort Moultrie fired the battle's first round, at the out-of-range *Weehawken*.[13]

As the *Weehawken* drew closer to Sumter, an explosion aside its bow threw up a large column of water. The captain, thinking a torpedo had detonated—it was actually a shell exploding next to the ship—ordered the *Weehawken* to veer away. The monitor's sudden course change, however, temporarily confused the line of battle. And as the tide had begun to ebb, the *New Ironsides* encountered difficult maneuvering in its rapid flow out of the harbor. Du Pont ordered his flagship to drop anchor and signaled the trailing warships to move up and open fire on Fort Sumter's right face. The frigate attempted to join the fight, but once again it couldn't overcome the tide and dropped anchor, this time directly over a submerged torpedo containing 2,000 pounds of powder. Confederates on Morris Island repeatedly tried to trigger the explosive's electric ignition system, but the torpedo consistently failed to detonate. (After the battle, the Southerners discovered that a wagon wheel

---

12 "Notes of the Fight of the 7th at Fort Sumter," *Charleston Mercury*, Apr. 11, 1863; Arthur Grimball to Father, April 10, 1863, and to Brother (Berkley), Apr. 14, 1863; Telegrams Sent 1863-64, War Dept. Confederate Records, Dept. of SC, GA & FL, NA/RG 109.

13 *ORN* 14:6, 98; Burton, *Siege of Charleston*, 137.

USS *New Ironsides* and monitors in action, *The Illustrated London News Supplement*, May 9, 1863. *FOSU*

had cut the line.) The *New Ironsides* and its 16 heavy guns, half of the squadron's firepower, remained out of the battle while the other ships continued to fight.[14]

Within Sumter, Lt. Col. Yates commanded the top tier while Maj. Ormsby Blanding defended the casemates. Colonel Rhett positioned himself on the parapet at the southeast angle near the regimental colors. The guns in the other harbor fortifications stood ready, and the CSS *Chicora* and CSS *Palmetto State* posted themselves near the harbor's interior obstructions. As they had in April 1861, civilian and military spectators crowded The Battery in Charleston and every other place with a view of the harbor's mouth. Frank Vizetelly, a British correspondent who was in Charleston that day, wrote that ambulances waited for the wounded near the wharves on East Bay Street.[15]

After Fort Moultrie fired the initial round, the *Passaic* responded. Soon after this shot, the *Weehawken* also opened on Fort Sumter. The monitor had reached the aiming buoy 1,400 yards from Sumter at about 3:00 p.m., and all nine guns mounted on the fort's right flank barbette that were trained on this marker opened fire. "We could see the shot crushing to pieces and glancing (against the turrets)," Arthur Grimball wrote to his brother after the battle, and "they came on as if saying fire ahead old boy we dont [sic] care a damn." After Sumter began firing, the guns on Morris and Sullivan's Islands joined the fight. Shells struck the ironclads and exploded next to vessels, throwing columns of water over the decks, pilot houses, and turrets.[16]

14 Wise, *Gate of Hell*, 30.

15 *OR* 14:265; Frank Vizetelly, "Charleston Under Fire," *Cornhill Magazine*, July-December 1864, 100-102.

16 *OR* 14: 264; *ORN* 14:9; Arthur Grimball to Brother (Berkley), Apr. 14, 1863.

Watching the "Ironclad Attack" from "The Battery," *The Illustrated London News Supplement*, May 16, 1863. *FOSU*

Though the Federals had heavier guns, they all had a slower rate of fire. The turrets of the attacking fleet were responsible for this. After firing, the turret was rotated to protect the guns during reloading. The turrets' cramped interiors, the weight of the projectiles, and the small aiming slits combined to slow the loading and aiming of the large guns—all this while under continuous fire from the Confederate batteries. Heavy, solid rounds slammed into or ricocheted off the turrets and the decks, and large shell fragments crashed into the ships. The pilot house, the duty post of both the ship's commander and its pilot, was situated atop each monitor's turret. Inside, the commander and pilot endured the same perilous conditions as the gun crews below their feet.

As Fort Sumter fired continuous rounds, soldiers inside the works raced up and down stairs to the magazines keeping the guns supplied. Some officers and men also carried messages and delivered orders. The *Weehawken*, the first of the monitors to come under fire, sent one of its first rounds through the center of the regiment's flag; another injured five soldiers when the ball struck the left flank's brick traverse, throwing out a shower of bricks and fragments. A shell exploding at the water's edge in front of the right flank wall sent a cascade of water onto the parapet over 50 feet above. It drenched the soldiers and guns there and filled the crown of Lt. Samuel C. Boylston's cap to overflowing.[17]

Another shell passed through the right flank wall at the second-tier level, exploded in the barracks, and set fire to some bedding, but the soldiers assigned as firemen quickly extinguished the flames. Another shell passed over the right flank parapet and exploded in the left flank barracks. In a letter to his father, Arthur Grimball reported that the enemy fired "15-inch solid shot and shell and the way they flew was terrific. Every time they struck the fort, the walls quivered."

Not long after the battle began, the fire from the right flank guns slackened by half. Some of these were 32-pounder smoothbores that had no effect against the monitors' 11-inch-thick iron turrets and 9-inch-thick iron pilot houses. And since the smoke rising from the first-tier guns obscured the view from the top tier, Rhett ordered them to cease firing so the larger smoothbores, rifled and banded guns, and two 7-inch Brooke rifles would have an unobstructed field of fire.

The Southerners' rounds repeatedly struck their targets. Arthur told his father that they had witnessed "some of our shot crushing to pieces against the turrets." The *Weehawken*, which had fired 26 rounds at Sumter, suffered at least 51 hits; some of its armor broke into "[s]plintered fragments" and pierced various areas of the deck, allowing water to pour inside. The *Nantucket* also took 51 hits. After firing three rounds at the fort, several shots struck near the monitor's 15-inch gun's port shutter, jamming it closed and taking the piece out of action. The 11-inch gun fired only 12 rounds: nine at Sumter, two at Battery Wagner, and one at Fort Moultrie.[18]

Along with the rest of the fleet, the *Nahant* fought "hotly committed" against fire from Forts Sumter and Moultrie, Battery Bee, and Fort Beauregard. It had been hit three dozen times, mainly on the turret and pilot's house. Confederate artillery shells struck with such force that bolts detached inside the ship, flew off, and fatally wounded one crew member while seriously wounding two and hurting four others slightly. The *Patapsco*, which opened fire 1,500 yards from Fort Sumter, moved up the channel another 300 yards, fired 10 rounds at the fort, and took 47 hits in return. One area of the deck took two or three direct strikes, breaking the

17 Wise, *Gate of Hell*, 27-28; *ORN* 14:3-112.

18 Wise, *Gate of Hell*, 51; *ORN* 14:3-112, 240-278; Arthur Grimball to Father, Apr. 10, 1863; Field, *1st South Carolina Artillery*, 9-11.

armor into "splintered fragments," and it appeared that "[m]uch [could] be picked off by hand and the wood exposed."

The *Passaic* survived 35 strikes and fired just 26 times at Sumter, including nine from its 11-inch gun and four from its 8-inch piece. Each gun fired one round at Fort Moultrie and directed 11 at Fort Sumter. After the fourth 11-inch round was fired, the turret absorbed heavy blows that rendered it inoperable. Substantial enemy rounds slammed against the base and "bulged" the plate and beams upon which the gun pivoted. The ring on which the turret rotated also jammed, and even after repairs it operated only "irregularly." Another round broke 11 iron plates on the top of the turret then ricocheted and hit the pilot house, leaving a 2½-inch dent. The round also bent the pilot house over, opened its iron plates, and "squeezed out its top," leaving a 3-inch gap that exposed its interior. The captain believed "the next shot would take off the top itself entirely." One of the ship's officers reported that "in a few seconds" he had counted 15 shots flying over his head just above the deck, and that at other times "the whistling was so rapid" that he couldn't keep count. At 4:10 p.m., the *Passaic* assumed a position below Fort Moultrie to assess the damage.[19]

The *New Ironsides*, unable to bring its guns to bear on Fort Sumter, fired eight rounds: a seven-gun broadside at Fort Moultrie from its 11-inch guns and one 8-inch Parrott round at Battery Wagner. Confederate shells hit the ship about 50 times, causing only minor damage. The *Catskill* suffered 20 strikes and the *Montauk* 14, but none of these caused damage. The two monitors fired a total of 49 rounds, all at Fort Sumter, while the *Montauk* fired from a range of 800 yards. The *Keokuk*, piloted by Robert Smalls, steamed to within 550 yards of Fort Sumter, closer than any of the other ships in the squadron, but it paid a tremendous price. Within 30 minutes, hostile shells hit the vessel at least 90 times, and 19 shots pierced its armor at or near the water line. The ironclad fired only three rounds, all at Sumter. Rhett reported that it "was completely riddled." The *Keokuk*, no longer able to defend itself or support the attack, dropped out of the battle and anchored in smooth water.[20]

At 4:30 p.m., after two and a half hours of intense combat and with his ships hit almost 400 times, Du Pont signaled the squadron to break off the assault. A half-hour later, the attack fleet anchored off Morris Island, out of range of the Confederate guns. Casualties totaled one mortally wounded and 22 wounded. The rear admiral planned to renew the attack the next day. When his captains reported the condition of their ships, however, Du Pont cancelled it. The damage reports

19 *ORN* 14:9-11, 21-24.

20 *ORN* 5-8, 13-14, 16-17, 25-27.

had been sobering. The *Keokuk* fought to stay afloat, and five of the monitors had holes smashed in their decks, damaged turrets and pilot houses, and loosened bolts. Captain C. R. P. Rodgers of the *New Ironsides* wrote after the war that "no one who witnessed it will ever forget. Sublime, infernal, it seemed as if the fires of hell were turned upon the fleet. The air seemed full of shot, and as they flew, they could be seen as plainly as a base ball."

On April 8, while the ships held their positions, Du Pont composed several letters. He reported to Secretary Welles that "five of the eight ironclads were partially or wholly disabled after a brief engagement." In a second letter to the secretary, he characterized the battle as "fierce and obstinate," but "the gallantry of the officers and men" on the vessels engaged had been "conspicuous." He told Hunter he was "now satisfied that [Charleston] cannot be taken by a purely naval attack." To this the general responded, "I cannot but congratulate you on the magnificent manner in which the vessels under your command were fought." In a private letter to a friend, Du Pont declared, "We attempted to take the bull by the horns yesterday—and had a very grand fight. It was a failure, but not a disaster."

The *Keokuk*'s crew worked all night to keep her afloat, but wind and rough water overwhelmed the ship. At 7:30 a.m., the ironclad sank upright in 18 feet of water about 1,300 yards off the south end of Morris Island. Admiral Du Pont watched it founder: "I got on deck in time this morning to see the *Keokuk* go down. . . . She was struck twenty-nine times on the water line, and her sides were perforated as if going through so many sheets of paper. She had [received] ninety shots in forty-five minutes." The same day Du Pont composed his letters, General Ripley telegraphed from Fort Sumter to headquarters: "Should Gen. Beauregard have time it might do for him to come down. . . .The '*Keokuk*' is a submarine battery." The squadron remained in position for five days after the battle, but by April 15 all the monitors had returned to Port Royal for repairs and provisions. Only the *New Ironsides* remained off Charleston as part of the blockading squadron.[21]

Of the 139 artillery rounds the U.S. warships fired, 113 (80 percent) had been directed at Fort Sumter. Most missed; only 34 (30 percent) found their mark. Still, scars marked the walls in 20 places, primarily from rounds grazing them or from shell fragments. Only 15 rounds produced any real damage. Eight of these came from 15-inch shells, two of which passed through the right flank wall. One of them exploded inside a casemate, and the other continued through a casemate, exited a window, and exploded in the center of the parade ground. An 11-inch solid shot penetrated this wall and continued into the barracks, where it lodged

21 *B&L*, 4:36-37, 39; *ORN* 14:3; Hayes, *Samuel Francis Du Pont*, 3:5-8, 10; Telegrams Sent, 1863-64, War Dept. Confederate Records, Dept. of SC, GA & FL, NA/RG 109.

in an interior wall. A 15-inch shell passed over the parapet and exploded inside the left flank barracks on the other side of the fort. The Southerners found an 11-inch solid shot and several 15-inch shells that failed to explode in various locations inside the fort. Every one of its windowpanes had been shattered.

These rounds fired by the U.S. Navy during the two-and-a-half-hour battle, which included the eight rounds fired by the *New Ironsides*, totaled about 16,000 pounds of iron. Seventy-seven Confederate guns and mortars on Sullivan's and Morris Islands and at Fort Sumter, plus a pair of 10-inch mortars at Fort Johnson (which each fired one round), delivered 2,229 rounds, about 73½ tons of ordnance, an average of five rounds every 12 seconds. Using 7,680 pounds of powder between them, Fort Moultrie fired 868 rounds, Sumter 831. Only 396 rounds, about 18 percent, struck the nine ships, twice the normal average of 10 percent in mid-nineteenth century engagements between ships and shore/land fortifications.[22]

At Fort Sumter, two embrasures had been destroyed and four were damaged. A 25-foot section of the right flank parapet "was breached and loosened." Also, part of the parapet wall fell, exposing the gun behind it. Rounds produced craters from a foot to 2½ feet deep, and about 3 feet in diameter. At one location, two or more rounds hitting close together created a crater 2 feet 7 inches deep, 6 feet high, and 8 feet wide. "The Iron Clads came up within 900 yards of the fort and did fearful execution," Arthur Grimball told his father, "The sea face of the fort was breached in three places, but is now fixed with sand bags and is all right[.]" He deemed the ironclads "very formidable things."

On April 14, 1863, Grimball reported to his brother: "The fire came hot and heavy. . . . One shot went right through the sea face of the fort. Two shell[s] burst in the parapet knocking it to flinders causing a crack in the wall of considerable size[.] The fort was breached in three places and if the fight had lasted 6 hours I believe the fort would have been Knocked to thunder."

Just one of Fort Sumter's guns was damaged by enemy fire: a 10-inch Columbiad was disabled when a round tore away part of its carriage. This gun had been assigned to Grimball, and he described the near miss in an April 10 letter. "I was given command of a gun . . . bearing on the City, but as I was called off to Signal . . . I was very glad of it afterwards, for my gun was soon after I left . . . . struck by a 15-inch shot and rendered useless, smashing up the carriage and tearing up the parapet[.]"

Another cannon, a rifled and banded 42-pounder, recoiled off its chassis after firing, and an 8-inch Columbiad on the right flank parapet burst when it discharged. The muzzle landed outside on the berm at the fort's base. The breech flew

22 *OR* 14:268; Wise, *Gate of Hell*, 30; Johnson, *Defense of Charleston Harbor*, 58-59.

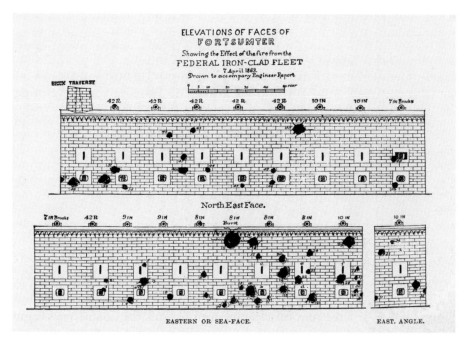

ELEVATIONS OF FACES OF
FORT SUMTER
Showing the Effect of the fire from the
FEDERAL IRON-CLAD FLEET
7 April 1863.
Drawn to accompany Engineer Report

North East Face.

EASTERN OR SEA-FACE.   EAST. ANGLE.

Engineer illustration of the effects of the "Ironclad Fleet's" guns on Ft. Sumter's walls.
The War of the Rebellion: A Compilation of the Union and Confederate Armies, hereinafter ORA

back over the roof of the barracks and landed on the parade ground. Remarkably, the gun crew was unscathed. Grimball wrote his father about the destroyed gun: "half of it [went] about . . . 100 feet out in the yard [parade ground], the other over the fort on the Birm [berm]."

The Confederates reported remarkably few casualties. In Fort Sumter, brick fragments injured five soldiers and a slave laborer. At Fort Moultrie, one soldier was killed, and at Battery Wagner an exploding ammunition chest killed three and wounded five.

With uncommon mastery of the succinct, Lt. Grimball described the battle in a letter to his sister Elizabeth on April 21: "To sum it up shortly, We fired They fired, they fired We fired. When they left we were glad. When they did not come back, We claimed a glorious victory." Earlier he had written that "the white flag will never hang over fort Sumter. All the garrison can die, but can not surrender."[23]

---

23 Johnson, *Defense of Charleston Harbor*, 56-58; Arthur Grimball to Father, Apr. 10, 1863, to Brother (Berkley), Apr. 14, 1863, and to Sister, Apr. 21, 1863.

Chapter 7

Defended at Any Cost

April–July 1863

After the guns fell silent on April 7, 1863, the Confederates began assessing the damage and repairing their fortifications to fend off another attack. Major William E. Echols, South Carolina's chief engineer, arrived at the fort and found E. J. White of the engineer department "busily engaged building in the casemates, first and second tiers, behind the damaged walls, with sandbags," which strengthened them considerably. The "work . . . continued all night and the next day by the garrison and the 50 negroes who had been employed at the fort and remained during the engagement."

Before noon on April 8 crews "replaced . . . two 9-in. Dahlgrens on the right flank parapet with two 10-in. Columbiads from the left." They also distributed sandbags to several places on the right flank and moved more to the terreplein and the arches over the upper magazines. The cracks in the right flank wall, the fallen parapet section, and damaged embrasures received "a heavy backing of sand, revetted with sandbags." As work progressed, 100 to 200 members of the 46th Georgia arrived to assist with the fatigue duty.[1]

Just two days after the battle, the South Carolina legislature passed a unanimous resolution thanking the "officers and men in Charleston Harbor" for their "gallant defense against the first onset of the foe." At a dress parade on April 12, the garrison commemorated the victory with a 13-gun salute. Ironically, the ceremony fell on the second anniversary of the 1861 bombardment. The *Daily Courier* noted that the "daughters of South Carolina" had sent a "magnificent

1 *OR* 14:249, 277; Johnson, *Defense of Charleston Harbor*, 78.

Maj. David B. Harris, Chief Engineer, Dept. of South Carolina, Georgia, and Florida. *LOC*

laurel wreath bound with palmetto" honoring "Col. Alfred Rhett and his gallant command."[2]

While repairs continued, chief engineer Maj. David B. Harris and Gustavus Smith inspected the fort and recommended enhancing the extensive defensive features. First, the first-tier right flank casemate guns were removed and it and the second-tier were filled with sandbags. On both tiers facing the parade ground soldiers coated the sloping revetments of sandbags with coal tar to hold them in place. Next, the powder in the second-tier magazines was removed, then they were filled with sand, providing additional protection to the first-tier magazines. In addition, their exteriors facing the parade ground were reinforced with laid brick. Outside the fort, the magazines' walls, already reinforced with 15-ft. high stone masonry after the April 1861 bombardment, were further fortified with a brick wall. Over four feet of sand, removed from the parade, filled the casemates and magazines, while tenders offloaded still more bagged and loose sand from the city to complete this work. General Ripley requested that the ladies of Charleston provide petticoats and pillowcases for sandbags. The spurt in activity spawned an advertisement in the *Daily Courier* for a "hundred ab[l]e bodied Negro Men" to perform labor at the fort for $26 per month plus rations.[3]

Crews experimented with methods of strengthening the parapet. They suspended bales of water-soaked "compressed cotton" on the exterior walls with ropes secured by eye bolts in the brick. The spongy bales would absorb the impact of artillery rounds and could be replaced easily. But a flaw in the plan soon appeared:

---

2 "A Garland of Honor," *Charleston Courier*, Apr. 13, 1863; Johnson, *Defense of Charleston Harbor*, 76-77.

3 Gustavus Smith's resignation as a major general was accepted Feb. 17, 1863. He then served as a civilian aide on Gen. Beauregard's staff until after the Ironclad Attack. No author. *Twenty-Eighth Annual Reunion of the Association of the Graduates of the United States Military Academy, at West Point, New York, June 10th, 1898.* (Saginaw, MI: Seeman & Peters, 1897), 13-22. It is unlikely that any of these black workers were even aware of their "pay and benefits"; slaveholders commonly "leased out" their slaves to perform just such miscellaneous jobs.

dried bales tore, exposing the highly flammable cotton to sparks from the fort's own guns. In spite of this setback, the fort's other new defensive measures had readied it for another assault. Grimball informed a correspondent that "working night and day" had rendered "the fort far stronger than before the fight[.]"[4]

*   *   *

Anchored just over 4 miles away off the southern end of Morris Island, the U.S. squadron posed a continuous threat. On April 8, 1863, Admiral Du Pont ordered the wreck of the *Keokuk*—about 1,300 yards off the southern end of Morris Island in 18 feet of water—destroyed, but rough seas prevented crews from reaching it. The Federals determined that its two 11-inch guns couldn't be salvaged and trusted that nearby U.S. blockaders would deter any C.S. salvage efforts.

The tops of the turrets, however, presented too tempting an opportunity. Colonel R. F. Graham, commanding on Morris Island, sent "parts of a signal-book picked up on the beach" to headquarters. After surveying the wreck two days later Ripley reported to Beauregard's chief of staff, Brig. Gen. Thomas Jordan, that he had retrieved a "signal-book of some kind from Keokuk." The Confederates broke the code and were doubtless surprised to discover the Federals hadn't changed it. Henceforth, this valuable piece of intelligence enabled the Confederate Signal Corps to read U.S. Army and Navy communications.

Visiting the site on April 19, Ripley and Harris agreed that the Dahlgrens should be salvaged, as they could substantially strengthen the harbor's defenses. Beauregard issued the necessary orders. As U.S. warships were only about two miles away, riggers, other specialists, and Sumter garrison troops began working at night without lights to open the turrets' tops. Each night they could only work about two and a half hours when low tide exposed the tops of the turrets. For two weeks, despite darkness and 70° water temperature, workmen labored to create holes large enough to accommodate the guns' removal. Cramped space inside the turrets also stymied efforts to free the massive 8-ton guns, which were submerged even at low tide. Workers freed the guns from their carriages. One was hoisted on a barge, and transported to the city, the second was removed in like manner. On May 5, Beauregard reported the successful completion of the project. Fort Sumter mounted one of the guns and Battery Bee on Sullivan's Island the other.[5]

Lieutenant Grimball (who wasn't a part of the salvage operation) explained to his sister, Elizabeth, that he was bored, ascribing it "to the spring heat and the

---

4 "Wanted By Engineer Department," *Charleston Courier*, May 14, 1863; Johnson, *Defense of Charleston Harbor*, 78; Arthur Grimball to Brother, Apr. 14, 1863.

5 Johnson, *Defense of Charleston Harbor*, 62-71; *OR* 14:890, 893, 926.

officers' close confinement . . . in this brick dungeon." He did report, though, that the fort had been sufficiently repaired to allow visitors and described a wonderful diversion when "Cousin Berkley came down . . . a few days ago chaperoning a number of North Carolina officers." "[S]ome young ladies from Florida" with "fresh complexions but faded and antique dresses" accompanied them. Dancing to the regimental band's music proved impossible: "the girls jumped so much, [and] were so very lively in their movements." They were, however, "highly delighted with their visit." In spite of this interlude, Grimball voiced his familiar refrain: "When will this war end? I am getting gray & valuable years are flying."

On May 7, 1863, patriotic Charlestonians hailed the sight of the first public display of the second national Confederate States' flag, which was raised at Beauregard's headquarters at 74 Broad Street. Newspaper announcements of the tragic death of Lt. Gen. Thomas J. "Stonewall" Jackson on May 10 overshadowed the good-news event. On May 13, Beauregard ordered the generals commanding the First Military District and District of Georgia to fire "a gun . . . every half hour" from sunrise to sunset. Plus "the flags at every Post in the Department will be hoisted at half-mast in token of this national bereavement." Similarly, First District commander Ripley ordered "a gun . . . fired alternately at each half hour from Fort Sumter and Moultrie, from sunrise to sunset." Flags would fly at half-mast at all posts on May 14 in Jackson's memory.

A week later, the South Carolina Executive Council passed several resolutions underscoring Charleston's significance in the war effort. All dated May 21, 1863, they resolved that the city "should be defended at any cost of life or property, and that in their deliberate judgment they would prefer a repulse of the enemy with the entire city in ruins to an evacuation or surrender on any terms whatever." [6]

*   *   *

Lieutenant Colonel Arthur L. Fremantle of Her Majesty's Coldstream Guards arrived in Charleston on June 8, 1863. Fremantle, an enthusiastic pro-secessionist, had come to the Confederate States to observe the war from the South's perspective. He had landed just south of the Rio Grande on April 2 and crossed into Texas to begin his journey across the Confederacy.

6 Grimball to Sister, Apr. 21, 1863; *Charleston Courier* articles: "Long May It Wave" and "A Ball and Ladies' Prize Dance" (May 7), "General Thomas J. Jackson" (May 11), "A Grand Ball and May Festival," "Grand Panoramic Mirror of the War," and "In Accordance With the Provisions" (May 14, 1863); *Charleston Mercury* articles: ". . . Death Of General (Stonewall) Jackson" (May 11), "The Guns of the Keokuk Raised" (May 7, 1863). Before the pall of mourning for Jackson settled on the city in mid-May, Charleston society had enjoyed several social events earlier in the month, including two balls at Hibernian Hall, a Mason-sponsored dance, a band concert, and more.

Upon reaching Charleston, Fremantle found a city suffering from the effects of two years of war. Its paving and lighting were in shambles. Most shops were closed, and those that were open offered few goods at famine prices. No attempt had been made to repair the "vast wilderness," a mile-and-a-half-long scar in the middle of town left by the great fire. It reminded the British officer of "Pompeian ruins." Deserted wharves presented a sad sight, as did the now-irrelevant "placards announcing lines of steamers to New York, New Orleans, and to different parts of the world."

Some of the city's population, however, still prospered. Fremantle observed an "immense amount of speculation in blockade-running" and a brisk market in slave trading. The papers were full of ads for slave auctions. Moreover, business boomed at the two "great hotels," where the food was good and "well-dressed, handsome ladies are plentiful."

On June 8, the Englishman met Gen. Ripley and described him as "jovial" [and] very fond of the good things of this life." Nothing, however, interfered "with his military duties," as he was "a red-hot and indefatigable rebel." According to Freemantle, Ripley deserved "[n]early all the credit [for] the efficiency of the Charleston fortifications."

Fremantle accompanied Ripley on an inspection of Fort Sumter on the 9th and particularly admired "a fine eleven-inch gun, which had just been fished up from the wreck of the Keokuk." He gave the fort a careful look, observing that generally it showed "but little signs of the battering" the Union monitors had reportedly administered recently. Fremantle also recorded his observations of conditions within and around the water that day, noting that "both sides of the harbor for several miles appear to bristle with forts mounting heavy guns." The presence of blockade runners also fascinated him: "[P]ainted the same color as the water; as many as three or four often go in and out with impunity in one night," but always "in cloudy weather. They are very seldom captured . . . and charge an enormous price for passengers and freight."

That evening he "dined with General and Mrs. Ripley," and the dinner was "a very sumptuous one, for a 'blockade' dinner, as General Ripley called it." On June 10, "Mr. and Mrs. H" drove him to The Battery, known as the gathering place for the well-dressed, who promenaded or rode about in carriages. But "Mr. and Mrs. H" lamented that "it is nothing to what it was. Most of the horses and carriages have been sent out of Charleston since the last attack."

On the 11th, Fremantle sailed with Ripley to Morris Island, which he termed "a miserable, low, sandy desert." He observed the wreck of the *Keokuk* and inspected the *Weehawken*'s torpedo raft, which the Confederates had dubbed a "Devil" or "alligator." It had drifted ashore after its crew cut it loose during the battle.

Maj. Gen. Quincy A. Gillmore

NARA

Eagle-eyed as usual, the Englishman recorded that at the island's extreme southern end, "a range of low sand-hills" formed "admirable natural parapets. And about ten guns were placed behind them."

The next day Fremantle called on Gen. Beauregard, who offered him the use of the horse he had ridden at both Manassas and Shiloh. The plan was to tour the Secessionville battlefield and James Island's defenses on June 13. The next day he attended services at St. Michael's Episcopal Church. "The Charlestonians . . . are very proud of it, and I saw several monuments of the time of the British dominion." That evening he dined at Mr. Robertson's, where he met still more military and political notables, among them Maj. William Norris, "chief of the secret intelligence bureau at Richmond." Fremantle left for Richmond on June 15, and while there was embraced as warmly by the citizens of the capital as he had been by the Charlestonians.[7]

*   *   *

Military and political leaders in Washington were not amused by the news of Du Pont's failed "ironclad attack" and the Confederate success in recovering the *Keokuk*'s guns. Least thrilled were Secretary Welles and Assistant Secretary Fox, who had fully supported the exclusive naval operation. They were now willing to support an Army-Navy expedition against Charleston and shake up the command structure. Du Pont's defeat, negative reports of his command during the assault, and the generally unfavorable opinion of ironclads were more than sufficient cause for Welles to replace Du Pont. He could "no longer be useful in his present command," Welles told his diary. He selected a 40-year Navy veteran, Rear Adm. Andrew H. Foote, to replace Du Pont. Foote had commanded the Mississippi River Squadron in 1862. He had worked closely with Brig. Gen. Ulysses S. Grant in the victories at Forts Henry and Donelson and had supported Brig. Gen. John

7 Arthur F. Fremantle, *Three Months In The Southern States* (New York, 1864), 8-202, *passim.*

Pope in capturing Island No. 10. Foote, still recovering from a wound suffered at Fort Donelson, was eager to return to active duty.

General-in-Chief Henry W. Halleck, equally dismayed by Gen. Hunter's lack of success, resolved to remove him from command of the Department of the South and chose Brig. Gen. Quincy A. Gillmore to replace him. Like Foote, Gillmore boasted a distinguished resumé. He graduated at the top of West Point's class of 1849 and had been the chief engineer in the operation to take Port Royal in November 1861. In April 1862, he had planned and directed the bombardment of Fort Pulaski, proving that heavily constructed brick forts could not deter rifled artillery. Many considered Gillmore the Army's leading engineer and artillery officer.

Brigadier General Truman Seymour accepted an appointment as an aide on Gillmore's staff and attended the May meeting at which Foote and Gillmore agreed to execute Welles and Fox's joint effort. Rear Admiral John A. Dahlgren, widely thought to be the Navy's best ordnance officer, had accepted command of the ironclad squadron and was also at the meeting. The straightforward plan charged the Army with quickly capturing Morris Island, repelling any counterattacks, and establishing breaching batteries on the island to bomb Sumter into submission. The Navy then would remove the obstructions, enter the harbor, and take Charleston.

On June 3, 1863, Halleck issued the order relieving Hunter and assigning Gillmore command of the Department of the South. Effective June 12, Gillmore assumed his duties at Hilton Head. Secretary Welles simultaneously appointed Foote to the command of the South Atlantic Blockading Squadron, replacing Du Pont. The infection of his Fort Donelson wound, however, prevented Foote's departure. On June 21, Welles awarded the command to Dahlgren. Foote died five days later. Dahlgren arrived at Port Royal and met with Gillmore on July 4. Two days later he formally relieved Du Pont.[8]

Gillmore commanded more than 24,000 men strung out from St. Augustine, Florida to Folly Island, South Carolina. Most were veterans of the department's operations, including the battles of Port Royal and Secessionville; other units had served in McClellan's Peninsula campaign. Gillmore's plan called for about half of his forces to capture Charleston. An infantry brigade, stationed on Folly Island since April 7, 1863, had built defenses on the island's southern end. Gillmore ordered the construction of gun emplacements at its northeastern end to assist in the attack. The Confederates, unaware of the Union works on Folly Island, labored tirelessly to erect their own defenses on the southern end of Morris Island, only 500

---

8 Welles, *Diary of Gideon Welles*, 1:288; Wise, *Gate of Hell*, 33-38; *OR* 14:464; *ORN* 14:230, 295-296, 311.

Rear Adm. John A. Dahlgren

LOC

yards across Lighthouse Inlet from Folly. Masked by trees and foliage and working only at night, Federal soldiers toiled at their earthworks, and by the end of June more than 4,800 troops occupied Folly Island, ready to begin the campaign.

Meanwhile P. G. T. Beauregard had to cope with diminishing troop strength. He lost nearly a third of his command between April and June when Richmond ordered 10,000 troops sent to other operational theaters. Only 20,780 men remained to defend the Department of South Carolina, Georgia, and Florida. About 8,000 infantry, artillery, and cavalry, all South Carolina units, manned Charleston's defenses, the core of Ripley's First Military District. Both Beauregard and Ripley believed the next attempt to take the city would occur sooner rather than later, on Morris Island.

Three positions on Morris provided defensive works: the incomplete "Inlet Batteries" at the southern end of the island; Battery Wagner, 3 miles farther up; and Battery Gregg at Cummings Point, about three-quarters of a mile beyond Wagner at the mouth of Charleston Harbor. Battery Gregg, formerly known as the Cummings Point Battery, had been renamed to honor South Carolina Brig. Gen. Maxcy Gregg, who had been mortally wounded at Fredericksburg the previous December.

The Confederate command ordered Lt. Col. Yates from Sumter to lead the island's artillery and assigned two companies of the 1st South Carolina Artillery to the Inlet Batteries. A detachment from Company H and several infantry detachments joined them. More than 400 troops now readied themselves and their defenses. Battery Wagner's garrison numbered 325 infantry and artillery. Nine heavy guns (three facing the Main Channel and six pointing down the island) were mounted within its walls, and 50 artillerymen from Company H who were directed to fire on the channel manned the four pieces at Battery Gregg. Twenty-

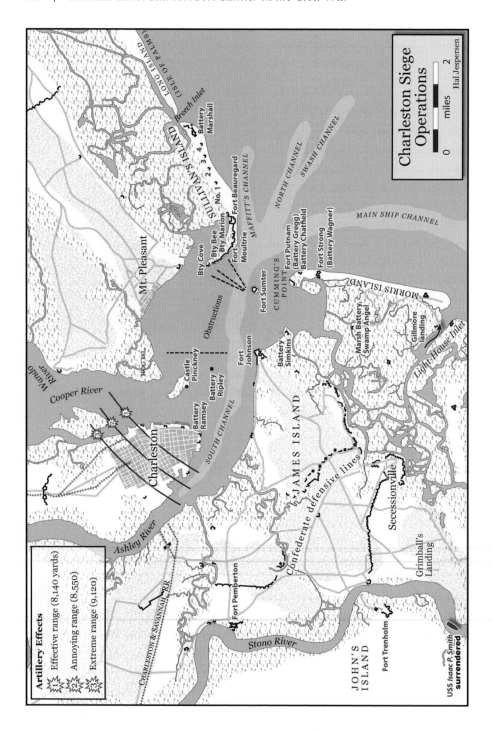

From the July 10, 1863, amphibious assault onto Morris Island ("Gillmore Landing") until the evacuation of Charleston's defenses and its occupation on Feb. 18, 1865, the city lay under siege—the longest of the Civil War. After Confederate forces evacuated Morris Island in Sept. 1863, Union troops would reconfigure Batteries Wagner & Gregg. Later, these and other fortifications would produce relentless and deadly fire upon Ft. Sumter, Charleston, and other C. S. installations.

six cavalrymen were stationed there to serve as couriers. The wharf at Cummings Point provided a secure landing for supplies, materiel, and troops.

On Folly Island, across Lighthouse Inlet from the Inlet Batteries, General Seymour positioned his men to deliver the upcoming assault. At daylight on July 10, 2,530 infantry, in row boats hidden in the tall marsh grass along the inlet, awaited orders. Another 1,360 men and a light artillery battery were ready to support the attack, and 1,450 more troops remained in reserve. The masked batteries comprised 15 mortars and 32 rifled field pieces, from 3-inch Ordnance Rifles up to 30-pounder Parrots. They opened fire just after 5:00 a.m.

The Confederate artillery responded quickly, and although the exchange of fire lasted about an hour, neither side suffered much damage until the *Catskill, Nahant, Montauk,* and *Weehawken* joined the fight. From the channel, off the Confederate left flank, they fired 15- and 11-inch shells and case shot. The roar of both sides' guns was audible 50 miles away in Port Royal. Exploding rounds rained fragments and shrapnel down into the batteries, reducing the now-irregular Confederate artillery fire. The Union infantry on barges emerged from the marsh grass, crossed the inlet, and engaged the Southerners in close combat. They quickly forced the infantry back. Federals with fixed bayonets moved into the batteries and confronted the cannoneers, who fought back with their guns' implements, and, after a brief hand-to-hand struggle, had to give way. The combined Confederate force, outnumbered five to one, retreated toward Battery Wagner.

Yates, commanding the Inlet Batteries, reported sending an order for Wagner's artillery to open fire on the enemy once "our column passed within range of our guns." The order was "promptly obeyed, completely checking the advance of the enemy for that day." But a new threat materialized when the monitors emerged, firing shells and grapeshot and enfilading Yates's command. The Federals turned some of the inlet batteries' guns and joined the bombardment. The Confederates retreated toward Battery Wagner, three miles away, but soft sand slowed their flight. They likewise had to endure the brutal July heat, ironclad fire on their flank, and fire from their rear from their own captured guns. The retreat quickly became a rout. Yates reached Wagner and reported the loss of almost 300 men, about half of whom had been captured. Two of them—Capt. J. Ravenel MacBeth and the mortally wounded Lt. John S. Bee—were scions of leading Charleston families.

The monitors arrived off Battery Wagner at 9:30 a.m. and engaged it as well as Battery Gregg. Some of their 15- and 11-inch shells skipped across the water, passed over the parapet, and exploded inside Wagner. Under covering fire from the Union warships, Gillmore brought the remainder of his troops onto Morris Island. Rhett watched the amphibious assault unfold from Fort Sumter's parapet and waited to order his artillerists into action. When he saw the U.S. flag raised over the far end of the island, he ordered the 7-inch Brooke gun at the parapet's southeast angle to open fire.

As the sun set, the monitors withdrew down the channel and the day's action ceased. Gillmore prepared to renew the attack the next day with the goal of driving the Confederates entirely off Morris Island. The successful U.S. joint assault had captured 11 guns, hundreds of prisoners, and 75 percent of the island. Beauregard began preparing the city for a prolonged campaign. These preparations included Special Orders No. 138, which organized the city's militia and had it report to General Ripley. More ominously, the "funds and valuables of the several banks of this city may be transported to the interior."[9]

9 Wise, *Gate of Hell*, 38, 39-40, 43, 44, 55-56, 59, 61, 67-72, 221-222, 227-228; *OR* 28/2:189; Field, *1st South Carolina Artillery*, 11; Johnson, *Defense of Charleston Harbor*, 92.

Chapter 8

Terribly Knocked to Pieces

July–September 1863

In Richmond, the disconcerting news of the Federal success on Morris Island, coming as it did after the disasters at Gettysburg and Vicksburg, cast the fate of Charleston in doubt. It was the nation's most successful blockade-running port; and of almost equal significance, it was the "cradle of the Confederacy." For the good of the fledgling nation, Charleston could not be lost.

Late on the morning of July 9, Lt. Col. Yates had sent a message from the Inlet Batteries on the south end of Morris Island. He had observed unmasked Federal earthworks and a large number of reinforcements on Folly Island, barges positioned in the creek behind the island, and four monitors nearby. Yates concluded that Yankees were about to renew the attack. Later that day in the threatened city, Mayor MacBeth met with Beauregard and issued a notice printed on July 10 in both Charleston papers: an assault on the city was "imminent," and with Beauregard's concurrence he was advising and requesting that "women and children, and other non-combatants leave the city as soon as possible." Two more proclamations appeared in both papers on the 10th. One suspended business in the city until it was safe. In the other, Beauregard called for volunteers "to work on some unfinished defences on Morris Island." All free African American males 18-60 years old who lived in Charleston would "be at once conscripted," taken to the police station, and would wait there for Beauregard's orders. Additionally, "every able-bodied male slave [would likewise] be subject to the general's orders." Later, Gov. Milledge H. Bonham informed Beauregard that a committee had been formed to assist, if necessary, with removing Charlestonians "who because of age, sex, or infirmity were unable to participate in defending the city."[1]

During the July 10 assault on Morris Island, First District troops had reinforced Battery Wagner; that same day Beauregard moved units from the Second and Third districts into the First. He also telegraphed for reinforcements from Wilmington, North Carolina, and Savannah. Troops in both cities boarded trains, and before noon, the first Savannah units entered Charleston. Eventually, 2,250 reinforcements arrived that day, most of which were dispatched to Morris and James Islands. At Battery Wagner, now manned by 1,700 men, torpedoes (mines) were sown in front of the works. On the morning of July 11, Gen. Gillmore, convinced that the rest of the island could be taken at the point of the bayonet, attacked the battery with 1,230 infantry. The assault failed; the Federals suffered 400 causalities, the Confederates only 24. After this defeat, Gillmore began converting his recently built works into a siege line, ranging 1,330 to 1,920 yards south of Battery Wagner.

As Mayor MacBeth addressed civilian matters, Beauregard continued to grapple with the fluid and critical military situation. By July 22, with more reinforcements arriving, the First District numbered more than 16,000 soldiers. Beauregard calculated that Gillmore planned to reduce Fort Sumter and instructed Colonel Rhett to prepare for a bombardment. Rhett in turn ordered most of his guns transferred to other harbor defenses to save them from being damaged or destroyed.

By July16, the completed Union siege line included four batteries. While it was under construction, Dahlgren positioned 21 warships and used the monitors to "pepper away at Wagner" and to provide covering fire. The various Confederate works responded in kind. Early on the morning of July 12, Rhett telegraphed that he had shelled Morris Island, and four days later had fired on the "new batteries" with the Brooke gun from the salient angle. One shell exploded prematurely over the parade ground and a fragment of it killed one of the garrison on the right face barbette.[2]

On July15, William Grimball wrote that on the previous day he had returned to Fort Sumter from Battery Wagner. Though he had been in the fight at the Inlet Batteries and Wagner, the young lieutenant didn't comment on those actions. He admitted to taking "a very gloomy view of affairs," and thought Sumter and Charleston would both be lost "ere two months. . . . The attack is a question

1 "The Duty of the Hour," "To the Citizens of Charleston and its Vicinity," and two "Proclamations," *Charleston Courier,* Jul. 10, 1863; three "Proclamations," *Charleston Mercury,* Jul. 10, 1862; *OR* 28/2:276.

2 *OR* 28/2:185, 186, 188, 189, 219; Wise, *Gate of Hell,* 74-76, 78, 79, 82, 229, 230; Johnson, *Defense of Charleston Harbor,* 93, n100.

of energy & engineering and where spades have become weapons, we are generally conquered."

Two days later, the Confederates began removing the guns, transferring a 10-inch seacoast mortar and 296 shells from the fort to Sullivan's Island. At 6:30 p.m., a Union battery fired on steamboats at the fort's wharf. Rhett reported, "This is the first shot fired from land in the direction of this fort," and it "replied by bursting 4 percussion shells on the island."

Lieutenant John Johnson had been preparing for the inevitable bombardment since he assumed command of the fort's engineer operations on June 21. He made several changes to Sumter's defenses, mostly at night. Ferried over to the fort in two shifts, 300 to 450 "blacks" helped to complete the improvements. On the gorge, they filled 17 rooms of the officers' quarters with 256 "bales of steam-compressed cotton . . . soaked in salt water." Others filled the guard rooms, cells, and additional rooms on the gorge with sand. The sally port was "reserved for future use" and efforts were made to protect its exterior. It took three weeks to complete this work, which included transforming the "lower quarters" on the left face into a hospital. Federal shells from Morris Island directed against the gorge wharf made it and the sally port too dangerous to use. Workers converted a left flank first-tier embrasure and casemate into a new sally port and built a new wharf. As the left flank wall faced Charleston, it allowed boats to "arrive under cover of the fort." The transfer of heavy guns and their chassis, carriages, implements, and ammunition began during this time as well.[3]

On the morning of July 18, five monitors and the *New Ironsides* steamed into position opposite Battery Wagner and began firing on it. At noon, land-based U.S. artillery also opened on the installation. The combined bombardment averaged almost a round every two seconds, and Rhett estimated that "twenty-seven shells a minute [were] bursting in and around the battery." Brigadier General William B. Taliaferro, who had replaced Col. Graham as the island's commander, reported from Wagner that the Union guns had fired for 11 hours, "without cessation or intermission." He estimated "that no less than 9,000 solid shot and shell of all sizes, from 15-inch down-ward, were hurled at the works."[4]

This massive bombardment ushered in a second assault on Battery Wagner. Two brigades totaling over 5,000 men from Seymour's division, spearheaded by the 54th Massachusetts, attacked up the steep incline of the sand and timber

3 Grimball to Mother, Jul. 15, 1863; Q. A. Gillmore, *Professional Papers, Corps of Engineers U.S.A., No. 16.-Supplement. Supplementary Report To Engineer and Artillery Operations Against The Defences of Charleston Harbor in 1863* (New York, 1868), 45-46, hereafter cited as Gillmore, *Professional Papers*; John Johnson File, NA/RG 109, CSRC; Johnson, *Defense of Charleston Harbor*, 109-111.

4 Johnson, *Defense of Charleston Harbor*, 100.

fortification while more than 1,600 infantry and cannoneers, with 14 guns, defended the battery. Hand-to-hand combat marked much of the fierce battle, and Union troops fought their way into Wagner before the Confederates finally repulsed the assault.

Sumter supported the defense, firing 125 rounds at enemy positions along their siege lines. Lieutenant Iredell Jones of Company B, 1st South Carolina Artillery wrote his father on July 20 that "[d]uring the fight" they had helped as "old Sumter" kept up a desultory fire against the Yankee batteries and occasionally lobbed shots at the monitors. Defeated a second time, Gillmore began siege operations against Battery Wagner.

Beginning at 2:00 p.m. on July 20, eight 30-pounder Parrott shells were fired from Morris Island to determine the fort's range. Rhett reported that the first round "struck the fort," and a shell fragment severely wounded drummer boy John Graham, who was standing in the original sally port. Graham, a New York native, had enlisted as a musician in the 1st South Carolina Artillery at Fort Sumter in September 1862 and was just 13 or 14 when wounded. He returned to duty by October 1863, Sumter's youngest known casualty.[5]

*   *   *

On the night of July 19 Gillmore, prompted by the arrival of the blockade runner *Margaret and Jessie*, ordered a resumption of the shelling. The ship had brought in "valuable cargo," including "Imported Liquors" such as "Hennesy and Martelle Brandy, fine old Bourbon Whiskey, Jamaica Rum[,] Gin, etc." Other goods from the vessel—barrels of "Mackerel," "Mess Pork," and "Crushed Sugar"; bags of "Choice Jamaican Coffee"; cases of "French Calf Skins"; "Indigo Blue Stripes & Plaids"; "Hoyle & Son's London Purple Prints"; "Black and White Mourning Prints"; "Steamboat Playing Cards"; "Brier Root Pipes"; and "Ladies Elastic Gaiters" would be made available at a "Private Sale."

On July 23, the *Daily Courier* reported that the blockade runner *Fannie* had arrived from Nassau with "fruit and several pounds of ice," which were liberally shared "among the sick." For several days after its arrival, the *Courier* advertised "Foreign Goods. . . . Just Received From London And Manchester." These included "Black silks, A large variety of Mourning and Fancy prints, Linen Cambric Pocket Hdkfs," note and letter paper, envelopes, "Tooth Brushes," "Hair Brushes," and

---

5 Iredell Jones to Father, Jul. 20, 1863, Cadwallader Jones Papers, SHC; Jones Papers, FOSU Research File; Gillmore, *Professional Papers*, 4; First Artillery, SC, John Graham File, NA/RG 109, CSR.

fine tooth and pocket combs. Of more use to the Confederate war effort were "Quinine, 100 one ounce bottles, Nitrate of Silver," and "Chloroform."[6]

*   *   *

The beginning of the siege of Charleston increased the number of proclamations, notices, and military orders in the newspapers. Of particular note, the *Mercury* printed a "Military Notice" from "Headquarters, Columbia, S.C." dated July 14 from Beauregard. It barred women, children, and non-combatants from entering Charleston. A guard stationed at Branchville would prevent anyone from going nearer the lines without passes from the commanding general. Additionally, all trains arriving at and leaving Charleston, Columbia, and Augusta would carry guards "to examine the papers of all officers and soldiers." Those with incomplete papers faced arrest and report to Charleston's provost marshal or the post commanders at Columbia and Augusta. Guards also would be instructed to demand the passports of all persons travelling, and "instantly report . . . all who are without them. All persons are, therefore, advised to obtain passports either, at Charleston, Augusta, or Columbia, or elsewhere . . . to enter this Department."

On July 27, the *Mercury* printed a proclamation entitled "Slave Labor For The Coast, Division No. 3," which expanded the area from which labor would be drawn. In response to Beauregard's call for workers "and [following] the orders of . . . Governor Bonham; the Commissioners of the Roads and Town Authorities of the incorporated cities, towns, and villages" in Barnwell, Fairfield, Lexington, Orangeburg, and Richland counties were "required forthwith to summon all persons in possession of slaves liable to Road duty to deliver *one-fourth* of their slaves . . . at the Depots nearest their residences on Friday, the fourteenth day of August prox., at 10 o'clock a. m., there to await transportation to Charleston for thirty days' labor on the fortifications." The *Courier*'s August 4 edition issued another call for citizens who wanted to "assist in the patriotic work of the speedy completion of our defences" to do so by providing a "laborer or two" to fill sandbags at the Commercial Wharf. It further reported that "urgent necessity" required men to row the filled bags to Fort Sumter.

On July 31, General Ripley forbade First Military District officers from providing newspapers with any type of information about military operations. He also declared it "unmilitary and prohibited" for them to make public their opinions on the merits of commanding officers and their commands. Rigid punishment was promised to those who ignored the order. Ripley also cancelled all fishing permits

---

6 Articles from the *Charleston Courier*: "From Nassau" (Jul. 21), "Very Commendable (Jul. 25), and "Foreign Goods" (Jul. 27, 1863); from the *Charleston Mercury*: "Imported Liquors" (Jul. 22) and "Private Sale" (Jul. 29, 1863).

in the harbor. The next day, the provost marshal revoked permits for all boats not in government service to operate within its waters. Harbor protocol was stiffened on August 11 when Beauregard ordered that anyone arriving there from the United States had to remain onboard ship until his headquarters specifically authorized their activity. Anyone boarding in a foreign port had to produce a pass issued by an agent of the Confederate government. Ships were forbidden to carry any U.S.-made cargo except for military goods and "articles of prime necessity." Finally, no one aboard outbound vessels (or inbound ones either, for that matter) could carry letters unless the Department or First District Headquarters had approved them.[7]

* * *

Work on Fort Sumter's defenses continued from July 21 to August 17, even as the garrison kept shelling U.S. forces on land and sea and transferring guns, ammunition, and powder out of the works. The fort fired for twenty days, mostly after dark, as the Union lines crept closer to Battery Wagner. During the night of July 23, despite the combined fire from Sumter, Batteries Wagner and Gregg, and the fortifications on James Island, the Federals completed a second siege line 470 yards in front of the first, only 870 yards from Wagner. During the first week of August, a third line was completed more than 300 yards closer. From August 12–16, most of the Union fire targeted Wagner and Gregg, though some guns also began focusing on Sumter.[8]

Seventeen 200-pounder Parrott solid bolts or shells struck the fort on August 12, six on the exterior and 11 inside. According to Lt. Jones, the enemy opened an accurate and destructive fire with a 200-pound Parrott gun. A single shot almost tore apart a docked steamer at the wharf. Another "unlucky (or lucky, as you may be pleased to call it) shot . . . tore up the bake-oven. Several others played wild in the company quarters. The shelling injured two soldiers and a wounded negro died."

Jones offered some interesting observations about the enemy, who in his opinion were "far ahead of us in skill and energy." In an open field fight, the Confederates would prevail, "but when you come to regular operations requiring engineering skill, we can't compare with them." He wasn't worried about Charleston, however. "I cannot express to you the pride I feel in and the love I entertain for the old city, the glorious mother of freedom."

---

7 Articles from the *Charleston Mercury*: "Military Notice,"(Jul. 20), "Slave Labor For The Coast," (Jul. 27), and "Headquarters First Military District," (Aug. 1, 1863); from the *Charleston Courier*: "Official Orders," (Aug. 1) and "Fill up the Sand Bags," (Aug. 4, 1863).

8 Wise, *Gate of Hell*, 141-143; Gillmore, *Professional Papers*, 49-76. In the same letter, Gillmore reported that work in the for fort was progressing "very rapidly."

Jones then addressed the continual removal of guns from the fort. "All the important guns have been moved out . . . and their places filled with dummies, or sham-guns, of the Brooke's pattern"; these were wooden "Quaker guns" painted black and mounted on the parapet that appeared real from a distance. Writing around 9:00 p.m., Jones reported the fort's casualties—three wounded, two badly—and noted that the damage was slight. He also offered a complimentary observation of the enemy gunners: in his opinion, "the world never witnessed better shooting." "It is a rare thing [when] they miss the fort."[9]

Two shifts of 470 laborers and mechanics now toiled on Sumter's defenses. Assistant engineers White and William E. Mikell were sent there to help Lt. Johnson supervise this labor force. The work included placing at least three sandbag traverses on the right face parapet and additional sandbags over the arches of the western magazine. A "blindage" (similar to a bombproof) was being built to provide "shelter under [the] gorge wall" of the fort's interior.[10]

*　　*　　*

By August 17, Gen. Gillmore commanded 12 breaching batteries that mounted 38 rifled guns and smoothbore mortars capable of firing over 3,000 pounds of projectiles in a single salvo; it was the war's largest concentration of heavy artillery. Twenty pieces were directed at Fort Sumter: two 10-inch mortars, two 5-inch (70-pounder) Whitworth rifles, nine 6.4-inch (100-pounder) Parrotts, six 8-inch (200-pounder) Parrotts, and one 10-inch (300-pounder) Parrott. All the rifled guns targeted the gorge wall, and at 5:00 a.m. on that day a 200-pounder Parrott opened on the fort from 3,560 yards. Soon, all 12 batteries pummeled Fort Sumter or Batteries Wagner and Gregg.

Dahlgren reported that he "moved up the entire available naval force." Six monitors, the *New Ironsides*, and seven wooden gunboats joined 18 other guns and mortars on Morris Island in firing on Wagner and Gregg. Twelve rained shot and shell on Battery Wagner while the *Passaic* and *Patapsco* steamed up the channel to within 2,000 yards of Sumter, where they targeted the gorge, right gorge angle, and right flank wall with their "8-inch rifles" (Parrotts).

These actions marked the beginning of the "first major bombardment" of Fort Sumter, which was divided into two phases. During the first phase (August 17-23), Col. Rhett stated that 5,702 rounds were fired at the fort, totaling more than 552,000 pounds of metal. On the 24th, Gillmore reported to Halleck "the practical demolition of Fort Sumter as the result of our seven days' bombardment

9 Jones to unknown, Aug. 12, 1863, Jones Papers.

10 *OR* 28/1:609.

Two of three 6.4-in. (100 pdr.) Parrotts in Battery Rosecrans, Morris Island. *LOC*

of that work . . . Fort Sumter is to-day a shapeless and harmless mass of ruins." The second phase began on August 24 and lasted until September 2. The rate of fire during this period, though reduced, was still formidable, and Lt. Johnson placed the number of shot and shell at 1,819.

Fort Sumter's complement of guns could not begin to compete with the Union's massed land and naval weaponry. At the beginning of the bombardment, Sumter boasted only 38 cannon and two mortars mounted within its works, the majority of which were on the parapet. Though in the most exposed position, these guns proved most effective, especially by pouring plunging fire onto the U.S. warships.

From within the fort, Jones provided a detailed account of the first day's shelling on August 17:

> We have been pretty severely pelted and shelled to-day. The enemy opened at daybreak . . . with their monitors and land batteries on Wagner and Sumter, and . . . continued with unabated fury until dark. It is now 8 o'clock P. M., and the land batteries are firing slowly on Sumter. Our fort did not reply this morning until 11:30 o'clock, when we opened a brisk fire on the monitors and gunboats, and in the course of an hour succeeded in driving all of them off. The land batteries, however, we could not silence, and they have given us bricks all day long. The casualties are one man killed and fifteen privates and three officers wounded. In all the enemy fired 910 shots at the fort, out of which 600 struck. The fort is badly used up— four guns dismounted. . . . We expect a renewal of the attack to-morrow.

Lt. W. Gordon McCabe: After leaving Charleston, he was adjutant of Col. William J. Pegram's Artillery Battn., Army of Northern Virginia. *Memories and Memorials of William Gordon McCabe*

Jones's report of casualties is correct. During the first day of the bombardment one member of the garrison was killed, 18 were wounded, and two were "slightly bruised by bricks." Johnson himself, with a flesh wound in the left arm, was numbered among the wounded.[11]

On the night of August 16, Lt. William G. McCabe arrived in Charleston. The Richmond Howitzers' officer, on detached service with the ordnance department, kept a diary while in the city. He had been ordered to report to Gen. Beauregard "to command a battery of long range Foote guns with which I have been experimenting in Virginia."

McCabe's arrival coincided with the first phase of the bombardment. He recorded on August 17:

> [W]as awaken[ed] this morning by the steady firing from our batteries and those of the enemy. However, I was too old a soldier to feel any excitement so I turned over and took my morning nap. After breakfast lit my cigar and strolled down to "the Battery". . . Old Sumpter, "grand and gray," loomed up in the centre through the haze that was vanishing before the ocean breeze. How proud and defiant the old fortress looked, the deep mouthed columbiads frowning down from her parapets, while the dear old battle-cross sallies to the fresh Atlantic breezes. The enemy have opened their heavy 200 pounder Parrott guns & their practice is admirable. Every few minutes comes the dull booming of their guns, and then the bricks fly from her south face [gorge wall], showing that she has been struck.[12]

11 Jones to Father, Aug. 17, 1863, Jones Papers; Gillmore, *Professional Papers*, 76-78; Wise, *Gate of Hell*, 159.

12 William G. McCabe, Diary, Aug. 17-Oct. 23, 1863, McCabe Family Papers, 1863-1972, Virginia Historical Society, Richmond, VA, FOSU Research Files.

Ft. Sumter's heavily damaged gorge and right flank, from Morris Island, 1863. *LOC*

McCabe then reported to department headquarters and as the guns had not arrived, he was instructed to return the next day. He went back to Ripley's headquarters on the 18th but was told to come back on the 19th. Using the free day to his advantage, McCabe accompanied Lt. Frank Markoe, First District Signal Corps commander, to Sumter:

> Ran the gauntlet . . . today under heavy fire. . . . The fort is badly breached, and I consider it exceedingly weak. The Parrott guns will soon render Sumpter a harmless wreck. Many, indeed, nearly every gun on [the] south face [gorge wall] has been dismounted, and the north face [left face] badly breached by these 200 pounder iron bolts, which graze the interior crest of [the] south face and strike over on the north [left face wall facing the parade ground]. . . . Though the firing was exceedingly heavy every thing went on as usual. Amid the crashing of timbers and the falling of huge masses of masonry the officers could be seen

coolly walking the parapet and the men could be heard laughing and singing. The colors were shot away, & several soldiers ran out immediately, though right in the line of fire, to fix the halyards. While talking to the Ordnance Officer just under the South wall, we heard rather a louder noise than usual, and looking up, after the fall of [a] mass of masonry over came a 32 pounder, carriage and all knocked entirely off the parapet into the parade by one of those huge 200 pounder bolts.[13]

*   *   *

Gillmore and Dahlgren continued to pelt Sumter with heavy fire. Rhett reported on the morning of August 19 that the original sally port was "covered with rubbish," and shells were "continually bursting near." By mid-afternoon the exterior gorge wall had "bulged out . . . in half a dozen places" and was "pretty well hammered." At 10:20 a.m. the first shot passed through the gorge wall. About two hours later, 20 feet of the wall fell and light shined through cracks or holes

13 McCabe diary, Aug. 19, 1863.

Soldiers on top of hot shot furnace chimney amidst interior ruins, right face (left), stair tower (center), and right flank barracks (right), probably after the First Major Bombardment, 1863. *LOC*

in several casemates. Seven other casemates were "badly shattered" as more shot and shell passed over the gorge and struck the left face interior. Several had "clean breaches," and almost all of the piers supporting the terreplein had "fallen in and more . . . [were] continually going." Gillmore also reported that half of the gorge wall had collapsed, "exposing arches and sand in rooms." At 6:45 p.m., Rhett raised the colors, manned the batteries, and fired two long-range shots. About 15 minutes later Union gunners reduced their fire to about one round every 30 minutes.[14]

Jones described the action on August 19:

> The bombardment still continues hot and heavy, and we are holding out as well as possible under the circumstances. It is useless [no]longer to conceal the fact — the fort is terribly knocked to pieces. Though there is no reason at present to abandon it, its fall is only a question of time. Many guns have been dismounted, and all the guns on the gorge face are unserviceable on account of the parapet's being knocked away. . . . They ceased firing last night, the first intermission since day before yesterday morning. The fort has not replied since day before yesterday, though our main battery is still in good condition. I cannot imagine the reason

14 Gillmore, *Professional Papers*, 79, 81-82.

. . . but the honor of our country, the honor of ourselves, and the reputation of the gallant old fort demands it. I trust we will remain and fight the fort to the very last extremity. If she falls, let her and her devoted defenders fall together and gloriously. It is now 12 o'clock M., and while I write the shells are bursting all over us and the bricks are flying wildly. Yesterday 895 shots were fired at us, but we had but few casualties. Only three men slightly wounded. To-day we have not been so fortunate. Already one man has been killed and five wounded.[15]

At 3:00 a.m. on August 20, two steamers left the fort under the cover of darkness carrying 35,000 pounds of powder, several hundred projectiles, and other items; the next day, another transfer of eight and half tons of powder along with 120 barrels of pork, 75 barrels of flour, and additional materiel was accomplished. Rhett reported "that at one o'clock to-day, Lieutenant Johnson . . . scaled the walls of Fort Sumter from the wharf, thus having the honor of being the first man in the breach." This "honor" was both dangerous and foolhardy for the engineer as 879 "projectiles were thrown" at the fort that day, resulting in the "greater portion of the gorge wall" falling along with the rubble, "revetting, in a manner, the lower rooms." The detritus formed a pile against the exterior of the gorge and provided additional protection for the east magazine. The left face terreplein had "fallen in" to a "greater degree" across the fort and nine embrasures were "shattered."[16]

At 7:40 a.m. on August 21, the Federal artillery opened on the right face and at 10:55 a.m. directed heavy fire on the "East Battery"—the right flank parapet guns. Rhett thought that if Northern warships moved in and opened fire his men would be unable to stay at their pieces. The bombardment ended at 7:00 p.m., and the damage inflicted by 923 rounds was substantial. The right face had been "pretty well battered," and several guns on it and the right flank were out of service, leaving only seven operable cannons on the parapet. Union rounds blew gaping holes in the left face wall; one of them measured 8 by 10 feet.

Lieutenant Jones wrote his mother about the day's action:

The firing continued all day yesterday with unabated fury . . . and . . . our flag-staff was shot away four times. The firing was concentrated principally on the eastern [right] face. . . . In the evening, the Ironsides came in, and we opened on her with considerable spirit . . . until she thought it best to retire. The casualties were few, but one of our best men had his leg shot off and afterwards amputated. General Beauregard came down about dusk, and General Ripley was here also

15 Jones to Father, Aug. 19, 1863, Jones Papers.

16 Gillmore, *Professional Papers*, 83, 84.

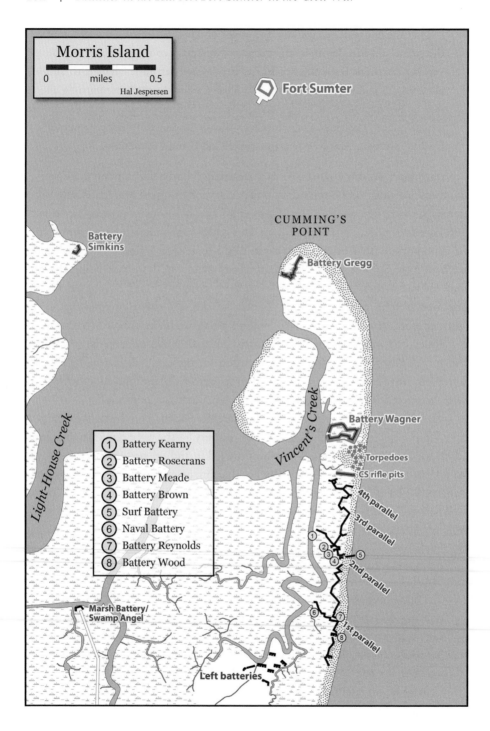

Morris Island

0 miles 0.5

Hal Jespersen

Fort Sumter

CUMMING'S POINT

Battery Simkins

Battery Gregg

Light-House Creek

Vincent's Creek

Battery Wagner

Torpedoes

CS rifle pits

4th parallel

3rd parallel

① Battery Kearny
② Battery Rosecrans
③ Battery Meade
④ Battery Brown
⑤ Surf Battery
⑥ Naval Battery
⑦ Battery Reynolds
⑧ Battery Wood

2nd parallel

Marsh Battery/
Swamp Angel

1st parallel

Left batteries

As Union siege lines moved closer to Battery Wagner, Federal batteries ranged in their guns on Ft. Sumter and other Confederate fortifications. In the 1st Major Bombardment, shot and shell from five of the "Left batteries" and seven in the siege lines pummeled Ft. Sumter. Union warships also targeted the fort and after the bombardment's first phase, the fort had been reduced to "a shapeless and harmless mass of ruins."

---

somewhat later. The former, while he appeared highly pleased and confident, could not help displaying a silent wonder and amazement at the ruined and dilapidated Fort. He says it must be held for one month yet.[17]

In a journal entry dated August 21, Rhett noted that the fort had been under "heavy and continuous fire" all day. Of the 943 shot and shell fired, 724 struck home and 219 "passed over." Accurate rounds disabled one 10-inch and one 8-inch Columbiad, as well as two rifled and banded 42-pounders. The flagstaff had been shattered and the garrison banner was "shot away" four times. Around sunset Beauregard and his staff, along with Col. Jeremy F. Gilmer, head of the Corps of Engineers, and Lt. Col. David B. Harris, chief engineer of the Department of South Carolina, Georgia, and Florida, visited the fort. Ripley and his staff followed at about 10:00 p.m. At 5:30 a.m. the next day Federal artillery opened up, and at 8:45 a.m. Rhett telegraphed that the fort's best gun, the 7-inch Brooke rifle, had been rendered unserviceable. The continuing bombardment also crippled a 10-inch Columbiad and a rifled and banded 42-pounder. The only functioning artillery pieces left were the 11-inch "Keokuk gun" and three 10-inch Columbiads. Before the shelling ceased at 5:00 p.m., the flagstaff at the salient angle was shattered once again and the banner fell to the parade ground. It was recovered and moved to the gorge. In all, the Federals fired 604 rounds at the fort, disabling all the barbette guns with the exception of the 11-inch and one 10-inch.

At nightfall, Lt. Johnson oversaw repairs to damaged areas and the restoration of disabled guns, tasks that were necessary every night. The workforce to accomplish these projects consisted of members of the garrison and 220 enslaved laborers.[18]

On August 20 McCabe, who had been placed on Ripley's staff as an acting assistant adjutant general until the Foote guns arrived, returned to Fort Sumter. Two days later it was still, according to McCabe,

---

17 Ibid., 85; Jones to Mother, Aug. 22, 1863.

18 Gillmore, *Professional Papers*, 87-88; *OR* 28/1:614-615; Johnson, *Defense of Charleston Harbor*, 128-129.

under very heavy fire [and I] . . . found the fort terribly used up; nearly all the guns [were] dismounted. I stood on the parapet a long time with several officers watching the fire of the enemy from their land batteries and the monitors. The shells (200 pounders) went screaming over us . . . [and in] walking on the brick pavement in front of the kitchens, I came very near being struck by several bricks & fragments of gun carriage, which were thrown up by a bursting shell. They fell all around me.

McCabe delivered dispatches to Battery Wagner and afterward "[g]ot home late and turned in as hungry as an elephant." The next day he recorded, "Firing heavy today. People more despondent here than we are in Virginia. Reason is because the horrors of war are new to them." That day he learned that "[e]very gun in [Company D, Capt. Francis H.] Harleston's Battery, Fort Sumpter, was disabled on yesterday by the enemy's fire, leaving only 4 serviceable guns on [the] parapet."[19]

Lt. Jones wrote his mother on August 22 that the bombardment

has resulted in considerable injury to us . . . dismounting guns. We have now only four guns fit for immediate service, though these are well protected by sand traverses. . . . Besides, several others are only temporarily disabled, and to-night, when the firing ceases, they can be repaired. One company was sent out of the Fort last night, and to-night another goes. This will leave three to keep the old machine going. No troops probably ever stood with so little concern and for so long a time such a terrific and constant shelling, and the more honor is due to them for such behavior when it is recollected that they do it without being allowed to reply. They have to sit quiet and take it the livelong day. You have no idea what a relief it is at night when the enemy stops pelting us; the feeling is delightful; we feel refreshed and rejoiced, and seem to breathe more freely an air that seems purer. The . . . Fort is still tenable, though no one expects it to be held any length of time. The object of holding now is to get time to build or complete batteries on James's Island. Powder is being moved out as rapidly as possible. . . . The Fort is so torn to pieces, and there is so much rubbish in it, that it would be a difficult job to get them [the guns] out.

The next day he described shelling from the monitors in a letter to his father:

They came up, five in number, about half-past three o'clock and opened on us, in our helpless condition, a most terrific and destructive fire. We had but one solitary gun amid the ruins, the remnant of thirty-five splendid barbette guns.

19 McCabe diary, Aug. 22 & 23, 1863.

. . . They were within 800 yards of the Fort . . . the other fortifications [couldn't see them] on account of the denseness of the fog . . . for some time our single gun was the only one on our side engaged. I could scarcely restrain my tears at our helpless situation. It was a sad reflection indeed to think that all our guns were disabled, and . . . that we had only one with which to fight the sneaking sea-devils. After awhile, however, Moultrie, Bee, Simpkins, Gregg, all opened, and, after a hot fight of two hours, in which we in the Fort were the only ones to suffer, the enemy retire[d]. I need not speak of the injury that we sustained, for we could scarcely be injured more than we already were.[20]

The monitors had opened fire at 3:15 a.m., lobbing 59 shot and shell before withdrawing about 5:30 a.m. Of these rounds, two 15-inch shells penetrated the right flank wall. Sumter's gunners responded by firing a total of six rounds from the "Keokuk gun" and a 10-inch Columbiad. These were the last artillery rounds fired in combat in the history of Fort Sumter. Throughout the day, the barrage from the land batteries and warships disabled three guns mounted in the second-tier and caused "very great" scaling of the right flank wall and southeast pan-coupé, and the right parapet was "very much shattered." In all, Union gunners fired 633 rounds at Sumter that day, twice cutting down the flagstaff.[21]

* * *

For weeks, Charlestonians safely watched and listened day after day as batteries on Morris Island and the guns of the U.S. Navy hammered the garrison at Sumter. They had no reason to consider that the city itself might become the target of the Federal bombardment until 1:30 a.m. the morning of August 22, when the night's calm was shattered by 8-inch shells falling on its fine houses and quiet streets. The shells came from a 200-pounder Parrott rifle in the "Marsh Battery" on the landward side of Morris Island 4½ miles away. The 8-ton gun dubbed the "Swamp Angel," fired sixteen rounds that night. Hours before the shelling, Gillmore had sent a message to Beauregard demanding "the immediate evacuation of Morris Island and Fort Sumter." If Beauregard refused or did not reply within four hours after the demand was received at Battery Wagner, Gillmore said, "I shall open fire on . . . Charleston from batteries already established within easy and effective range of the heart of the city." Wagner received the ultimatum at 11:15 a.m., and from there a courier took it to Battery Gregg, which in turn signaled a vessel to pick it up and transport it to Beauregard's headquarters. The ultimatum reached

20 Jones to Mother, Aug. 22 and Jones to Father, Aug. 23, 1863.

21 *OR* 28/1:615-616.

Charleston almost twelve hours later at 10:45 p.m. When it was delivered to Brig. Gen. Thomas Jordan, Beauregard's chief of staff (Beauregard was out of the city on an inspection), he observed that Gillmore had failed to sign the demand and returned it for official verification. By the time Beauregard returned and received the signed document, it was 9:00 a.m. on August 23, and the firing was long over.

Outraged, Beauregard fired off a message to Gillmore. "Among nations not barbarous" it was normal practice to provide one to three days' notice before attacking a city of non-combatants so "at least women and children" could evacuate. And since the Union commander general could not reduce Fort Sumter and Batteries Wagner and Gregg he had resorted "to the novel measure of turning your guns against the old men, the women and children, and the hospitals of a sleeping city, an act of inexcusable barbarity." Gillmore responded that his actions were justified as the city was "not invested" and "its avenues of escape [were] open and practicable," and by Beauregard's "own computation" he had had "forty days' notice" of any such danger. The assault on Charleston's defenses had steadily progressed, and the "ultimate object of that attack has at no time been doubtful." Gillmore concluded, "I shall suspend the bombardment until 11 p.m. tomorrow, thus giving you two days from the time you acknowledge to have received my communication of the 21st instant."[22]

Lieutenant Jones echoed Beauregard's fury:

> The garrison had been ordered previously to turn out with small arms to defend the mothers and daughters of our noble old city, against whom (for it was meant for no others to suffer by it) the atrocious demand was made had the effect to increase, if that were possible, the deep feeling of disgust and revenge that I already harbored in my breast, from witnessing on Saturday morning the unprecedented act that he threatened, [then] actually performed. And now, before God, I vow that if such an act is repeated, and I am ever placed in a situation to take revenge, I shall neither give nor ask quarter, but slaughter every wretch that comes within my power. . . . Such an act forewarns us what we may expect at the hands of General Gilmore; and, while it demonstrates his brutality, it demonstrates still more his weakness and recklessness. . . . The enemy's battery in the marsh, from which the shots were fired on the city, can be seen plainly from here, and has only one gun mounted, and at such a distance (five miles) no one thinks that it can injure the city materially. We cannot imagine any other object that General Gilmore could have had, save malicious spite. He could not have supposed that by firing on the city he would compel the surrender of Morris's Island and

---

22 Wise, *Gate of Hell*, 149-150, 169-171; *OR* 28/2:57-60.

Sumter. He is chagrined that he cannot, with his all-powerful combined force, make two poor little batteries crumble before him; that Sumter, though knocked to pieces, still continued to show fight; and that he has expended on the latter alone 100,000 pounds of powder and 1,000,000 pounds of wrought iron. But, though he cannot boast of having whipped us at all, much less in six hours, he cannot injure us much more than he has already.[23]

The Swamp Angel resumed firing on the evening of August 23, but the breech burst on its twentieth discharge; the shell continued its arc toward Charleston. On August 25, the *Courier* reported that six buildings had been struck, but no fires broke out and no one was injured. In response to the shelling, M. H. Nathan, chief of the fire department, issued a notice requesting citizens to have a tub of water immediately at hand to quickly douse any flames kindled by the shellfire.[24]

An experienced artilleryman, Lt. McCabe commented on the shelling's effect in Charleston:

[T]hese fiery messengers occasioned considerable consternation among the citizens, & people are leaving the city as if we had the plague here instead a few 200 pounder shell[s]. The enemy's battery . . . demonstrates that Parrott's guns are inferior to none, not excepting Armstrong's or Whitworth's. . . . I hope it will not sound unpatriotic for me to say that I went to sleep during the performance (because I knew there wasn't much danger). . . . Just as we expected the marsh battery commenced shelling the city last night. Frank Markoe and I had a good laugh at the absurdity of the Yankees in supposing that a few 200 pounder shells could begin to bully us into even thinking of surrendering [the] city.[25]

"I told you in my last that we had but one serviceable gun," Lt. Jones wrote his father. "Since then, however, we have rigged up two others that were disabled, which we expect to fight in case the Ironclads try us again. . . . [T]he Fort is to be held for the present, [but its] best guns are being removed. It is a slow and difficult work, however, and it is only at night that we can do anything at all." The firing that day had not been as heavy as the day before and the removal of Sumter's guns, both disabled and serviceable, continued. "[O]nly two of our own companies [remained] in the Fort—Captain Harleston's [Company D] and Captain [David G.] Fleming's [Company B]." Following the transfer of Companies C and F, 150

23 Jones to Father, Aug. 23, 1863.

24 Jones to Father, Aug. 23, 1863; "The Bombardment" and "Incendiary Shells," *Charleston Courier*, Aug. 25, 1863, 1.

25 McCabe diary, Aug. 23, 1863.

men from the 27th and 28th Georgia arrived on August 22. With infantry now forming the majority of Sumter's garrison, the fort had been transformed from a powerful artillery installation into a defensive infantry outpost.[26]

* * *

While the Southern infantry faced the challenges of Gillmore's siege and the U.S. Navy's blockade, the Confederate Navy considered means by which it could provide relief. On July 31, 1863, Adm. Franklin Buchanan, head of naval operations in Mobile, Alabama, wrote Cmdr. John Tucker, Charleston's naval commander, that he may have found such means. "To judge from the experiment of yesterday I am fully satisfied it can be used successfully in blowing up one or more of the enemy's Iron Clads in your harbor." "It" referred to a submarine dubbed the "fish boat." Buchanan had witnessed a test dive of the submersible, which successfully destroyed a barge in Mobile Bay. He informed Tucker that two of the vessel's owners were en route to meet with Beauregard and discuss the possibility of the "sub-marine iron boat" being deployed in the waters around Charleston. Franklin wrote that under proper conditions, "I can recommend it to your favorable consideration."

After the August 5 meeting, an enthusiastic Beauregard telegraphed Mobile. "Have accepted their submarine boat. Please assist them to get it here as soon as possible. The *Fish Boat* (later named the *H. L. Hunley*) arrived in Charleston only seven days later. C.S. commanders wanted the submarine operating against U. S. warships as soon as possible, but the crew from Mobile moved too slowly and Beauregard seized the vessel and turned it over to the Navy. On the 29th, operating with an inexperienced crew it sank killing five of its eight crew members. A few days later the *Fish Boat* was recovered and training with a new commander and crew resumed in September.[27]

* * *

During the bombardment's second phase, Union gunners continued the inexorable brick- by-brick destruction of the fort and the disabling of Sumter's guns. On August 24, they heard reports that the 11-inch Dahlgren (Keokuk gun) was the only serviceable piece on the right flank parapet. That night the Confederates used sandbags to fill "four penetrations" of first-tier embrasures on the right face. More sandbags were placed to strengthen the western

---

26 *OR* 28/1:617, states that Companies C and F transferred on the night of the 24th. The Aug. 26 Fort Sumter Journal entry reads, "Cos. 'C' and 'F' left fort last night."

27 Tom Chaffin, *The H. L. Hunley, The Secret Hope Of The Confederacy* (New York, 2008), 111, 113, 116, 121, 134, 139. Hereafter cited as Chaffin, *H. L. Hunley*.

magazine and repair the traverses on the barbette. The next day, 175 projectiles were fired at the fort. Only 36 rounds struck inside, but they caused significant damage as they slammed into the right face casemates. An understated entry in the fort's journal for August 25 declared: "The shock of the 10-inch Parrott shell is very great." Throughout the 26th, 130 more rounds were sent over, but this fire was reported as "slack and inaccurate" and the resultant "damage not very perceptible," though a rifled and banded 42-pounder on the right face barbette was dismounted and hurled backward into the parade ground. With no casualties, the garrison worked all night to seal the first-tier casemate embrasures with bricks.

With the exception of four shots directed at the flag, no other Union guns fired at Sumter on August 27. Consequently, the garrison and laborers worked through the day and night, completely "bricking up" the casemates. Efforts to remove and relocate materiel from the fort continued unabated despite the shelling of the previous days; 12,000 pounds of powder and "50 damaged muskets" were among the items sent away during that time.[28]

Lieutenant Johnson wrote about the transfer of these and other guns in his memoir. "Though often completely covered up on the dangerous crest of the shattered walls or protruding through caving, treacherous slopes of ruined casemates," the heavy artillery was "invaluable . . . for the defense of the inner harbor," so the garrison recovered as many pieces as possible. Fraser Mathewes, a civilian assistant engineer, was given this task. During the night, the guns were dropped one at a time "down from the parapet, upon a cushion of sandbags . . . on the berme at the water's edge . . . to be removed on a float." This remarkable operation was accomplished under the most extreme circumstances. Mathewes and his men scaled the ruins where sections of a wall, casemate arches, or brick piers could collapse at any moment, and they also were subject to Union solid shot landing or shells exploding in their midst. Often the guns had to be hoisted "up the hill of ruins" to the parapet, or what was left of it, and then made to "plunge thirty or forty feet . . . to the sandbags." From there the "tedious work of moving the gun from the tide-washed rocks to the float, "rising and falling with the swell of the sea," had to be overcome. The effort continued for six months, and about two dozen guns and mortars left in this manner. Lieutenant Julius M. Rhett supervised the removal of another six or seven pieces by this method.[29]

On August 28, only six shots hurtled toward the fort; three struck the outside and three missed. During this brief period of calm, laborers completed a traverse on the parade ground to protect the entrances to the

---

28 *OR* 28/1:616-617; Gillmore, *Professional Papers*, 91.

29 Johnson, *Defense of Charleston Harbor*, 138-140.

magazine and hospital located at the fort's southwest angle, and repairs and improvements were made to the right face barbette battery. Efforts to return disabled or dismounted guns to service continued nightly.

The Federal guns stayed silent again the next day. Lieutenant Jones wrote to his mother:

> I am happy to inform you that we have been spared the disagreeable whiz of 200 and 300-pound Parrots for the past few days. . . . I would not be surprised if the next attempt is a combined attack between their monitors and land batteries with redoubled fury. But whatever their mode, or whenever they see fit to make another attack, I hope and trust that our fortifications in the harbor will be sufficient to repel it. As to ourselves in the poor old fort, I hope we will give them the best we have got.

That night Company D departed Sumter, leaving Jones's Company B "the only one of the regiment now left here to guard the honor of the fallen fortress." Jones made no reference to the 150 soldiers from the 27th and 28th Georgia infantry regiments that were now serving at the fort. He continued:

> We have three barbette guns to fight, but of these one has its trunnion cracked, and the other two have the parapet knocked away from in front of them. . . . [O]n the night of the 26th . . . the detested monitors came sneaking close up to the fort, and it would have made the blood boil in the coldest hearted coward to have seen the men rush to battery to man their disabled guns. The night was very dark and foggy, and before we could see them to open, they sneaked out again and left us to surmise, as usual, as to their object. . . . [Y]ou may rest assured that the fort is to be held for the present, at least until the guns are gotten out, at which we are now working hard.[30]

Despite Sumter's growing inability to defend itself, many still believed it should be held. On August 29, Col. Rhett received a letter from Beauregard's chief of staff outlining the opinions of the department's two senior engineers, Maj. Gen. Jeremy F. Gilmer (who had received a temporary promotion on August 25) and Lt. Col. David B. Harris, concerning the advisability of abandoning Fort Sumter. The letter included the department commander's endorsement "approving the same" and stated that "Fort Sumter [should] be held to the last extremity, i.e., not surrendered until it becomes impossible to hold it

---

30 Jones to Mother, Aug. 29, 1863; Comstock, *Organizations at Fort Sumter*, 25.

longer without unnecessary sacrifice of human life. Evacuation of the fort must not be contemplated one instant without positive orders from these headquarters."[31]

The garrison's respite from the bombardment ended at 6:15 a.m. on August 30, when Gillmore's guns roared back into action; they "did not abate in the least until 5 P. M." Sumter was hit with 634 shot and shell, and Rhett reported that the damage was "very great." The parapet stood "all shaky, and partially demolished"; three right face casemate arches had "fallen in on [the] casemate containing commissary stores"; the right flank wall had three breaches; and a solid shot had "penetrated the gorge wall." As for the guns, the 11-inch Keokuk gun lay "badly shattered," a 10-inch Columbiad had its muzzle shot off and dismounted, and two more pieces wobbled with "carriage[s] broken." The only remaining serviceable gun on the barbette was a 10-inch Columbiad.[32]

August 1863 closed tragically for the Confederate military at Charleston. At 3:30 a.m. on the 31st, the CSS *Sumter* had picked up about 600 infantry and artillerymen who had been relieved from duty on Morris Island and, on its way into the harbor, was mistaken for a U.S. warship. The guns at Moultrie opened fire, and before realizing the error, the *Sumter* had been hit three times, run aground, and sunk in shallow water near Fort Sumter. The friendly fire killed two soldiers and wounded one. Rhett dispatched rescue boats, and the survivors took refuge in the fort. The next day, they went to Charleston by steamer.[33]

Union Army and Navy gunners targeted Sumter on the first day of September; 564 rounds rained onto the 2½-acre fort. By 2:00 p.m., what remained of the left face terreplein had fallen in; only the two casemates used for commissary stores survived, and later, two shells exploded in the stores themselves. According to Rhett, the right flank wall appeared "badly scaled, and in all probability will come down to-morrow as low as the first tier of casemates." No guns on the third-tier could be fired, and the only remaining piece in service was mounted in a casemate. September 2 marked the last day of the first major bombardment; shelling had begun at 11:40 p.m. on September 1. The *New Ironsides* and six monitors moved into position 700-1,500 yards from the fort and pummeled it for five hours with 185 shot and shell. Colonel Rhett escaped injury while crossing the parade ground, a 15-inch shell exploded a dozen feet in front of him, slightly wounding his orderly, Pvt. Robert B. Foshee.

The ships retired about 5:00 a.m. under fire from guns on Sullivan's Island. After they withdrew, the artillery on Morris Island opened up, but fired

31 *OR* 28/1:618.

32 Gillmore, *Professional Papers*, 96; *OR* 28/1:618-619.

33 *OR* 28/1:619, 687-712.

only three dozen shots at Sumter the entire day. While the fort's journal read, "No material damage," a round did penetrate the gorge wall, allowing daylight into the east magazine. The journal added, "Negroes worked all day repairing previous damage" and strengthening the magazine at the west end of the gorge. The garrison also filled the right face with sandbags. Lieutenant Johnson, whose August 17 wound had become "aggravated," was relieved of duty, and Lt. Francis M. Hall took over as the fort's engineer officer. Also, William Mathewes arrived to assist Hall and Mathewes's brother, Fraser, to remove the guns from the berm.[34]

Remarkably, the number of causalities suffered at Fort Sumter during the bombardment was surprisingly small. Only four soldiers were killed, as well as two African Americans, one from wounds and the other from "heart disease." At least 48 officers and soldiers and five "negro laborers" were wounded, and six were "hurt" or "bruised" by falling or flying bricks. Colonel Rhett reported one such incident on August 23. While at the dinner table, a shell burst just above the messroom with fragments from it "coming through on the dinner table and throwing down brick." In the casualty list, Rhett was "slightly hurt," Capt. David G. Fleming "bruised," Lt. Samuel C. Boylston "seriously bruised," Lt. Charles A. Scanlan had a bruised arm, and Lt. Eldred S. Ficklin was "slightly hurt." Captain Fleming had also had a close call two days earlier when he "was struck, though not hurt, by a shell."[35]

The first major bombardment culminated in significant damage to the fortification and effectively destroyed it as the principal defensive installation at the entrance to Charleston Harbor. The heavy guns that had been transferred were posted in new fortifications built on Sullivan's Island, James Island, and other harbor defenses. Fort Moultrie now served as the primary installation protecting the harbor's mouth. Four new sand and timber/log fortifications (two each on either side of Moultrie) now augmented Moultrie's firepower, and the whole presented a formidable line of works bristling with heavy guns and mortars. The harbor's entrance remained secure. Throughout both phases of the shelling, the U.S. Army averaged 78 percent accuracy striking Fort Sumter. Gillmore's most accurate gun, the 10-inch Parrott rifle firing 250-pound percussion shells, gouged and bore through its walls. The reliability and toughness of this gun was demonstrated on August 20, when one of its shells exploded prematurely and took 18 inches off the

---

34 *OR* 28/1:619-620; Gillmore, *Professional Papers*, 100-103.

35 *OR* 28/1:615; Confederate States Army Casualties: List and Narrative Reports, 1861-1865, List and Reports of Casualties In Individual States, South Carolina, Fort Sumter, NA/RG 109.

muzzle. Engineers simply chiseled off the ragged rim and filed down the rough edges. The monster gun resumed firing, its accuracy undiminished.[36]

On September 1, 1863, the *Mercury* printed a message from Beauregard to Ripley dated August 27:

> The Commanding General has witnessed with genuine pride and satisfaction the defence made of Fort Sumter by Colonel RHETT, his officers, and the men of the First Regiment of South Carolina Regular Artillery, noble fruits of the discipline, application of their duties, and the soldierly bearing of officers and men, and of the organization of the Regiment. In the annals of war no stouter defence was ever made, and no work ever before encountered as formidable a bombardment as that under which Fort Sumter has been successfully held.[37]

---

36 Wise, *Gate of Hell*, 156, 157-158; *ORN* 14:448-449, 452-453; Johnson, *Defense of Charleston Harbor*, 119, 143; Gillmore, *Professional Papers*, 89; *OR* 28/1:222, 598-599.

37 "Head Qrs. Dept. of So. Ca, Ga and Fla," *Charleston Courier*, Sep. 1, 1863.

Chapter 9

"When He Can Take It and Hold It"

September–December 1863

On September 3, Col. Rhett reported the results of the previous day's bombardment to Beauregard. The left and right face of the terrepleins had fallen in, the left flank wall was cracked from top to bottom, a large portion of the gorge was down, and the right gorge angle magazines had been penetrated, with the lower one cracked. The right flank was "very nearly shot away . . . the ramparts gone . . . nearly every casemate breached, and the remaining wall [was] very thin." Rhett observed, though, that the sand-filled casemates had sufficiently protected the garrison from shells. He also believed it was no longer possible to mount guns on the parapet. The "fort in its present condition [was thus] unserviceable for offensive purposes." Rhett's report confirmed Beauregard's belief that Sumter had lost its offensive capability. On August 31, Beauregard directed that "a large number of torpedoes [mines] [be placed] in front of the obstructions between Forts Sumter and Moultrie." He also ordered the mining of the inner harbor in the Hog and Folly Island Channels and of the channel east of Castle Pinckney.[1] Lieutenant Francis Hall, who had replaced the wounded Johnson on September 2, supervised the ongoing activities, including the shipment of the last two guns mounted on the parapet. Sumter's only serviceable gun, a smoothbore 32-pounder, was mounted aside the new sally port in the left flank's first-tier, facing the city.

An often overlooked event in Fort Sumter's history happened the evening of September 4: its final transition from an artillery to infantry post. Col. Rhett ceded command to Maj. Stephen Elliott, Jr. Rhett and Company B, 1st South

---

1 Gillmore, *Professional Papers*, 103-104; *OR* 28/2:323-324.

Carolina Artillery departed the fort; Company D had transferred a few days before. Lieutenant Jones "had the pleasure of being among the very last to leave the Old Fort," but his feelings were complicated. Pride was tinged with "deepest feelings of regret and sadness on my part." Six companies of the Charleston Battalion arrived that night, replacing two Georgia companies. Sumter's infantry now numbered 320 officers and men.[2]

Stephen Elliott, a native of Beaufort, South Carolina, had been captain of the Beaufort Light Artillery when the state seceded. A participant in the April 1861 bombardment, Elliott commanded the artillery and was wounded at Fort Beauregard during the November 7 battle at Port Royal Sound later that year. After his promotion to major in April 1863, he served as the Second Military District's chief of artillery and supervised torpedo placement in the Stono River and Lighthouse Inlet. Five months later, Elliott accepted command of Fort Sumter.

In his first report, Major Elliott noted no "direct fire on the fort" and only 18 days of rations on hand. After dark on September 5, two monitors took up position and "kept up a continuous fire" of case shot upon the harbor's entrance, which had been supporting fire for the failed Union amphibious assault on Battery Gregg and also was meant to discourage Confederate reinforcements from reaching Morris Island. Elliott also submitted a "Final Report" of Sumter's ordnance. Of the 64 cannon and four mortars installed on June 30, just 27 remained "uninjured" and seven were listed as "injured." The other pieces had been shipped to Charleston and its neighboring fortifications.

In the city, Beauregard continued to receive reports on worsening conditions at Battery Wagner, which was under heavy artillery fire. Large numbers of Federal troops had been transferred to Morris Island, and they made a failed attempt to take Battery Gregg. At midnight on September 5, the advancing Union siege line reached Battery Wagner's moat. According to a report the next day, 100 of the 900 men in its garrison were casualties. The salient parapet had been badly breached, and the entire battery "much weakened." Such continuing shelling would certainly court "ruin." Beauregard ordered the island evacuated. On the night of September 6-7, the Confederates retired under heavy fire from land and sea. Fort Sumter thereby became the forward installation in Charleston's defenses and continued issuing almost daily operations reports on Morris Island and the positions of enemy warships.

Four sharpshooters who had served in Battery Wagner were now assigned to Sumter. The specialists carried Whitworth rifles with telescopic sights and took up positions in the fort's ruins. Johnson observed that they proved very effective

2 *OR* 28/2:621-622; Comstock, *Fort Sumter Organizations*, 27.

Lt. Col. Stephen Elliott

LOC

against the Union artillerists 1300 yards away at Cummings Point.[3]

* * *

Fort Sumter's appearance of being totally destroyed presented a tempting target to Adm. Dahlgren. On September 7, he messaged Maj. Elliott demanding the fort's surrender, and four days later, he told Secretary Welles that the evacuation of Morris Island "offered an opportunity for assaulting Fort Sumter," which was so beaten up on the gorge and southeastern (right flank) faces that he would be able to pass the Main Channel's obstructions and enter the harbor. Elliott, not even in command of Sumter for half a week, forwarded the demand to P. G. T. Beauregard.

"Inform Admiral Dahlgren that he may have Fort Sumter when he can take it and hold it," the Creole general replied curtly. "[S]uch demands are puerile and unbecoming." Dahlgren was unphased and called for a group of volunteers to prepare for a nighttime amphibious assault. Neither Dahlgren nor Gillmore expected much resistance. Sumter's guns had been silent since August 23. Dahlgren told the assault force's commander that a mere "corporal's guard" manned the fort, and "all we have to do is go in and take possession."

The *New Ironsides* and six monitors engaged Fort Moultrie and lobbed a few rounds at Fort Sumter on September 7, taking another piece out of the "left face parapet." One of the monitors, the *Weehawken*, ran aground in the narrow, shallow channel between Sumter and Cummings Point. Elliott ordered the stranded vessel fired upon, and Moultrie soon began executing this directive. Shortly afterward,

---

3 Stephen Elliott, Jr., File, and South Carolina, Capt. Stuart's Company (Beaufort Vol. Arty), Stephen Elliot, Jr. File, NA/RG 109, CSR&SO; Gillmore, *Professional Papers*, 106; *OR* 28/1:87-90, 622, 669; Johnson, *Defense of Charleston Harbor*, 173; *OR* 28/2:344.

the *New Ironsides* and the remaining five monitors moved up to fire on the Sullivan's Island fortifications and covered the *Weehawken* as it fired in its own defense—first at Moultrie then at Sumter. At high tide the monitor floated free, and the U.S. warships withdrew.[4]

The September 12 issue of the *Daily Courier* reported details of the engagement, embellishing the artillery duel of September 7 as "one of the most remarkable acts ever recorded in the history of war." Two Charleston photographers, George S. Cook and J. M. Osborne, took photographs of the damages of the first major bombardment from a parapet gun carriage while the ships hurled 11- and 15-inch shells "against and into Sumter." Despite the obvious danger, Cook and Osborne continued documenting "the dilapidated old pile," then turned the camera on the warships. The photographers, according to the *Mercury*,

> had the good fortune to secure, amid the smoke of battle . . . a faithful likeness of the *Ironsides* and two Monitors. . . . Thus, our citizens and country . . . had preserved . . . a valuable memorial of a defense almost unequalled in its obstinacy—one worthy to be transmitted to the future generation. The feat is unparalleled, as far as we know.[5]

While Dahlgren continued preparing for his attack, communications with Gillmore disclosed that he too was planning an assault for the same night. Though each unsuccessfully requested the other's support, they at least agreed upon a password to avoid mistaking each other for the enemy during their separate advances in the darkness. Gillmore ordered his infantry to return to Morris Island if the naval forces landed first (which they did).

Elliott, anticipating a nighttime amphibious assault, had been positioning his command to meet one. On September 9 at 1:00 a.m. he observed that he had seen "a fleet of barges approaching from the eastward." One company of the Charleston Battalion defended the gorge wall, another supported its right, and a third covered its left. Twenty-five men and a lieutenant held the northeast angle; a company was stationed at the large breach in the left face wall and a second supported them. Yet another defended the left flank wall and the new sally port and wharf, while members of the signal corps and remaining infantry were "posted at three points on the wall" to throw hand grenades and fireballs. Additionally, the old wharf had been mined to discourage a landing.

The garrison withheld fire until the Federals drew within a few yards. When they "attempted to land on the southeastern [right flank] and southern faces

4 Gillmore, *Professional Papers*, 108; OR 28/1:714-716; Johnson, *Defense of Charleston Harbor*, 156-158.

5 "Ironsides and Two Monitors Taken–A Bold Feat," *Charleston Mercury*, Sep. 12, 1863.

Fort Sumter's garrison firing on the U.S. Navy and Marine night amphibious assault.
Battles and Leaders of the Civil War

[gorge]; [they were] received by a well-directed fire of musketry, and by hand-grenades, which were very effective in demoralizing [them]; fragments of the epaulement were also thrown down upon [them]." Those who landed "sought refuge in the recesses of the foot of the scarp." From their rowboats, many sailors and Marines fired muskets or revolvers, but were soon ordered to retreat. The "brief and decisive" fight lasted about 20 minutes. Of the 320-man strong garrison and the Signal Corps detail, only "80 riflemen and 24 men detached for service of the grenades and fire-balls" were engaged. Sumter received supporting fire from artillery in and around the harbor, and Lieutenant McCabe recorded that "Dan Lee Midshipman on the 'Chicora', sent them . . . compliments in sundry stands of grape from his 7 in. rifle Brooke gun, while Ft. Johnson, & the batteries on Sullivan's Island also sent their remembrances."

Elliott reported that numerous shots struck the fort. "Not one of [his] men [was] hurt" although the U.S. forces lost four killed, 19 wounded, and 102 captured. The garrison recovered five stands of colors and five barges. At around 4:00 p.m. the Northerners sent over a flag of truce to convey the captured officers' "baggage" and "conveniences for the wounded." About two hours later, under a truce flag from the fort, the Union dead were sent to the fleet. McCabe wrote that around 8:00 p.m. the prisoners were taken to Charleston. Colonel Rhett's regiment assumed guard duties and, once organized, marched the captives off to prison.[6]

*   *   *

The Federals, in full control of Morris Island, soon began improving existing works, constructing new ones, and rebuilding Confederate fortifications. Battery Wagner was renamed Fort Strong in honor of Brig. Gen. George C. Strong, who had been mortally wounded in the July 18 attack. Battery Gregg became Fort Putnam, named after Col. Haldiman S. Putnam, who was killed in the assault on the 18th. Midway between the two they built Battery Chatfield, so named for Col. John L. Chatfield, who also had been mortally wounded on July 18.

Morris Island remained a powerful Federal artillery site. The proximity of the big guns at its north end, from three quarters of a mile to just over a mile and a quarter from Fort Sumter, had a greater impact on the citadel than the artillery below Fort Strong. This also allowed nighttime Federal surveillance of the fort. On September 17, for example, the Confederates reported that rays of "a large calcium light" were "directed" on the fort and "its approaches" from Cummings Point.[7]

*   *   *

From the beginning of September until near the end of October, Union guns fired only sporadically upon Sumter. This respite of sorts allowed its garrison, engineers, civilians, and enslaved laborers to put in long hours of work strengthening the crumbling citadel. Many of the slaves got sick, and the engineer recommended their transfer. Captain J. T. Champneys, who had replaced Lt. Hall as the fort's chief engineer, report to department headquarters said that most of the black men working there had arrived during warm weather. What little clothing they had was worn out, many were "nearly nude," and not one in ten had a blanket. The shortage of available shelter mandated housing them in "splinter proofs," which were similar to bomb proofs, on the damp and sometimes wet parade ground. Though Champneys requested clothing for them to "facilitate the work," preserve their health, and ward off illness, 115 of them were transferred out three days

6 Wise, *Gate of Hell*, 206-209; Gillmore, *Professional Papers*, 109; Johnson, *Defense of Charleston Harbor*, 161-164; *OR* 28/1:724-728; McCabe diary, Sept. 9, 1863.

7 Wise, *Gate of Hell*, 158, 210; Frederick Denison, *Shot and Shell: The Third Rhode Island Heavy Artillery Regiment In The Rebellion, 1861-1865* (Providence, 1879), 194-195. No official records record 10-inch seacoast howitzers on Morris Island; *OR* 28/1:625. The 3rd Rhode Island Heavy Artillery's regimental history states that on Oct. 26, those three fortifications mounted over 30 pieces of heavy artillery: 19 Parrotts (a 300-pounder, a pair of 200-pounders, a dozen 100-pounders, and four 30-pounders), a 10-inch Columbiad, four 10-inch seacoast howitzers, an 8-inch seacoast howitzer, six 10-inch seacoast mortars, and four 12-pounder Napoleons.

U.S. gun crew preparing to fire, Battery Chatfield, Morris Island. *LOC*

later and replaced by 147 others and two overseers. This workforce converted surviving first-tier casemates and areas of the gorge into quarters or bombproofs and built other defensive structures. Harbor steamers ferried in timbers, thousands of sandbags (filled and not), and other materials and supplies at night. They also repurposed salvaged items from the ruins of interior buildings, as well as rubble and debris. The original sally port survived under the ruins of the gorge wall, from which quarters for 100 men were created. Ventilated galleries were built out from the wall. The left flank casemates on the first-tier were converted to a hospital, and a bombproof was built to shield the men from "exploding fire from the sea." The latter was located at the entrance to the southwest angle stairs where the gorge and left flank met.

Stone collected from the rubble replaced protective sandbags that had been washed away. The perpetual demand for sandbags plagued Champneys, who complained that those received were only half the size of the earlier ones. Plus, "so fragile" was their construction that "the bags decayed after only one or two

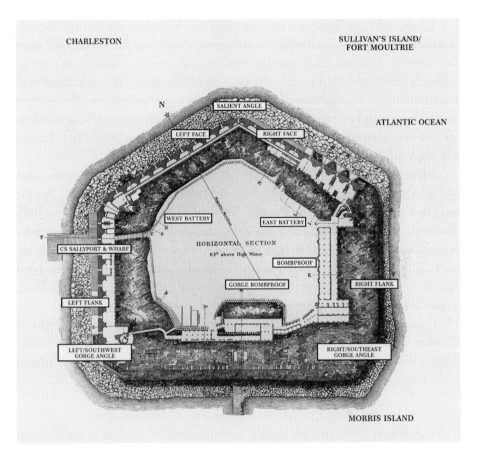

Diagram of C.S. modifications of Fort Sumter, September 1863–February 1865. *AC*

weeks" in the weather, a waste of valuable time, labor, and materiel. He expressed a preference for "gunny bags" made of burlap.

On the evening of September 19, 250 officers and men of the 11th South Carolina relieved the Charleston Battalion. Six days later, six "sub-terra torpedoes" exploded in the rubble along the fort's exterior. Mistaken for an attack, the explosions were the result of the rising tide and surf that rolled fragments upon them, causing them to ignite. The new garrison members joined the others in stabilizing the fort and transferring more of its guns. By September 26, three guns and two 10-inch mortars had been shipped from Sumter.[8]

8 J. T. Champneys, "Fort Sumter Letter Book," Sep. 12, 1863-Oct. 28, 1863 (specifically Sep. 12, 19, 20, and 23); Gillmore, *Professional Papers*, 114; Comstock, *Organizations At Fort Sumter*, 34. Champneys reported that 11 cannon remained in the fort: two 10-inch and two 8-inch Columbiads,

Elliott told Gen. Ripley on September 21 that he judged the fort still capable of offensive operations and proposed mounting cannon in the undamaged right face first-tier casemates. These emplacements would create a crossfire with guns on Sullivan's Island and help protect the channel obstructions. The right flank wall would "partially" protect them, and "masses of the upper arches" would shield the spaces above it and to the rear "to a great extent." Furthermore, only U.S. warships off Sullivan's Island could bring them under fire; shelling from Morris Island could not reach them.

Gilmer and Harris visited the fort to consider the plan's implementation and on October 27, Champneys was ordered to prepare three casemates "for the reception of guns" and to devise a plan for their protection on the exterior wall. The work progressed rapidly and two days later, a rifled and banded 42-pounder occupied one of the casemates. By October 14, the remaining two guns, both 10-inch Columbiads, had also been mounted. Masses of rubble and debris were piled against the casemate arches to protect against reverse fire from Morris Island. Later, a cribwork of pine and palmetto logs was added to strengthen the exterior.

Company K, 1st South Carolina Artillery Regulars arrived on the night of October 5. These artillerymen served the "three-gun battery" and the 32-pounder next to the new sally port. Fort Sumter now had four heavy guns mounted and ready for service, though none would ever be fired in combat.[9]

*   *   *

The citizens of Charleston eagerly read the news of activities at Sumter, and sometimes became part of the news itself. A September 23 *Daily Courier* article reported that a "patriotic young lady of South Carolina" presented the Charleston Battalion with "an exceedingly handsome laurel wreath," which honored the "noble and gallant services [it] rendered to the cause of freedom in the recent battles at Battery Wagner and Fort Sumter." When Beauregard ordered a salute fired to celebrate the recent Confederate victory at Chickamauga, it "thundered forth from the each of the batteries of the harbor entrance. Even old gray Sumter joined her voice in the chorus of heavy ordnance, and sent forth from her ruined arches a poem for the victor."[10]

---

two rifled and banded 42-pounders, one 8-inch shell gun, and four 32-pounders (two rifled and banded and two smoothbores). Most had no carriages.

9 Johnson, *Defense of Charleston Harbor*, 169-170, cxlv; Champneys, "Fort Sumter Letter Book," Sep. 29, 1863; Comstock, *Organizations At Fort Sumter*, 35.

10 From the *Charleston Mercury*: "Presentation to the Charleston Battalion" (Sep. 23) and "Operations of the Siege" (Sep. 24, 1863).

The "three-gun battery"/"East Battery." *ORA*

While on a train to Charleston, Edmund Ruffin recorded that he heard "heavy & frequent cannonading" 18 miles away from the city, which he assumed to be combat-related. Arriving at the Charleston Hotel, he learned the sound was instead the Chickamauga salute. Ruffin had not visited Charleston since 1861, and he felt a need to return. After securing the necessary permissions, he visited Ripley's headquarters near The Battery and with an "excellent spyglass" examined the harbor, fortifications, and vessels. The "side of Fort Sumter next to the city" remained virtually undamaged. Charlestonians had become so used to artillery fire, he observed, that it seemed to pass "unnoticed & scarcely heard."

Ruffin stayed at Dr. John Bachman's home and made day trips to the surrounding area, including James Island and Battery Simkins. Deserted plantations and homes and ragged, weed-choked fields abounded. On September 28, he visited the harbor's forts, including Sumter, "the chief object of my expedition." He found the left flank "but little shattered" and the right face the "next best preserved," while the gorge and right flank were "entirely broken down." As for the interior, the extensive damage seemed worse than the outside.

In summary, Ruffin noted that "the whole may be said to [be] made up, in fragments of various sizes, of everything that constituted the structures & their contents. Amidst the principal mass . . . of crumbled masonry, are seen large masses of fallen walls, portions of chimney, . . . timbers, cannon & carriages partly protruding, with portions of wheelbarrows, furniture &c."[11]

11 Scarborough, *Diary of Edmund Ruffin*, 3:148, 150-151, 153-156, 158, 159-160, 162-164.

And the destruction was far from over. Union artillery in Forts Putnam and Strong opened on Sumter at 1:45 p.m. on September 27. Known as "the first minor bombardment," the shelling lasted just six days. The guns fired 597 times, taking 11 seconds (according to Champneys) from muzzle blast to impact. He also reported, "Many shot fall within a few feet of each other." Elliott stated that the shelling "cut the top of the gorge wall slightly in one or two places," bored holes in the parade ground, extended the breach in the left face wall, and left it vulnerable to possible future damage. The existing "direct breaches" could be secured if a thousand or two sandbags were delivered every night, but that didn't happen. Overall, however, damage to Sumter was limited.[12]

The shortage of sand in the fort and its infrequent delivery caused Champneys to complain that he would have to fill bags with sand and broken bricks. On the night of October 19, though, so much sand was delivered and deposited on the wharf that it was useless until the piles were moved to the fort. But for every problem solved, another begged attention. The shipment of water to the fort presented problems. Shelling had destroyed Sumter's cistern system of draining rainwater from its five terrepleins, so the men relied on boats for its delivery. Elliott called the boat's commander "an arrant coward" and urged military seizure of the vessel to assure the garrison's "full supply."[13] On October 23 Champneys reported that no water had been supplied for three nights, and the fort was thus in severe danger.

Amidst the shelling, operations continued as usual. Troops cycled in and out and saw to their assigned tasks. Artillery pieces were moved and provided appropriate protection, with sandbags in some cases. Soldiers discovered a rifled and banded 42-pounder in good condition buried in the rubble and "exhumed" it for further service. Several casualties were sustained during the six-day shelling: one enslaved person was killed, four were wounded, and a brick fragment broke a soldier's jaw.

The Union artillery fell silent once again, and in the 20-day interlude, Champneys and his crews continued work on the "three-gun battery" and other engineering projects. Elliott, meanwhile, sent daily reports to his superiors in Charleston, including missives on the duel between Confederate guns on Sullivan's and James Islands and Federal artillery on Morris Island, plus the positions of U.S. warships. On the night of October 10, the fort's "post-boat," on its way to Sumter, captured a boat with two Union soldiers aboard who were sent to Charleston after

---

12 Gillmore, *Professional Papers*, 116-119; Champneys, "Fort Sumter Letter Book," Oct. 2, 1863; *OR* 28/1:140, 627.

13 Champneys, "Fort Sumter Letter Book," Sep. 29, 1863, and Oct. 23, 1863; *OR* 28/1:626; Gillmore, *Professional Papers*, 123.

questioning. That same evening the Confederates released "four floating torpedoes" from the fort, and though a "heavy explosion" occurred at about the "proper time in the fleet," the mines failed to damage any U.S. vessels.

Near the end of October, Sumter's surgeon, Dr. A. W. Bennett, informed Champneys that typhoid fever threatened 200 enslaved workers, and advised their transfer. Champneys agreed but requested that it be done "as soon as practicable." Another 200 replaced them two days later.[14]

* * *

Fire from the Morris Island batteries resumed on October 26, commencing the "second major bombardment" of Fort Sumter. The shelling lasted 41 days and ended on December 5. General Gillmore had received credible reports from prisoners and deserters that the fort was remounting artillery on its right face—the "three-gun battery." Gillmore intended to "cut down that face" and shell those casemates from the rear.

Champneys reported that the shelling "led off with a 200 Pounder" from Fort Putnam and was quickly followed by fire from Battery Chatfield and Fort Strong, including a 300-pounder and 10-inch mortars. The gorge wall "received many blows" and "the reinforce . . . [was] much injured." On the left flank, a monitor's 15-inch shell struck the traverse in a second-tier casemate above the hospital. The shell "penetrated 15 feet through" the top of the traverse. The various batteries threw 198 rounds at the fort until falling silent near dark. In spite of overnight labor to repair and reinforce the traverse and relocate 1,000 pounds of powder, a shot from one of the monitors bored almost completely through it the next day. Fortunately, the medical facility escaped damage.

Union gunners targeted the right flank and gorge almost exclusively when the barrage resumed, and Champneys estimated that shells struck both the southeast and southwest angles about a hundred times. The southeast angle, the section closest to Morris Island, took so many 300-pounder shot and shells that it was crushed, and the rubble fell onto the parade ground. Over the next few days, additional damage rendered both sections "perfectly accessible from the outside." He reported that a large enemy audience on Morris Island observed the bombardment.

Inside Sumter men continued to clear rubble and reinforce the interior. The bombproof at the old sally port and at the one extending from it into the parade

---

14 Comstock, *Organizations At Fort Sumter*, 35; Champneys, "Fort Sumter Letter Book," Sep. 29 and 30, and Oct. 22 and 26, 1863; Gillmore, *Professional Papers*, 117, 120, 121-122, 123. Champneys reported that many of the replacement workers had "deficient" or summer-weather clothing, and others had no shoes. He was concerned that since the parade ground was "always wet and often covered with water" and cold weather was coming, they would suffer. Presumably this situation was addressed, but no available evidence indicates when and how.

Interior, Fort Sumter's southeast (right) gorge angle, 1864. *ORA*

ground were the "only safe place[s]." While shelter for enslaved personnel was adequate, Champneys fretted about sufficient shelter for the garrison. Once sand covered both shelters, they would serve as "admirable bombproofs." Champneys continued to express concern and offered suggestions for the garrison's safety in a note to Elliott.[15]

In the predawn hours of October 31, members of the garrison assumed their customary duty stations, wary of a possible assault. The roof, third floor, and most of the second floor of the right flank barracks had been destroyed during the various stages of the bombardment. A large volume of rubble from those areas had accumulated over the surviving sections of the ground floor, creating a bombproof-like shelter. Because iron girders had been used in the barracks' construction, the first floor rooms on their northern end paralleling the right flank were considered safe for positioning men who could respond "in case of an alarm." A dozen soldiers were stationed there, as was William Mathewes, the slaves' civilian overseer. All were crushed and died when "a Parrott shot struck an iron girder" and brought down the roof. Eleven of the dead were members of Charleston's Washington Light Infantry (Company A, 25th South Carolina); Mathewes and a member of the

15 *OR* 28/1:30; Champneys, "Fort Sumter Letter Book," Oct. 27, 1863.

The gorge bombproof with right/southeast gorge angle beyond, 1865. *LOC*

12th Georgia Artillery Battalion were the other two. The local papers reported the tragedy. According to the *Courier*, the "painful news" arrived early Saturday morning and created "a general feeling of sadness and depression." The deceased were "mostly natives and residents of this city and their deaths have brought mourning to a large number of households and distressed families and friends."

After this tragedy, Beauregard ordered that "all walls threatening to fall and injure [the] garrison be pulled down or shot down." He would dispatch "an iron field piece" to facilitate the work if needed. At least one attempt was made to implement the order. Repeated tries early on the morning of November 21 failed to pull down a broken arch on the gorge wall. It finally came down at 5:00 a.m. when a Parrott shell struck it, killing "2 negroes and wound[ing] 6" along with two soldiers, who were also wounded.[16]

16 Johnson, *Defense of Charleston Harbor*, 171-172; "Bombardment of Fort Sumter," *Charleston Courier*, Nov. 2, 1863; *OR* 28/1:632, 640; Gillmore, *Professional Papers*, 143.

Over the next 10 days the garrison incurred two killed and four wounded, all from mortar fire. October 27, however, produced the greatest number of casualties in Sumter's history to date: 15 killed, three wounded, and one injured. Lieutenant Andrew P. Brown of the 12th Georgia died after being struck in the head by a brick after a 15-inch shell exploded; he was the first officer to lose his life at Fort Sumter. From October 26 to 31, the Confederates lost 18 killed or mortally wounded and 11 wounded or injured. Between October 26, when the second major bombardment began, and the 31st, Union artillery hurled 5,606 projectiles at Sumter. By the 30th, Battery Barton on Morris Island (four 10-inch mortars) and Battery Seymour (four 13-inch mortars) had been completed near Fort Chatfield and joined the shelling. The 15-inch Dahlgrens, 30-pounder Parrotts, and 10- and 13-inch mortars fired with 85 percent accuracy. Though 822 shots missed the fort, 4,784 struck their target. During this period, Sumter's "Second National" garrison flag flew at the southwest angle of the gorge, which at 55 feet above the water was the fort's highest point. The garrison had erected the staff in a massive mound of sand over the spiral stair and much of the firing from Morris Island focused on it. On October 29, the flagstaff was "shot away after retreat." Two days later, the flag was cut down twice more. After the third time it was so "cut up . . . it was necessary to raise" the 12th Georgia's battle flag until a new flagstaff could be obtained for the national colors.[17]

The bombardment continued with varying ferocity through November. On the 2nd, 837 rounds were fired, while only 24 were shot on November 30. An average of 405 rounds were fired per day, 13,505 in all. Of this number 9,496 struck the fort's exterior or interior (69 percent accuracy) while 4,209 missed the mark entirely. Morris Island's guns continued to pummel the gorge, with the southeast and southwest corners their principal targets. The monitors, meanwhile, maintained their fire on the right flank. Many of the rounds that arced over or passed through the walls landed in the parade ground or struck the interior walls. Even with reduced accuracy the Union gunners still inflicted casualties and structural damage. On November 6, a mortar shell exploded at the eastern entrance of the main bombproof, killing two soldiers, wounding seven, and concussing seven more. The Confederates believed that the shelling served as a prelude to another night assault, and on October 30 Beauregard ordered Ripley to ready all batteries bearing on Sumter at night to "sweep its exterior faces at a concerted signal from Elliott, or whenever the approach of hostile boats shall be evident." This wariness proved prudent on the night of November 3, when a small boat with four enemy "scouts" landed at the fort's southeast angle. In the darkness sentinels mistook it

---

17 *OR* 28/1:632, 668; Gillmore, *Professional Papers*, 127, 128-129.

for a friendly picket boat and hailed the vessel. It did not respond and pulled away under a spray of musket fire.[18]

On November 1, Beauregard telegraphed Adj. Gen. Samuel Cooper in Richmond regarding the threats to the fort, proclaiming that the "[r]uins will be defended to [the] last extremity." Several days later he issued Special Orders No. 22, which decreed that as of November 6 Sumter's garrison would consist of no more than 300 infantry, and about 100 men would relieve part of the garrison every fourth or fifth night. Beauregard visited the fort on the night of November 5 and reported to Pres. Jefferson Davis the next day that it was "all right at present" and that the garrison was "in fine spirits." He also recommended that Elliott be promoted. He then ordered Ripley and Taliaferro to keep 200 men each "in readiness nightly, to be thrown to the assistance of the garrison" should the enemy attempt "to assail" Sumter. On November 7 Beauregard requested that Cmdr. John R. Tucker, commanding the naval squadron, position one or two ironclads nightly to "sweep with their fire" the areas between Fort Johnson and Cummings Point and Battery Simkins and Johnson, or if enemy ironclads tried to remove or run past the "obstructions between Sumter and Moultrie."

*   *   *

In addition to the artillery trained on Fort Sumter, a 100-pounder Parrott at Fort Putnam targeted Charleston on October 27. At a range of 7,440 yards, the gun fired three shells with 35-second fuses. Beauregard telegraphed Adj. Gen. Cooper that one fell short, and the other two landed in Charleston with no damage and but "little excitement produced." The *Mercury* reported that the firing began at 11:00 a.m., and one round passed through a vacant house without damage to "life or property." An unexploded shell was recovered and "found to contain the celebrated greek fire."[19]

Six days later on November 2, Davis stopped in Charleston on his way back to Richmond after a high-level meeting with Gen. Braxton Bragg and senior officers of the Army of Tennessee. Widespread excitement greeted the president. A number of senior officers and politicians greeted him, and a 15-gun salute marked his arrival. A crowd of thousands cheered and ladies waved handkerchiefs as he made his way to City Hall, while a wreath proclaiming welcome hung at the corner of Meeting and Broad streets. The 1st South Carolina Artillery's band saluted him

18 Gillmore, *Professional Papers*, 130-131, 133, 147; *OR* 28/2:463, 466, 486, 489, 491-492.

19 "Jan-Mar 1865, Report of the Bombardment of Charleston, January 1st, 1864 to January 1st, 1865," Gillmore, Quincy A. File, NA/RG 94; *OR* 28/2:446; "Siege Matters-One Hundred And Ninth Day," *Charleston Mercury*, Oct. 28, 1863; "News from the Islands," *Charleston Courier*, Oct. 28, 1863.

with "Hail to the Chief." Davis addressed the crowd, praising the state's patriotism and devotion and the valor of the city's defenders. He said he did not believe the enemy would ever capture Charleston. Should that happen, though, Davis wanted only "rubbish" to remain, and no "prey for yankee spoils." He also "paid warm tribute" to Major Elliott and Fort Sumter's garrison. Davis retired to the home of ex-governor William Aiken after the speech and spent the next couple of days inspecting fortifications and reviewing troops on Sullivan's and James Islands. He also witnessed the bombardment of Sumter and the other harbor defenses being shelled before departing on November 5.[20]

* * *

The previous night Edmund Ruffin returned once again to Fort Sumter, riding out on a slow, quiet steamer while watching timed fused shells fired from Cummings Point fall on their targets. Ruffin stood on the upper deck as the steamer shielded itself between the fort and U.S. artillery fire. Within 300 yards of Sumter, "a brilliant & broad flash from [Ft. Putnam] announced a coming shell, . . . I felt . . . a sort of shrinking, or effort to contract my body into a smaller space. But the shell came no nearer to me than to announce its near passage by louder singing than I had ever heard before."

While at the fort, he observed a "strong guard" who he thought "were mostly sleeping, in every posture of reclining . . . with their muskets within their grasp." To his surprise "almost every man was up & awake, as if it was day time." Elliott appointed an officer to escort Ruffin around the works. The Virginian observed the widespread destruction and the fact that the "three-gun battery" was the sole area seemingly "well protected from the enemy's fire . . . by timbers & thick bulwarks of sand-bags."

While a good portion of the exterior of the gorge remained solid, Ruffin could "see the sky through it in some places . . . & all was so thin & weak" that his guide told him "every ball or shell which struck there, passed through the area, or beyond through the opposite Channel or North [right or left] Faces." Returning to Elliott's casemate shortly before boarding the steamer to return to the city, Ruffin observed the major and "some of his officers & guests" partaking of a "supper of cold meat & bread."[21]

* * *

20 *OR* 28/1:155-156; Burton, *Siege of Charleston*, 202; "President Davis In Charleston," *Charleston Courier*, Nov. 3, 1863.

21 Scarborough, *Diary of Edmund Ruffin*, 3:215-219.

From November 1863 to February 1864, five regiments of Brig. Gen. Alfred H. Colquitt's Georgia brigade and a couple of South Carolina regiments served as Fort Sumter's infantry garrison. During the first two days of November members of the 25th South Carolina and 12th Georgia Battalion left the fort, and the 210 men of Colquitt's command plus 96 more from the 25th South Carolina arrived. Elliott began assigning units to specific areas of the fort, as well as to specific guns. For instance, from November 4-12, various companies of the 1st South Carolina Artillery served the fort's heavy guns and 12-pounder mountain howitzers. In a report dated November 3, Elliott recommended that a 10-day furlough be promised the "garrison in the event of their repelling a heavy assault upon this work." He couldn't think of anything better to ensure a successful defense.[22]

On November 4 Elliott reported the firing of 92 time-fused 30-pounder Parrott shells during the previous night, with 77 exploding "over and within the fort." The "practice with these projectiles is beautiful; the adjustment of the time being so perfect that the occupants of the gorge wall are secure from the effects of the explosion, which rarely fails to occur during the passage of the shell over the parade."

During late October the flag was cut down three times. On November 5 it was moved from the southwest to the southeast angle of the gorge, closest to the Union positions on Morris Island. There the staff was somewhat protected by a parapet of sandbags, which also provided a modicum of cover for the sentinel stationed at that point. Nevertheless, the next day artillery fire cut it down for a fourth time and once again it was re-raised under fire. Union gunners struck the flagstaff a fifth time on the 12th. On the 27th it was shot down a sixth time and Private James Tupper, on duty as a "shot marker" at the southwest angle to record the number of rounds that hit or missed the fort, witnessed the last strike. While under fire he covered the entire length of the gorge parapet and retrieved the flag. When he tried to re-raise it, however, he found the staff was too short. He, Pvt. C. B. Foster, and Cpls. W. C. Buckheister and A. J. Bluett spliced a piece of spar to the staff but when they attempted to replace it, a shot cut it from their hands. The soldiers persisted and after about 15 minutes, amidst bursting shells and clouds of sand thrown up around them, they succeeded. Two of them stood on the parapet and waved their caps at the Federals. In his report dated November 28, Lt. Col. Elliott, who had been promoted seven days earlier, called their actions a "most distinguished display of gallantry." On December 15th, Beauregard issued Special Orders No. 272, which recognized the men, all from the 27th South Carolina, for their bravery and the "gallantry displayed by them that day." He granted them 15-day furloughs and invited them to his headquarters to receive his thanks.[23]

In addition to assigning units to defend specific areas of the fort, Elliott added other defensive devices to the mines already in place. Each evening 12-pounder mountain howitzers, fraises (wooden spikes), and wire entanglements were positioned. The guns were mounted on the parapet, the "bristling array" of fraises was placed below the crest of the exterior of the right flank and gorge so as not to block the infantry's field of fire, and the wire was strung near the base of the sloping ruins of each wall. Every day at dawn the guns, fraises, and wire were removed. About 30 yards from the fort, Confederates floated a boom of logs and chains to impede boats attempting to land, and every night two or more guard boats watched the waters around the fort. In spite of these precautions, small Federal boats came close to the right flank and gorge at night and rowed completely around the fort on more than one occasion.

On the night of November 6-7, John Johnson, now a captain, returned to Sumter to relieve Capt. Champneys as Sumter's senior engineer. Johnson described the fort's appearance, defensive measures, and the effects of the Union spotlight. He noted that at 8:00 p.m. on November 12, the "calcium light" at Fort Putnam illuminated "our works." And although not as bright as a full moon, the "large capitals of a newspaper" could be read by its light at Sumter. The beam lit up the crest of the gorge, revealing the "jagged pinnacles" of the left face "in bold relief against the midnight sky above and the gloomy crater of the fort below." It also proved a "great annoyance," blinding the sentinels watching for activity on the dark water.

Johnson wrote that at night Sumter presented a "most impressive . . . strange, silent grandeur." The interior appeared "dark and gloomy" and occasionally a shower of sparks from a fire on the parade ground would briefly illuminate "rugged blocks of brickwork and the stagnant pool of water." Lanterns "carried by unseen hands" moved across the "spacious enclosure," lighting the way for "long files of men" carrying heavy timbers or sandbags over the "steep, crumbling, dangerous slopes" to repair areas damaged by the shelling, or reinforce or construct new shelters for the garrison. Others could be seen "through . . . crevices" of damaged casemates, "burrowing deep and mining their way slowly under hills of rubbish to give unity to the work and confidence to its defenders." About halfway up the interior slopes were the guard posts, where soldiers wrapped in blankets sat around small fires

---

23 Johnson, *Defense of Charleston Harbor*, 179-180; Gillmore, *Professional Papers*, 132, 146; *OR* 28/2:555.

Two 12-pounder Mountain Howitzers and fraises (wooden spikes) on the fort's parapet, 1865. *LOC*

while at the crest, sentinels peered into the night. One "lookout," perched atop a ladder at the "most critical breach," was fully exposed "to the dangers of the firing."

According to Johnson, if an assault succeeded in driving the defenders from the walls, the garrison was to fall back to interior positions and contest "every foot of the parade and casemates." "Every quarter" with a view of the interior was "carefully loopholed for infantry fire," and near the corner of the left face and left flank, the muzzle of a 12-pounder mountain howitzer "protruded every night . . . to sweep the parade with grape and canister." Upon a signal from the fort, Confederate batteries would fire into the interior "until they [the Federals] were forced to leave."[24]

The new defenses were tested on the night of November 17 when several small boats were reported near the fort and the alarm was raised four times. Then at 3:00 a.m. on the 19th, a "number of enemy barges" approached within 300 yards and opened fire with muskets. The garrison's infantry responded, wounding three of

24 Johnson, *Defense of Charleston Harbor*, 173-174, 175-177, 182; Gillmore, *Professional Papers*, 137-138.

Maj. John Johnson, Fort Sumter's longest serving CS engineer and author of *The Defense of Charleston Harbor*. *The Defense of Charleston Harbor*

the estimated 250 Federals, who were conducting a reconnaissance in force to determine Sumter's strength. In support, heavy guns on Sullivan's and James islands sent rounds ricocheting across the water's surface near the gorge and right flank walls.[25]

At this time, Company D, 1st South Carolina Artillery, commanded by Capt. Francis H. Harleston, manned the garrison's guns. The men were stationed at the "three-gun battery" in the right face first-tier casemates. Harleston was also assigned command of the right flank. At 4:30 a.m. on November 24, a sentinel reported to him that waves threatened to wash away some of the fraises. As Harleston exited the fort to inspect them, a 30-pounder Parrott shell from Morris Island struck both his thighs and one arm. Elliott wrote that Harleston "bore his sufferings most manfully, and was averse to taking any opiates," but "on account of his great pain" they were administered despite his objections. His only anxiety was for his mother, and he "was perfectly calm, and as cheerful as his great sufferings would permit." Harleston died six hours after being wounded, just two weeks shy of his 24th birthday. The highly respected officer was a Charleston native and an 1860 Citadel graduate.[26]

On December 3, Edmund Ruffin made a final trip to Fort Sumter and arranged to spend the night. He met both Lt. Col. Elliott and Capt. Johnson, the latter of whom "gave up the use of his cot & Mattress, & the larger share of his blankets" for Ruffin's stay. The two officers shared a casemate in the first-tier left flank next to the postern, which was divided by a "board partition." The section toward the parade ground was the "eating room," and the other half, which faced

25 Gillmore, *Professional Papers*, 140, 142.

26 Johnson, *Defense of Charleston Harbor*, 111-178.

Charleston, was the "sleeping room." The "only window" was the gun embrasure, and Johnson's cot lay "immediately under & alongside of this porthole."

That evening a military brass band arrived and, according to one eyewitness, "played a number of spirited airs, outside the wall, & just under my window. This unusual occurrence was one of few things serving to indicate to the enemy that demolished Sumter is not only alive, but lively." The December 5 issue of the *Daily Courier* reported that the "Fort Sumter Band . . . discoursed some excellent music for about an hour," including, "for the benefit of the Yankees, 'Dixie's Land.' The enemy made no reply to this demonstration, not firing a gun." The group was likely the regimental band of the 1st South Carolina Artillery Regulars.

The next morning, thick fog prevented the Union gunners from firing, but since it was clear at Sumter, Ruffin examined the fort's exterior. He was astonished by "the great number of the enemy's shot & shells lying . . . on the berm & slopes of rubbish" and stated that while many of the shells were whole, "more were broken by explosion." He then walked around the fort and attempted to make "some rough sketches" of it. By 8:30 a.m., as the sun rapidly burned off the fog, Ruffin returned to the fort's interior. Assisted by two soldiers he carried off two "memorials of Sumter," an unexploded case shot and a shell fragment. He also was allowed to "cut off a small piece of the flag . . . which has so often been struck down by the enemy's fire."

Federal guns fired with long intervals between rounds and after breakfast Ruffin repaired to the parade ground, where he sat against the sandbags covering the gorge bombproof and began drawing. After being warned that the Federal mortars had joined the bombardment and that these shells might strike anywhere, he joined the laborers and soldiers "in the bomb-proofs, passages & apartments." While under cover a mortar shell "sunk into the ground near where I had been [and] exploded," gouging "a hollow some 6 feet across." At noon the mortar fire ceased; Ruffin went back to the parade ground to resume his sketching but was interrupted once again by falling shells.

Later Johnson, using a lantern, led Ruffin through "the bomb-proofs, the narrow & dark passages . . . the winding staircases, & . . . lower casemates" that had not been rendered "impassable by the rubbish." He also observed "lines of casemates . . . so full of crumbled masonry, [and] blocks of fallen wall" that it was "like going through . . . a limestone cavern."

The next day, Ruffin observed that the firing from the rifled guns seemed to be directed at the corner where the gorge and left flank walls met. These "shots cause no danger, except, when striking near the top, scattering fragments of bricks are thrown over into . . . the fort." Most of the errant shots passed "close by the corner . . . & by [the] now opened . . . window by which I am now writing. The pattering on the water of the shower of finer rubbish driven by the striking shells, & more rarely of the fragments of missing shells which explode before striking the water, is quite exciting." Ruffin felt little danger "in my position—unless a shell should happen to explode when immediately opposite the open port-hole."

When the firing ended around sunset Ruffin "followed several . . . soldiers in climbing up the inside face of the City wall . . . to the top of the adjacent West corner, on which the rifled shot had been directed all day." There the sandbag traverse "was well demolished, & the entrance therefrom, down the narrow winding stone stairway was choked by the split & loose sand, so as to be impassable. . . . The sand was cut up in deep & broad trenches made by the passage of the shot. . . . These damages, as usual, will be repaired tonight." As the onset of twilight obscured his view, Ruffin returned to his "apartment." Shortly afterward the shelling was renewed at 15-minute intervals and after 1:00 a.m. on December 6, he returned to Charleston. Eight days later, Ruffin left for his home in Virginia.[27]

Edmund Ruffin had witnessed the last day of a prolonged bombardment. Johnson wrote that after 41 days of shelling, both day and night, the "second great ordeal was passed." Three walls had received the majority of the damage from 13,649 shells and solid shot that struck Fort Sumter out of 18,677 fired. The Union gunners were accurate about 73 percent of the time. They almost entirely destroyed the right flank (ocean facing) second-tier casemates. On both sides the wall presented the appearance of a mass of rubble averaging 20 feet high, with a "rugged crest" about 6 feet wide. With the exception of some exterior damage, the first-tier casemates, filled with sand, had survived. The wall's corners stood near their original height.

Johnson corroborated Ruffin's observations. The damage to the gorge was concentrated about midway between the old sally port and southeast angle. At that point "converging fire" from the front and rear had produced a "large semicircular gap in the crest." The "heavily battered" left face now averaged a height of 25 feet. Multiple rounds that passed over the gorge and struck the side facing the parade ground gave the wall the appearance of "a range of rocky mountains." On December 4, Elliott reported what might have been the only good news on Sumter's condition when he noted that the "slope is exceedingly steep and the footing very insecure. Nothing like a rush can ever be made up these slopes as long as they retain their present inclination."

The objective of the bombardment—to destroy the "three-gun battery"— had failed. Only three mortar shells struck that area, and they inflicted limited

---

27 Scarborough, *Diary of Edmund Ruffin*, 3:253-258; "Siege of Charleston," *Charleston Courier*, Dec. 5, 1863, 1.

The fort's destroyed left face interior, 1863. *LOC*

structural damage. Five soldiers were wounded in the first explosion, one suffered a concussion in the second, and "several" were wounded in the third. The casualty count during the 41-day bombardment was 89 men: 31 killed, 45 wounded, and 13 injured. Of equal or greater importance to the Union failure was the Confederates' success in perfecting Fort Sumter's interior defenses and the improvement of the garrison's and enslaved workers' quarters.[28]

28 Johnson, *Defense of Charleston Harbor*, 180, 182; Gillmore, *Professional Papers*, 132, 133, 147.

Chapter 10

Confident and in Fine Spirits

December 1863–April 1864

The second major bombardment of Fort Sumter ended on December 5, 1863. It had reduced large portions of the once-mighty fortification into a mass of debris and rubble. Lieutenant John R. Key, Confederate Corps of Engineers, and Sgt. Conrad Wise Chapman, on detached service from the 59th Virginia, arrived at Sumter the night of December 7. According to Captain Johnson, they were under orders "to execute sketches and take views of the historic ruin." Two photographs of one made by Key, grandson of Francis Scott Key, were mounted and autographed by General Beauregard. One was presented to Lieutenant Colonel Elliott and the other to Johnson. Chapman's paintings of the fort, other area defenses, and the *H. L. Hunley* are among the war's most famous.

General Beauregard optimistically reported the next day, "The enemy appear to have altogether ceased any further attempts against Sumter," though "an occasional shot" struck Sullivan's Island and Battery Simkins, "which responded with a few shots." Johnson noted that "the fort had begun to settle down into something like quiet, and even comfort." From within the ruins, the Signal Corps detachment observed and reported on the U.S. Army's and Navy's activities, while sharpshooters peered through telescopic sites ready to fire. The absence of chaos brought on by enemy shelling allowed for the easy rotation of the garrison and laborers, as well as the delivery of supplies. Laborers worked in daylight repairing damage and improving defenses, while carpenters converted casemates' interiors into more comfortable quarters for the winter. Some of the garrison even took the opportunity to sun themselves with "great enjoyment."

The buildup of rubble and debris continued to pose problems, as did reconfiguring the fort's interior. Casemates were used for quarters, offices, the hospital, and other purposes. Storage for powder and other explosives, however, was problematic. Three powder magazines, one original and two improvised, housed Sumter's explosives and ordnance materiel. On the right face, a casemate had been converted into a service magazine for the three-gun battery, and another was located on the gorge in the center bombproof. The "southwest magazine" or "small-arms magazine" located next to the southwest circular stair was the only original magazine still in use. Located at the southwest end of the gorge wall, it had been constructed with two rooms, one inner and one outer, both lined with wood. Several feet of wreckage produced by Union artillery fire provided additional protection. The rooms of the original magazine were separated by a 6-foot-thick brick wall with a passage between them 8½ feet tall and 32 inches wide, but only the innermost room served its intended purpose. Captain Johnson said it held an "incongruous assortment" of rifle cartridges, 12-pounder mountain howitzer ammunition, hand grenades, "fire-bottles, signal-rockets, sensitive tubes for priming, shells, torpedoes, etc." These items, plus the 150 pounds of powder stored there, may have totaled 300 pounds of explosives. The outer room functioned as the fort's commissary.[1]

In the quiet of the morning on December 11, soldiers waited for rations in a line extending from the commissary into a timbered gallery, thickly covered with sand, which opened onto the parade ground. At 9:30 a.m. the "incongruous assortment" of materials and powder in the inner room exploded. Both rooms "were immediately ignited . . . the occupants killed, and those stationed in adjoining passages either killed or burnt with greater or less severity." Much of the blast raced through the gallery out to the parade ground, and simultaneously the passages to the lower and upper left flank casemates became "filled with most dense smoke, introduced by a blast of great strength." In total darkness the occupants abandoned their arms and personal belongings and rushed from the stifling smoke to the open embrasures. The blast, heat, and smoke "prevented any prolonged attempt to obstruct" the fire's progress. Flames funneling up the stair tower ignited a "chest of hand-grenades and combustibles" positioned there to "assist in repelling surprise attacks." In the second-tier casemates, which had been converted into quarters, the conflagration briefly trapped soldiers, who escaped by ladder down the exterior wall through an opening for firing muskets.

Crew members with water buckets from one of the gunboats provided the first assistance, but because of the intensity of the blaze and the lack of firefighting

1 Johnson, *Defense of Charleston Harbor*, 187, 188-189; *OR* 28/1:176.

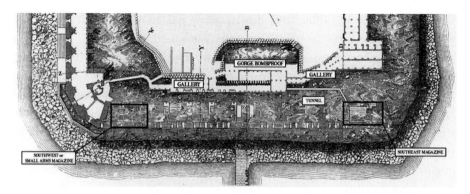

C.S. 1864 conversions on the gorge: the southwest/small arms magazine, the gorge bombproof and galleries, and the southeast magazine. *AC*

equipment, fire fighters decided to seal off the flames, eliminating the air flow where possible. Embrasures, the stair tower's top door, the southwest angle postern door, and the gallery to the parade ground were closed or blocked, possibly with wet sandbags. "[It] was all that could be done, and the fire was left to expend itself," Johnson noted sadly.

The flames forced Elliott to move his headquarters from the first-tier left flank to the right face. The telegraph had to be relocated, which interrupted communication with the city, and the Signal Corps detachment was unable to contact Sullivan's Island or Fort Johnson until late in the day. At 4:40 p.m. telegraph operator William R. Cathcart re-established the line and reported the explosion. He then requested provisions, 100 muskets, buckshot cartridges, 50 men, telegraph instruments, and 200 yards of wire. After that, telegraph communication was lost again until 4:00 a.m. on the 13th.

By noon two days later, nearly everything flammable on the left flank of the second-tier, except the timbers over the stair tower and its upper steps, continued to burn. About half the timbers of the gallery to the parade ground collapsed, effectively smothering that portion of the fire. The flames devoured everything combustible in the left flank first-tier casemates. They finally stopped at the wooden platform next to the sally port, but not before its gates burned and rendered the bricks "as hot as though in an oven." With access to the wharf cut off, the ladder on the second-tier exterior provided entry to and exit from the fort; an additional ladder on the second-tier's interior allowed for a 30-foot descent over sloping rubble to the parade ground. Every man labored to end the crisis. On December 12, Elliott reported that Capt. Johnson had been "everywhere, doing everything that [a] man could do." Lieutenant L. A. Harper, 25th South Carolina, "showed great gallantry in rescuing burning bodies from the smoke and flames."

Eleven officers and soldiers were killed and 41 were wounded or injured. The 25th South Carolina suffered the greatest losses, with 20 killed or wounded. The trio of Georgia regiments, the 6th, 19th, and 27th, lost 23 killed or wounded. The 1st South Carolina Artillery and White's South Carolina Artillery Battalion suffered six casualties, while the staff and Signal Corps lost one killed and two wounded. Union troops on Morris Island noted the smoke and flames rising from Sumter on December 11. As the garrison worked to reorganize itself, the Federal artillery resumed its bombardment, firing 220 rounds. Johnson referred to this as the "second minor bombardment." During the shelling, fragments struck Lt. Col. Elliott in the head and ankle. Though slight, these injuries were the second and third wounds he had sustained in the war. He reported the ankle wound as a "slight temporary injury." His acting adjutant and cousin, Pvt. Percival Elliott, was also hurt. More soldiers were killed or wounded in this tragic accident than on any other day in Fort Sumter's history.

The day after the accident, heavy winds and rain hampered the garrison's efforts to restore normalcy. From December 13-15, Elliott reported that the passages and casemates had begun to cool, and the gorge wall was "much sunken in over the exploded magazine." The blast's upward force had collapsed about an 18-foot square above the magazine nearly 10 feet into the room. Little evidence of the explosion showed on the exterior of the gorge near its crest.

By December 14 only one place in the fort still burned. Elliott reported that his men "penetrated . . . to the . . . commissary store house" where only a "small amount of burning material" remained. Water buckets extinguished it. With the fires out, Elliott pronounced the day one of "extreme quiet." Beauregard had inspected the fort immediately after the accident and returned on December 15 with Col. Alfred Rhett and Lt. Col. Harris for further inspection. He telegraphed Richmond reporting the "explosion and fire less considerable than supposed" and that the damage had been repaired quickly. He added that "Colonel Elliott and garrison are confident and in fine spirits." After the inspection he ordered that the "most vigorous measures" be "immediately taken to restore the burnt quarters and communications of the interior."

As an indication of adherence to established routine, the rotation of troops in and out of the fort continued as usual. During the night of December 11, 100 members of the 32nd Georgia arrived. The next night, however, the "regular relief" was ferried to Sumter and the Georgians returned to James Island. A week later, except for White's Artillery and the Signal Corps detachment, all the garrison's units had been relieved.

On December 18, Elliott reported that Capt. Johnson had departed on sick leave with a high fever. Assistant Engineer Francis M. Hall, who took over the work of repairing the damage, replaced him temporarily. In the overheated passage to the magazine, a long wooden pipe funneled water into the still-smoldering ruin. Once inside the commissary, Hall found the most telling testament to the explosion's force. The 6-foot-thick partition between the magazine's inner and outer rooms had been thrust forward about 2 feet at the top and 1 foot at the bottom. The roof was cracked in numerous places, and the entry way's copper door was bent and twisted. They also discovered charred bones, both human and animal.

On December 20, soldiers' remains discovered near the "foot of [the] southwest stairway" were transported to the city that night. Harris reported that "cleaning the passage from [the] lower casemates into the commissary room" was almost finished. The following day, three more bodies were discovered near one another in the southwest arched brick entry. In both cases, the remains were "boxed up" and sent to Charleston.

Elliott reported on December 22 that Sumter's condition was "much the same as usual, all changes being for the better." Repairs to the commissary included dividing it "into two halves of a triangular section." Heavy logs set diagonally from the top to the bottom of the upper half of the room were covered with sand; the lower half became an ordnance storeroom. Thirty-four feet of "rubbish, broken stone steps, charred timbers, and sand" in the 112-foot southwest stair tower were cleared out and "capped with the heaviest timber roofing and covered with six feet of sand." In the second-tier casemates, four of the five burned casemates were narrowed to 8-foot-square timbered rooms surrounded by sand. According to Johnson, these changes produced quarters "superior to those in use before the accident." On the first-tier interior, "[s]tout planks and heavy timber" replaced the sandbags as a buttress and the pier arches were "strengthened with timber frames and lumber." The casemates and sally port returned to service.[2]

* * *

While Federal artillery units concentrated on Fort Sumter during the second major bombardment, they also dueled with fortifications on James and Sullivan's Islands. On November 16, 1863, Union gunners began targeting the city and continued to do so into December 1864. Over 260 days they fired more than 12,300 rounds at Charleston.

From November 16 to December 31, 1863, the rifled guns fired 316 shells—150 of them on Christmas Day— of which 134 reached the city. "Twas the night before Christmas," a December 24 entry in the 3rd Rhode Island Heavy

2 Johnson, *Defense of Charleston Harbor*, 189-194, 198; *OR* 28/1:177-178, 643-644, 646, and 28/2:546-548; Gillmore, *Professional Papers*, 149-153.

Artillery's history reads, "but all in the house was stirring as a cat for a mouse. We were hurling our shell and Yankee sort of Greek fire into the city of Charleston. This music kept up an animated dance among the rebels, and they answered us to the best of their ability." Two-hundred pounder Parrotts fired a shell every five minutes, and Beauregard wired Richmond the day after Christmas to report casualties of seven wounded and half a dozen houses burned.

On January 6, 1864, Maj. Henry Bryan, Beauregard's inspector general, reported the number of shells fired and the damage to life and property. Between August 22, 1863, when the "Swamp Angel" fired on Charleston, and January 5, 1864, about 440 shells struck the city. Of this number, 145 had hit houses, 19 fell in yards, 61 dropped onto streets, and many reached "the edge of [the] burned district." Bryan speculated that a considerable quantity struck inside the burned district, but he couldn't determine the exact number.

About half of the buildings hit showed severe damage and the other half were only slightly damaged. Bryan presumed three-quarters of the homes could be repaired. He also reported four deaths. A "Mrs. Hawthorne" died six weeks after being "wounded by a shell." "Miss Plane" died six days after a shell crushed her left foot. Four days after a shell took off his right leg, William Knighton died, and Rebecca, "Mr. Lindsay's slave," was killed outright when a shell struck her.

Not surprisingly, shells falling on the city created, in Maj. Bryan's words, "considerable social distress." Fearful citizens fled the lower part of the city for the relative safety above Broad Street. When newspapers began listing them as relocated or their homes closed, their empty properties became easy targets for thieves and vandals. Abandoned property notices soon filled a column and a half of newsprint. Colonel Rhett reported frequent, almost daily, fires, and lauded the fire department's quick responses despite the increased danger when the flames drew the attention of Union gunners. John Doscher of the German Fire Company died after being wounded fighting a fire on Christmas Day. The continuing artillery fire wounded another fireman, a policeman, and four soldiers.

As a "matter of prudence" nearly all "military headquarters, offices, and hospitals" in the lower portion of the city were "moved out of range to the upper portions of the city." The Signal Corps office, out of direct line of fire, remained in the "Bathing House" extending out over the Ashley River at The Battery. Beauregard had to relocate his headquarters from Broad Street to ex-governor William Aiken's home on Elizabeth Street.[3]

*　　*　　*

3 Denison, *Shot and Shell*, 206-207; *OR* 28/1:682-687; *OR* 28/2:581; "Removal," *Charleston Courier*, Dec. 2, 1863, 2; "Removal," *Charleston Mercury*, Dec. 1, 1863, 2.

Over the final days of 1863, the rotation of Fort Sumter's manpower continued, with each new unit assuming the duty of defense and observation of Federal military activities. About 1:00 a.m. on December 22, lookouts spotted enemy barges taking soundings then retiring toward Morris Island. "The condition of the fort is very much the same as usual," the report closed, "all changes being for the better." On the morning of December 23, "all was quiet," and the U.S. fleet inside the bar consisted of the *New Ironsides*, four monitors, a mortar boat, three wooden gunboats, and 14 sailing vessels. Four blockaders and 16 other craft were at Lighthouse Inlet. On Christmas Eve, Elliott reported one or two monitors on picket duty within 1,400 yards of the fort.

On Christmas, while Union guns on Morris Island bombarded Charleston, Capt. Johnson, who had returned to duty two days earlier, recalled the festivities of the day. "[S]ome extras were arranged for the soldiers, and the several messes of the officers were gladdened" to receive "well-packed boxes and hampers from their homes." In the three-gun battery, Company K, 1st South Carolina Artillery enjoyed "an elegant dinner" served on a 10-inch Columbiad chassis. The chairs "to match this improvised table" consisted of "carpetbags, sandbags, stands of grape and round shot." The men made "an assault . . . on a plentiful supply of roast turkey, wild duck, oysters and sweet potatoes." The headquarters casemate boasted a centerpiece that perfectly represented the spirit of the garrison: half of a 15-inch shell, presumably delivered by a Yankee cannon, "set in a flattened sandbag [serving] as a punchbowl!" Sadly, the unexpected explosion of an old shell tarnished the merriment, wounding two and reminding everybody of their continuous peril.

The Confederates observed similar activity on Morris Island the following week. On December 30, "indications of a parade of ceremony" with music, batteries firing their guns, men thronging the southern end of the island, and a heavily decorated steamer "at the landing at Lighthouse Inlet" captured their attention. The garrison heard an enemy musket volley at 8:00 p.m. on New Year's Eve and "two enemy shots over us at sunset," at which point the enemy "respectfully dropped his flag at the report of our evening gun." Beauregard mentioned this singularly unique event in the headquarters journal—[an] "unusual and unexpected piece of courtesy on the part of the Yankees."

The immediacy of work after the magazine explosion soon gave way to projects to restore order amid the ruins. Captain Johnson cataloged the damage to be repaired. Except for the right face's three-gun battery, the continual bombardment had destroyed or significantly damaged the remaining first- and second-tier casemates and reduced the third, or upper tier, and the ones on the left face. He described those as "[h]uge masses of brickwork or concrete, tons in weight, splintered and broken beams of wood, bars and rails of iron." Mixed in were heavy guns, carriages, chassis, and platforms, plus "wrecked" quartermaster or commissary stores. All this, he declared, "constituted as chaotic a pile as could be conceived."[4]

Johnson determined that a protected line of communication between the sally port through the left face's "long ridge of ruins" was necessary, and excavation soon began of a 275-foot tunnel from the sally port to the three-gun battery. Communications across the parade ground became dangerous for multiple reasons. After the ironclad attack of April 7, 1863, most of the parade ground's sand had provided the fill for the right flank first- and second-tier casemates. Moreover, shell craters and debris now pockmarked and littered the parade ground. These were hazardous to cross during the day and attempting to do so in the dark of night presented even greater challenges to life and limb.

This project, undertaken alongside other ongoing work, took four weeks, probably from December 1863 to January 1864. Work on the passageway and in other areas in the fort continued in earnest despite various obstacles. Most of the passageway was little more than a 3-foot-wide and 6-foot-high tunnel built with heavy planks. At crushed casemate arches, heavy timbers replaced planking, and blocks of solid masonry, gun carriages, and chassis were left in place and cut through.

A similar tunnel was being constructed at the same time on the gorge. Fifty feet long, it bored through the ruins of the officers' quarters from the center bombproof (the original sally port) to the southeast powder magazine. Workmen cleared a path through the rubble, debris, wet cotton bales, and sand previously used to fill the rooms before the first major bombardment. At one point they gouged their way through a 5-foot-thick solid brick pier. The two-room magazine, now safely accessible, stored provisions until the fort's evacuation.

Another ongoing project involved improving the stability of the right flank. A sloping mass of rubble protected what remained of this wall, in some places only 20 feet above high tide. In bad weather heavy spray from breakers washed over the crest and the omnipresent, relentless ocean waves eroded and washed away the rubble at the base. To stop the erosion, workers wedged iron floor joists from the ruins of the quarters and barracks in the stone crevices of the fort's foundation at the water's edge. Other joists, laid horizontally and piled on top of each other, acted in concert with the wedged iron to retain debris and prevent further erosion. After adding solid masses of brick masonry, Johnson observed, the wall stood about 4 feet high and "proved . . . a durable adjunct to the stability of this much

---

4 Gillmore, *Professional Papers*, 155-157; Johnson, *Defense of Charleston Harbor*, 196-198; *OR* 28/1:189.

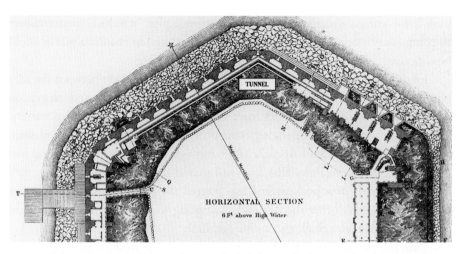

Tunnel from the C.S. sally port through the left face and salient angle to the right face "three-gun battery"/"East Battery." *AC*

exposed flank." Wire strung on the upright girders created a galling entanglement for any amphibious attackers.

Amidst this activity, Johnson reported "an occurrence as unexpected as it was agreeable." On a clear, moonlit night, when Union guns were silent, a "small party of ladies" arrived, escorted by an "officer of high rank." They explored the "labyrinth of galleries and damaged casemates, clambering over ruined arches up to the very crest of the battered walls." Delightful as it was, the surprising visit soon ended, and Sumter quickly returned to its usual state of military solemnity.[5]

In a letter to his sister dated January 13, 1864, Lt. William Grimball described the officers' living conditions:

> [Y]ou must not suppose that Sumter is a very disagreeable place. We live in the casemates on the North side of the Fort. There are a small number of bunks here and the sleepers being numerous [Capt. Kosinski] Kemper & myself occupy one bunk together in very close proximity. We divide the night together every twenty-four hours. One of us staying away until two o'clock and the other from two to day break. This occurs every night and is very disagreeable to one who is obliged from his inability to read at night to pass the weary hours in walking, whistling & singing out of tune. Humming, or any other mechanical act which an ennuied [bored] mind uses to pass time.[6]

5 Johnson, *Defense of Charleston Harbor*, 196-198.

6 Grimball to Sister, Jan. 13, 1864.

Right flank wire entanglements at base (lower right), fraises (upper left), two cannon barrels (midground), 1865. *LOC*

*   *   *

Lieutenant Colonel Elliott returned from leave on January 27 to find another project completed. The parade ground, riddled with craters from mortar shells, was often filled with "stagnant and offensive water," and the garrison was threatened with an "epidemic of cerebrospinal meningitis." Johnson had ordered two ditches cut across it to drain the water into a shallow well in its northwest section. The water was then pumped out into the harbor through an embrasure. Elliott reported that by evaporation much of the water was removed, and the parade ground had "been in a great measure covered with brick and lime" and gradually filled "to within two and a half feet of its former level."[7]

7 Johnson, *Defense of Charleston Harbor*, 205; Gillmore, *Professional Papers*, 164.

On January 29, 1864, the "third minor bombardment" of Sumter began and continued for several days. Union artillery on Morris Island fired continually, throwing 583 rounds at and into the fort. Both angles of the gorge wall took the brunt of the shelling, and on the 30th, the garrison flag at the southeast angle was cut down for the fifth time. Private Ferdinand Shafer of Lucas's Artillery Battalion and two other soldiers returned the colors to their post under heavy fire. Shafer then stood atop the parapet and repeatedly waved his cap at the Federals in both a show of bravado and patriotism.[8]

Shafer's actions didn't reflect the morale of the entire command. By the end of February some members of the garrison were complaining, possibly spurred by the implementation of the third conscription act on February 14, 1864. Beauregard was aware that some soldiers' terms of service were about to expire and encouraged them to re-enlist like their "brothers in arms of the veteran Armies of Northern Virginia and Tennessee." In Beauregard's view, the defenders of Sumter, Moultrie, and Wagner should follow their example. On February 29, Lt. Col. Elliott reported that 16 members of Capt. David G. Fleming's Company B, 1st South Carolina Artillery, who were close to the end of their three-year enlistments, refused to answer to their names at roll call, fearing that if they did so they would "virtually re-enlist." They did, however, continue to perform their duties.

Nothing further is known about their situation until August 14, 1864. A report indicates that these men, along with soldiers from other units, were incarcerated "under sentence of ball and chain for a term." They had been offered "every inducement consistent with good discipline to persuade them to return to . . . duty." But all had refused, citing their rights as citizens. Some recommended that they remain incarcerated until their cases were referred for trial, in which case there should be no compromise if they continued to hold to their beliefs. Additionally, they would not be allowed to return to their company lest their attitude "destroy" the regiment, as the rest of the unit was "in the like position" and awaiting the result. Furthermore, the courts-martial decisions should be "liberally carried out . . . [and] the convict should wear ball and chain in his company's camp." The punishment should serve "not only to reform the offender, but . . . deter others from the commission of the like offense." Neither the names of the soldiers nor their sentences were revealed in subsequent reports.[9]

* * *

8 Gillmore, *Professional Papers*, 165.

9 *OR* 35/1:193, 577 and 35/2:608.

Federal warships didn't engage Sumter in February 1864, but Morris Island guns occasionally lobbed desultory fire toward it; only 31 rounds were detonated that month. Amidst this nuisance fire, garrison life continued as usual. On the night of February 1, a musket shot "seaward of the fort" triggered an alarm that spurred the "parapet . . . [to be] manned very satisfactorily." The next day Elliott reported that several Parrotts, including a 300-pounder and four monitors, opened fire on the blockade runner *Presto*, which had run aground near Fort Moultrie. Several shells exploded within the ship and by that afternoon it was ablaze. As the flag was lowered on the evening of the 14th, the only round fired by Union gunners that day cut off the staff close to the top. It was a strike that "was regarded generally as being a good shot." Two days later another shell exploded near the flag, and three fragments tore into it.[10]

A late winter storm blew in on February 18. The *Courier* reported the biting cold that day, "with a piercing Easterly wind" that brought a rare event—snow. For two hours that night it snowed in Charleston, "giving the streets and roofs something of an Artic appearance." On James Island, Maj. Edward Manigault noted in his journal, "Afternoon bitter cold. Wind a little East of North. . . . At 5:30 P.M. Snow commenced falling in beautiful Star Crystals (6 rayed). After dark, a slight fall of snow sufficient merely to make the surface of [the] ground quite white." The next day he added, "Wind N. East and very cold & Keen. . . . Wherever water fell it froze in a few minutes."[11]

On February 17, 1864, several miles from Sumter, the *H. L. Hunley* sank the USS *Housatonic*, a seminal event in naval history. Of its aftermath, Elliott wrote, "[O]ther aspects of the fleet remain the same except that a three-masted propeller appears to be sunk outside in about 5 fathoms of water." That same night two U.S. picket boats approached within 500 yards of the fort. After they left, Elliott reported that if they returned, he would "open with [a] boat howitzer." On February 26, he recorded, "Our picket-boat . . . captured [a] Yankee picket-boat." This incident and others like it led to reinforcement of the fort's defenses given the prospect of another night assault. General Beauregard suggested a bell-ringing system with bell pulls placed at "four points on the crest of the ruins" that would immediately sound the "alarm in the soldiers' quarters down below in the cavernous recesses of gallery and casemate," reducing the garrison's response time. After the bell sounded, the sentinel would fire his musket to reinforce the alarm.

10 Johnson, *Defense of Charleston Harbor*, xvi.

11 "Snow," *Charleston Courier*, Feb. 19, 1864; Warren Ripley, ed., *Siege Train: The Journal of a Confederate Artilleryman in the Defense of Charleston* (Columbia, SC, 1986), 122.

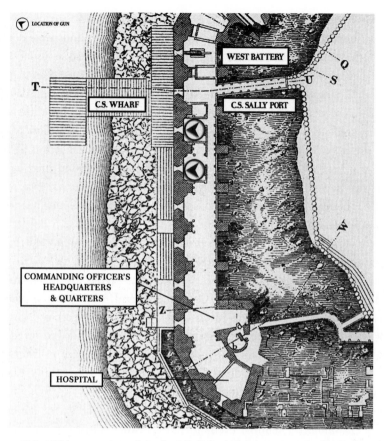

C.S. 1864 conversion of the fort's left flank first tier: A new sally port, flanked by the gun "West Battery" (arrows designate two of its guns), the commanding officer's quarters/headquarters, and a left gorge angle casemate hospital. *AC*

The system was implemented and "maintained in perfect working order" until the fort's evacuation a year later.

Three heavy guns were mounted to defend the sally port and wharf. A rifled and banded 42-pounder replaced the smoothbore 32-pounder "evening gun." In the casemate to its left, a second rifled and banded 42-pounder was mounted, and in the casemate "south of the sallyport" a rifled and banded 8-inch Columbiad was "duly installed." These guns were known as the "West Battery," and the three-gun battery in the right face became the "East Battery."

A 10-foot-deep "cribwork or grillage," composed of pine timber and palmetto logs and filled with debris, reinforced the exterior of the East Battery. The work was

Right face "cribwork" for the "East Battery" with outhouse, 1865. *LOC*

completed and went undetected by U.S. monitors patrolling near the right flank's eastern angle until March 15, 1864. Shortly after its discovery, Parrott rifles on Morris Island opened on the site. Of the 143 rounds fired, 100 found their mark, "cutting away" a part of the crib work. Five soldiers were injured and "1 negro dangerously" wounded. Captain Johnson referred to this brief but concentrated barrage as the "fourth minor bombardment."[12]

* * *

On February 12, 1864, 53 members of the 25th South Carolina arrived at the fort. The officers and soldiers were members of the Washington Light Infantry,

12 *OR* 35/1:191-192, 197; Johnson, *Defense of Charleston Harbor*, xvi, 202, 205.

founded in 1807 and one of Charleston's oldest militia units. On the evening of February 22, following tradition, they held their annual observance of George Washington's birthday. Joined by the regimental band and a few guests, the festivities were held in the refitted left flank casemates. According to Johnson, they "banqueted with toasts, songs, speeches, and the music of their favorite band." Private William R. Greer, a member of the unit, reminisced years later that the "menu on this occasion insofar as the private soldiers were concerned was indicative of the period; simplicity itself, for each one a baked sweet potato with the accompaniment of some very fiery, potent corn whiskey, contained in a tin cup."

The *Mercury* provided details of the toasts. First, the men saluted Washington. "May we as soldiers of the South, ever strive to emulate that devotion to duty, that consistent piety and sacrificing patriotism, which rendered him the hero of the first Revolution." The band then played the "Eutaw Banner Song." The second drink toasted the fort's commander, whose "chivalric bearing and soldiery demeanor justly entitle him to the confidence and esteem of his countrymen." Elliott responded in kind, and the band played "Hail to the Chief." Next came a toast to *"The Engineer Corps of Fort Sumter*— Who, with energy, courage, and skill, have continually met and overcome, apparently, insurmountable difficulties." After Johnson's response, the band struck up "Root Hog or Die." The next one honored the fort's medical staff. "Surgeon's Call" was sounded, and Dr. Lewis C. Hasell spoke followed by another musical piece. The fifth toast saluted *"Our Departed Comrades*—Their names are now inscribed on the Rolls of the Martyrs of Liberty. Their sacrifice will ever impart to us a sacredness to the cause of Southern Independence." All stood and drank in silence as the band played "Rest, Spirits, Rest." The final toast honored *"The Women of the South*—Whose heroic fortitude, patriotic devotion and Christian virtues have rendered *unconquerable* the armies of their country." The band followed with "Am I Not Fondly Thine Own." The evening ended with several "volunteer sentiments and songs by the 'Glee Club,' all highly pleased with the entertainment."

The Confederates weren't alone in honoring the first president. The *Courier* reported that the Union warships "celebrated Washington's birthday Monday by displaying all his colors from his fleet and firing national salutes at sunrise, noon, and at sunset."[13]

*　　*　　*

13 Comstock, *Organizations At Fort Sumter*, 53; Johnson, *Defense of Charleston Harbor*, 201; "Siege Matters—Two Hundred And Twenty-Ninth Day," *Charleston Mercury*, Feb. 23, 1864, and "Washington's Birthday," Feb. 26, 1864.

Winter was winding to a close. At his Hilton Head Island headquarters, General Gillmore received a short message from Maj. Gen. Henry Halleck. Dated March 26, 1864, it read, in part, "General Grant directs that all of the available force in your department not required to hold your present positions be assembled and prepared for orders to another field." Other Union commanders received similar notifications.

Earlier that month, Lt. Gen. Ulysses S. Grant, now commanding all the armies of the United States, had begun planning joint campaigns to hasten the war's end. The plan included transferring as many troops as possible from Gillmore's command, which had been designated the X Corps in September 1862. Before the end of April 1864, almost 18,000 of them were at Yorktown, Virginia, assigned to Maj. Gen. Benjamin F. Butler's Army of the James. Grant ordered Butler to advance on Richmond from the east while he directed the Army of the Potomac, north of the Confederate capital, in an attempt to destroy Robert E. Lee's Army of Northern Virginia. On May 1, 1864, Gillmore left the Department of the South to command the X Corps.

Gillmore's guns had fired on Sumter for only 10 days during March, and the "fourth minor bombardment" occurred within that time. On May 14, 143 rounds were fired, and five members of the garrison were wounded. Throughout April, while Gillmore was transferring troops to Virginia, the fort endured 12 days of shelling. On April 13 Fort Sumter celebrated its three-year anniversary in Confederate hands. The *Mercury* reported that "the embrasures of the stately old ruin belched forth their defiant salute of thirteen guns." Other Confederate fortifications joined in the salute; those on Sullivan's Island fired "by battery." That day, 17-year-old Signal Corps Pvt. Joseph P. Huger stood on Sumter's southwest angle observing the exchange of fire between Cummings Point and James Island. When a Confederate round struck, he waved his cap, drawing the attention of Union artillerymen. In short order, a 30-pounder Parrott shell exploded aside Huger and blew his head off. Fifteen days later Federal gunners opened on Sumter in earnest. In this "fifth minor bombardment," from April 28 to May 4, 510 rounds were fired at the fort.[14]

For nearly the entire month of May, 1864, Brig. Gen. John P. Hatch served as the department's new commanding officer, and his reports offer additional insight into the shelling of both Fort Sumter and Charleston itself. On May 13-14, the Union batteries maintained "heavy fire . . . from our mortars, columbiads, and rifled guns on Sumter," Hatch wrote. "A few shells are daily thrown into the city

14 OR 35/2:29; Manigault's Artillery Battalion, Pvt. Joseph P. Huger File, NA/RG 109 CSR, SC.

. . . not with the expectation" of doing severe injury, "but with the hope of annoying them and delaying the movements of the railroad trains."[15]

At nearly the same time Hatch took command of the Department of the South, Capt. John C. Mitchel, Jr., Company I, 1st South Carolina Artillery, arrived at Sumter and assumed command of fort and garrison from Elliott. On April 20, 1864, Elliott was promoted to colonel and took command of Holcombe's Legion of Brig. Gen. Nathan G. "Shanks" Evans's brigade, which had been ordered to Virginia. Evans did not accompany his troops, as he had been seriously injured in an accident in Charleston. His replacement, Brig. Gen. William S. Walker, was wounded and captured on May 20, 1864, during the Bermuda Hundred campaign, and four days later Elliott was promoted to brigadier general and brigade command. A little more than a month later, his troops occupied a section of Petersburg's defensive line, including "Elliot's Salient." On July 30, 1864, the Federals exploded a mine under the salient and in the resulting battle of "the Crater," Elliott was seriously wounded by a bullet that passed through his left arm and lung. He survived this fourth and fifth wounding, but unable to fully recover, he returned to Charleston in temporary command of the Third Sub-District in December. When the Confederates evacuated Sumter on February 17-18, 1865, his troops served as a brigade in Brig. Gen. William B. Taliaferro's Division. Elliott was hit in the leg, his sixth and final wound during the March 19-21 fighting at Bentonville. The injury was severe and did not heal well. He was in Camden, South Carolina, that June trying to regain his health, and later that year returned home to Beaufort. He succumbed to complications from his various wounds on February 21, 1866.[16]

Captain John Mitchel was the son of a convicted leader of the 1848 Irish Rebellion who had been sentenced to 14 years of exile on Tasmania. John accompanied his father and, after the rest of the family joined them in 1851, they escaped to the United States. Prior to secession, Mitchel, an engineer by training, lived in Alabama. He traveled to the Palmetto State when it left the Union and was commissioned a lieutenant in the South Carolina Artillery Battalion. During the 1861 bombardment of Fort Sumter, Mitchel served in Fort Moultrie, and in 1862, with the battalion's expansion to create the 1st South Carolina Artillery Regulars, he was promoted to captain and commander of Company I.[17]

---

15 *OR* 35/2:80; Johnson, *Defense of Charleston Harbor*, n206; "Siege Matters-Two Hundred and Eighteen Day," *Charleston Mercury*, Apr. 14, 1864.

16 Johnson, *Defense of Charleston Harbor*, 206.

17 1st Artillery Regt. Regs., Mitchel File, NA/RG 109, CSR, SC; Johnson, *Defense of Charleston Harbor*, 208-209; John C. Mitchel, Jr., FOSU Research File.

Capt. John C. Mitchel, the only officer to die while commanding Ft. Sumter. *AC*

Not long after Mitchel assumed command of Sumter, Union gunners directed another concentrated minor bombardment, the sixth, from May 13 to 16. The heavy cannonading previously reported by Hatch was part of this barrage. Two monitors off the right flank also joined in the shelling. Eleven hundred forty rounds were fired during this four-day span; at least three soldiers sustained wounds, one "negro workman" was killed, and two others were slightly wounded. Captain Johnson noted some weakening to the right flank and that two arched passages next to the east angle stair tower were filled to prevent them from being breached; the fort's interior had received but "trifling" damage. On June 13, Capt. Mitchel reported that a small rifled gun on the deck of a "picket monitor" fired 17 shots, but only two struck the fort. The next day, he observed heavy firing from Sullivan's Island on the monitors. These few days of shelling marked the end of U.S. warships firing on Fort Sumter.

After midnight on May 20, 1864, Union barges reconnoitered between Forts Sumter and Johnson, and Mitchel reported that they reached the telegraph poles between the two fortifications at 1:30 a.m. He ordered a 12-pounder "boat howitzer" to fire on the enemy and as the Federals withdrew, a howitzer on a barge returned fire. At 1:00 a.m. on May 28, the fort took hits from an "enemy barge" that fired a boat howitzer round and small arms at the fort.[18]

On May 26, Maj. Gen. John G. Foster replaced Hatch as commander of the Department of the South. Between April 1858 and April 1861, then-Captain Foster had commanded engineer operations in Charleston Harbor and was thus intimately familiar with Fort Sumter. By July 1862, as a major general of volunteers, he commanded the Department of North Carolina, then the Department and Army of the Ohio. After recovering from a fall from his horse, Foster returned to active duty as Department of the South commander. He longed to take the fort

18 Johnson, *Defense of Charleston Harbor*, 209-210; OR 35/1:210-211, 212, 214.

and city, but Grant preferred him to "act purely on the defensive" and prevent Confederate forces from transferring to Virginia or other theaters of operations.

The task outlined for Foster proved difficult. In April and May, 1864, major changes in the Department of South Carolina, Georgia, and Florida took effect. On April 20, Beauregard left to command the Department of North Carolina and Southern Virginia. Major General Samuel Jones, the department's second in command, replaced him. More importantly, Foster learned that a significant number of troops had been transferred, including four infantry brigades and one cavalry brigade, to the Army of Northern Virginia. Three of the infantry commands—Shanks Evans's, Brig. Gen. Johnson Hagood's South Carolinians, and Brig. Gen. Alfred H. Colquitt's Georgia regiments—each had provided detachments that had served as part of Fort Sumter's garrison.[19]

19 *OR* 35/1:7, 117; 35/2:168, 427, 453, 462.

Chapter 11

Progress of Demolition

June 1864–February 1865

In June, 1864, Union artillery hurled more than 375 mortar and Parrott rounds at Fort Sumter, some of them remarkable enough to be noted in Captain Mitchel's reports. He stated that on June 24, seven mortars fired a salvo and five shells either burst over or struck the fort. The accuracy of the Parrotts, however, elicited the most comments. On June 2, a 300-pounder shell dismounted a 24-pounder howitzer, and from June 20-25 Sumter's flagstaff was downed or splintered repeatedly by the Federal gun crews' accurate fire. After the flag was cut down on June 20, Lt. Charles H. Claiborne of the 1st South Carolina Regulars and two civilians serving with the fort's engineers raised it once more. They displayed "exceeding gallantry" and "at a most imminent personal risk." Four days later another Parrott shell "cut away the flag-staff," and the colors were replaced with the "storm flag." On June 25, the flagstaff was twice cut down within two minutes and Pvts. Walter Steel and D. E. Badger re-raised it amid "sharp fire." Artillery fire splintered the staff later that day, bringing down the Confederate standard yet again.[1]

The shelling's intensity increased and on July 7, the third and final "major bombardment" began. Five days later, General Foster informed Washington that he was convinced the enemy was "making arrangements for [a strong] defense" of the fort. Necessity demanded a more effectual demolition of its walls. Foster reported that the bombardment had begun "to breach the wall in a horizontal line on that part . . . now standing vertical." After "a good cut" had been opened,

1 *OR* 35/1:214-220.

large torpedoes would be floated down to explode against the wall until they were "shaken down and the surrounding obstructions . . . entirely blown away." This activity would be continued "until the walls [were] demolished as far as possible." Foster confidently asserted that boats could then assault the fort and the men could take and hold it "without any great loss of life." Once occupied "it would afford a shelter or starting point by which boat expeditions" could attack Fort Johnson or Mount Pleasant. In June, Foster had proposed to Halleck that 5,000 men on "six assaulting rafts or boats, each . . . with a very large scaling ladder" could simultaneously surmount the fort's wall. Nothing came of the proposal.

Captain Mitchel understood the Union objective was to destroy the boom and defenses against an assault, as well as to "break through the gorge wall." The current bombardment was "as damaging as any . . . since the year commenced"; shelling again cut down the fort's flag and tore it to pieces three times. Mitchel requested an additional 50 men to bolster the garrison, but General Ripley replied that he had no "laborers or soldiers to send." The next day, however, Ripley sent 150 "workmen and mechanics" to Sumter. Troops that could be spared had been sent to repel Foster's attempt to cut the Charleston and Savannah Railroad. Beginning on July 2, about 9,000 troops along with naval support landed on James and Johns Islands, most moving up the Stono and North Edisto rivers. The Federals withdrew in the face of stiff resistance on July 11.

By mid-month the fort began taking fire, but no damage, from 8-inch Parrotts "loaded with incendiary composition"; this was the dreaded "Greek fire." On July 13, when the Parrotts began their cannonade, the fort received "very little assistance" from Sullivan's Island and none from Fort Johnson; but the next day both joined in and "measurably annoyed . . . and interfered" with the fire from Morris Island. On July 17, shells from Forts Strong and Putnam pummeled the southeast and southwest angles. Foster reported "nothing of interest" since July 12 to Halleck in Washington, but fire on Sumter had "slowly" continued "with marked effect." On July 17, for example, after taking 450 rounds the battered fortress appeared to have been breached "near the right gorge angle."[2]

*   *   *

Throughout the bombardment, laborers and mechanics under Captain Johnson cleared, repaired, or reworked the damage. Three reports dated July 19-26, from Johnson to Maj. William H. Echols, provided details. The fire had been "unusually heavy" but had "slackened" off. Both gorge angles had been the primary targets, and he recorded several noteworthy events. A 13-inch mortar shell "struck

2 *OR* 35/1:15, 17, 221; Johnson, *Defense of Charleston Harbor*, 214-222.

immediately over" the sally port's arch on July 19, and though covered with 7 feet of fill, it was visibly marred. It and adjacent arches displayed "wear and tear" and cracks in various directions from previous bombardments, and engineers responded by adding more fill over the sally port arch.

Nightly mortar attacks occasionally sank small supply boats at the wharf. On July 20, Johnson reported that 8-inch Parrott salvos against the southwest angle had been "particularly destructive, carrying away large masses of brick from [the] scarp and sand from the angle's slope." Though the angle itself remained "in large part unhurt," the shelling had begun to undermine the "mass above it," and the "west end of the heavy parapet over [its] stairway" had been "shot away." Johnson feared the 12-pounder mountain howitzer next to it could no longer provide "raking fire along the gorge slope" but hoped the gun's "plowed up" position could be restored that night. Despite the mortar fire Johnson's crews labored to restore the parapet works. Measures to discourage a night-time amphibious assault—fraises, mountain howitzers, and sandbags—continued and were removed each day before dawn.

By July 22, the "battering in reverse" of the southwest angle had expanded the old crack on the left flank near the postern. This crack, a result of the "first major bombardment" of August-September 1863, ran from the top of the wall to its base, and although worrisome, other fissures in the southwest angle were more serious. Three sizeable new cracks indicated the alarming "progress of demolition" and the imperative need to fill the casemates with sand. But even then, the exterior wall on either side of the postern would probably collapse, causing "a disastrous loss of material from top to bottom of the present towering southwest angle."

The "arch and crest of [the gorge] wall over . . . [the enslaved workers'] quarters . . . were brought down without any harm by a chance Parrott shell," Johnson noted on July 24. The rubble added to its strength, and the crest's height remained about 25 feet above the parade ground. But the repair routine was wearisome, to say the least. As many times as Johnson and his crews effected repairs at night, Union guns destroyed them in the daylight. A likely frustrated Johnson wrote two days later that "heavy firing . . . entirely carried away" the southeast angle parapet by noon, and "[f]or five successive days" artillery fire had "swept away . . . the work it took all the previous night to reconstruct."

Johnson also outlined the division of labor. The garrison worked in two reliefs of 40 men each, one from noon to 3:00 p.m. and the other from 3:00 to 6:00 p.m.; the "negroes" labored throughout the night from 7:00 p.m. to 5:00 a.m. From July 20-26, two enslaved laborers were killed and a dozen wounded; five soldiers were also wounded. Johnson reported 2,135 rounds fired at the fort, more than 300 every 24 hours. Only 505 missed: nearly 80 percent found their mark.[3]

*   *   *

As the end of July approached, Foster ordered the "Marsh Battery," the site of the "Swamp Angel," repaired. A 30-pounder Parrott had been mounted there to fire at Sumter's wharf and left flank to "prevent the enemy landing materials at the sally-port" and from "receiving re-enforcements and supplies." Theoretically, the gun should have caused significant damage, but reports from Sumter indicate that few projectiles struck either target. According to one report, one of the 13 shots hit a "flat at the wharf, but did not sink her."

On July 27, Lt. Col. William Ames, Morris Island's Northern District Chief of Artillery, reported his guns had been firing with "good effect" and cutting away much of the southeast gorge angle—where all fire should be directed, he believed. On the opposite end of the gorge, about "8 or 9 feet of the southwest angle" also had been "cut away." On August 1, Ames observed that fire from Fort Putnam "on the gorge wall to the left of the old breach" had "cut or combed off for about 7 feet." Battery Chatfield's guns had "cut down" about 5 feet of the center of the left flank.[4]

The stress placed upon some of these guns was evident in reports of their damage or failure. The first such incident was recorded on March 19 during a bombardment of Charleston when a 30-pounder Parrott at Fort Putnam burst while firing its 4,606th round. The next gun, also a 30-pounder directed against Sumter, burst on May 15. It had fired 2,400 rounds prior to being mounted in Putnam, and upon firing its 500th round there, the gun "burst into eight pieces," its reinforcement band broken into "halves longitudinally."

From May 7-27, five more Parrotts at Putnam, all targeting Charleston, burst. On May 7, the 401st round of a Navy 30-pounder exploded in its bore and destroyed 16 inches of the muzzle. Two days later a 100-pounder burst on its 241st round, and an "oblong piece" of the right side of the barrel was blown off from the right half of the trunnion to 6 inches "under [the] reinforce." The breech behind the vent was "blown out." On May 15 a second 100-pounder barrel cracked on its 1,086th round; four days later the barrel of a 100-pounder "burst into 8 pieces" on its 1,100th round, to the rear of the trunnions, and its band broke "in halves longitudinally." The last gun failure, another 100-pounder at Putnam, occurred on May 27. The 34th round detonated inside the gun and "an oblong piece" of

---

3 *OR* 35/1:243-247.

4 Ibid., 35/2:187-188, 190-191, 207.

A breach burst Parrott in Battery Brown, Morris Island. *LOC*

the barrel, about 1/3 of its circumference, was blown out about 4 inches in front of the reinforcement band "to a point 20 inches forward of the trunnions." At Battery Chatfield a 100-pounder burst firing its 1,590th round and all "of the gun [behind] the trunnions was broken into a large number of pieces and [the] reinforce broken in halves." Astonishingly, no casualties were reported in any of these accidents.

No other accidents occurred until July and August, when five more guns shelling Fort Sumter failed. On July 23 at Putnam, a 200-pounder Parrott's breech was "blown to the rear" on the firing of its 1,456th round, followed on the 30th by failure of another 200-pounder as it fired its 573rd round. The latter gun suffered a "fracture across the right side of the breech toward the vent and continued on a line under the reinforce to the left trunnion." The shell in a 300-pounder firing its 1,200th round exploded prematurely in the bore and "blew off" about 24 inches of the muzzle. Members of the 3rd Rhode Island Heavy Artillery serving this gun recalled, "Our men often used, in a single day, shot, shell, and powder, to the value of $1,500, which should be regarded as costly gunning, and was so viewed by the rebels." In modern currency, that one gun used approximately $20,000 in materiel daily.

At Chatfield on August 1st, a shell in a 10-inch Columbiad that had fired "200 rounds before being brought to the Depart. of the South" exploded prematurely on its 1,007th round and lost 26 inches of its muzzle. Yet it remained in service and was expected to be used "for short range." Four days later, a 200-pounder cracked from the left trunnion to under the band on round 296. The failures continued. The reinforce of 200-pounder at Fort Putnam was "broken into four pieces" while firing its 1,063rd round and the "left side of the gun from in front of the left trunnion to the base of [the] breech was broken into many pieces," most "blown . . . out of the battery." As before, no casualties were reported in this series of gun failures.

Procuring sufficient ammunition and replacement guns proved challenging. Only one 300-pounder and a few 30-pounder Parrotts were available within the department, and as the supply had not kept up with demand, the stockpile of ammunition was depleted. Foster was unwilling to reduce his rate of fire and on July 30 asked Adm. John A. Dahlgren to "borrow" six 100-pounder Parrotts and the ammunition for them.

Given previous antagonism between the two services, Dahlgren's response was uncharacteristically cooperative. He simply wrote, "Conformable to your request, six 100-pounder Parrotts will be loaned to you, and are at your disposal." He also offered some 11-inch Navy guns that were not immediately available but would be made so when they arrived. Dahlgren then notified Foster on August 5 that he could lend him three 200-pounder Parrotts and 200 barrels of powder. The same day Foster wrote to Brig. Gen. Alexander Schimmelfennig, commanding the Northern District of Morris Island, that the Navy was loaning the Army six 11-inch smoothbores with carriages, implements, ammunition, officers, and crews. Four 100-pounder Parrotts and ammunition for 100-, 200-, and 300-pounders were included in the loan. By September 21 the 11-inch guns had been "ready to open for a week" but had not fired because their battery was incomplete.[5]

The Federals undertook a night reconnaissance of Sumter on August 1. Three boats pushed off from Morris Island and the crews rowed completely around it. Passing between Sumter and Fort Johnson, they saw the dock and a sentry, then floated on the tide past the left flank, clearly seeing lights through the embrasures. They observed three ironclads in the harbor but detected "no signs of life" on the left face. While passing the right face, they saw a light "very plainly" from the "East Battery" embrasures and "glimmering" lights through several others. At the wall's base, where it joined the right flank, a dim lantern shone, possibly a "signal lantern

5 Gillmore, *Engineer and Artillery Operations Against the Defenses of Charleston Harbor in 1863* (New York, 1865), Plates XI-XXXIII; *OR* 35/2:191, 207-208; Denison, *Shot and Shell*, 262.

for their boats." Undiscovered, the reconnaissance returned to Morris Island before the ironclads moved into position and launched patrol boats for the night.[6]

* * *

Throughout July, Sumter's garrison suffered from both heat and withering artillery fire but their continued observation of Federal activity, though perilous, was imperative. Mitchel reported the number of rounds fired at the fort early on July 20, adding that one soldier had been wounded and a "negro killed, 2 severely wounded, [and] 5 slightly wounded." Around 1:00 p.m. he ascended the southwest angle's stairs under heavy Parrott fire to watch the Federals on land and sea. Mitchel left the relative safety of the stair tower's massive, chest-high earthwork and took a more exposed position in order to make his observations.

Sergeant Milton M. Leverett described the next few seconds in a letter home. A mortar shell exploded, sending "a large fragment right through [Mitchel's left] thigh and hip mutilating and mangling it horribly [and] taking out the bone clean." When Captain Johnson arrived at the hospital, the Irishman said to him, "They have killed me captain, but I ought to have been a major." (Only four days earlier, General Ripley, with General Jones's endorsement, had written to Richmond recommending both Mitchel and Johnson for promotion to major). Mitchel lived for about four hours. Leverett "fanned him with a hat until he died, [and] assisted in laying him out and dressing him in his full uniform." He helped place him in his coffin, and after "putting a large flag . . . over him, [sent] him off by boat to Charleston." The next day, numerous Army and Navy officers, including Ripley and Colonel Rhett, attended the funeral. Captain John C. Mitchel, Jr., the only officer to die while commanding Fort Sumter, was then buried in Magnolia Cemetery, where he rests to this day.[7]

News of Mitchel's mortal wounding arrived in Charleston shortly after it occurred. Later that day, Capt. Thomas A. Huguenin of the 1st South Carolina Regulars assumed command. An 1859 graduate of The Citadel, Huguenin spent the following year as an assistant mathematics professor at the school, then traveled to Europe to study civil engineering. He returned to Charleston in view of the deteriorating political climate, and by October 1860, the 20-year-old "was soon engaged nightly in drilling the various new companies being organized." Commissioned a first lieutenant, Huguenin served on Sullivan's Island during

6 *OR* 35/2:210-211.

7 *OR* 35/1:226; Johnson, *Defense of Charleston Harbor*, 227-228; Frances Wallace Taylor, Catherine Taylor Matthews, and J. Tracy Power, eds., *The Leverett Letters: Correspondence of a South Carolina Family, 1851-1868* (Columbia, SC, 2000), 345-346; *OR* 35/2:589; "The Friends and Acquaintances," *Charleston Courier*, Jul. 21, 1864.

Capt. Thomas A. Huguenin, Ft. Sumter's last C.S. commanding officer. *FOSU*

the April 1861 bombardment. The following July, he was promoted to captain of Company A. Until September 1863, he spent most of his service at fortifications on the island and as Fort Moultrie's commander from April to August 1863.

In September 1863, Huguenin and his company were ordered to Morris Island, where he served as the chief of artillery. While at Battery Wagner he was wounded twice by shell fragments. The second time, on September 7, severely injured his left knee. That night Beauregard ordered the island's evacuation and directed Huguenin to spike Wagner's guns and blow up the magazine. Under heavy fire, he lit the magazine's fuse, which failed; then he, the three remaining officers, and a sergeant evacuated the battery to join the rest of the command at Cummings Point, about three fourths of a mile up the island. Slowed by his injury, Huguenin struggled toward the boats. His comrades, fearing the captain had been captured, were relieved to see him limping out of the darkness. He was the last Confederate to leave Morris Island.

Huguenin returned to Sullivan's Island and served there for nearly a year. On July 20, 1864, he was commanding Battery Marshall when he received orders from Ripley stating that Mitchel was dead and he was to be the new commander at Sumter. Ripley succinctly added, "I need not tell you to hold it." En route to Sumter, shell fragments struck the rowboat several times and knocked a crewman's oar out of his hand. Upon his arrival, "the first thing I saw was a coffin containing the dead body of my gallant predecessor"; this was hardly "an inspiring sight," and a hint perhaps of "my own fate."

After meeting the garrison's officers, Huguenin and Johnson "visited every portion of the Fort." The next day, he mustered the garrison: three infantry detachments and two artillery companies, about 300 men; 45-50 members of the "Engineer corps"; and around "200 Negro laborers." The new commander then inspected all of the fort's departments. He noted the well-supplied hospital and the common practice of evacuating casualties to the city nightly. He closed his report by observing, "The garrison appears to be in good spirits." [8]

Huguenin had "found the fort not seriously damaged by the present bombardment," though the rifled guns' fire on the southwest angle was "cutting away the exterior crest," with the fallen debris "making [an easier] ascent." Also, the left flank's southernmost first- and second-tier casemates were "being filled up," resulting in the loss of their use as quarters. As some "incendiary" shells had been fired "upon this point" the southwest magazine's ammunition was moved "for fear some incendiary matter may be communicated by the ventilator." Firing on the gorge had stopped, and Huguenin hoped it and the broken boom near the southeast angle would "soon be repaired." He repeated Captain Johnson's request that 1,000 sandbags be delivered every night; they would be "required in large quantity" if the bombardment continued. He asked that the Signal Corps detachment be increased from two to six. In the event of a night assault, one would be stationed on the parapet to request supporting artillery fire from Sullivan's and James Islands.

Huguenin's permanent garrison consisted of his staff officers and the engineer, adjutant, quartermaster, commissary, and ordnance officers who "never went to bed until daylight"— as did the surgeon who tended the wounds and injuries, which occurred mostly at night. The new commander ate breakfast at noon, dinner at sunset, and supper at midnight, and never removed his clothing at night and seldom during the day, except to bathe or change clothes. In July, after the transfer of units to Virginia or Georgia, the department reported 11,790 troops present for duty with approximately half of them serving in Charleston's defenses. These units provided Fort Sumter's rotating garrisons with "fresh" soldiers after about two weeks and "Negro laborers" every 10 days. Basic necessities for the soldiers were met, Huguenin recalled. Water was stored in three of the fort's cisterns. The supply in the original sally port cistern was held in reserve, the cistern at the right face was saved for emergencies, and the one on the left flank was intended for daily use. Weather permitting, the garrison received the "best provisions . . . fresh bread, meat and water," and the fort maintained a 90-day reserve of commissary supplies. Charlestonians supplied many luxuries, and since blockade runners had to report their arrival at the fort, they often "sent presents of ice, fruit, liquors, etc." As the blockade became increasingly effective, the flow of delicacies diminished.[9]

8 Thomas Abram Huguenin, "A Sketch of the Life of Thomas Abram Huguenin," FOSU Research Files, n.d., Part 1:18-20, 35, hereafter cited as "Huguenin Journal"; Thos. A. Huguenin File, NA/RG 109, CSR.

9 OR 35/1:227 and 35/2:598; Huguenin Journal, 2:4, 5.

A nighttime amphibious assault continued to pose the fort's greatest threat, and the new commander altered the garrison's routine to meet it. The guard mounting took place with the firing of the sunset gun. One infantry detachment was posted on the parapet all night, the second "sheltered behind the parapet," and the third, "expected to be awake," remained in their quarters uniformed and under arms. The detachments rotated every evening. Most of the garrison slept in their quarters during the daylight hours.

Every day after dark, Huguenin and Johnson inspected the damage and ordered repairs. Over the course of the night the fort buzzed "like a hive until morning." Supply boats arrived with engineer materials, water, and commissary supplies. Soldiers unloaded the vessels, and laborers made repairs. After the unloading, any casualties were placed on board and taken to Charleston. Around 10:00 p.m. the "post-boat" arrived, carrying "official correspondence and small packages," garrison officers leaving or returning, and visitors on official business. While the boat was tied at the wharf, Huguenin prepared daily reports, answered letters, and attended to "all necessary office work." After the other boats left, the post-boat remained until just before daylight, returning with the commander's reports and dispatches and with the wounded, injured, or sick.

Late summer heat and humidity wore on everyone, and to provide some relief, the gun embrasures were left open. They were quickly secured with sandbags stacked behind the covers when an alarm sounded. The sally port's "iron door" was closed and sandbags were placed against it also. Soldiers assigned this duty were ordered to defend these locations if the Federals forced their way into the fort. A 12-pounder mountain howitzer stood at the ready, loaded with grape or canister to rake the entrance. The remaining casemates, interior entrances, bombproofs, and galleries also had "iron doors, with loopholes for musket fire onto the parade ground." In the event of an assault, everyone was "expected to do his duty, even the officers' servants."

At the sound of an alarm, Huguenin, his staff, and the officer of the day assembled at the southeast angle parapet, Sumter's most vulnerable location. From there they delivered orders and contacted supporting fortifications. If the fort came under assault, three rockets would be fired signaling the batteries and forts to provide ricochet fire and solid shot close enough to destroy attacking boats. The Federals couldn't land enough men to drive his soldiers from the parapet, Huguenin believed, and if they held the parapet, the greater the number "sent against us the greater would be their discomfiture." The defenders possessed a "great advantage" in that they knew "every inch" of the fort and "every man knew his post and duty

Southeast (right) gorge angle: Meeting place of Capt. Huguenin, his staff, and officer of the day when the fort's alarm bell rang. *LOC*

. . . while the enemy in darkness would approach an unknown fortification" and it would be "almost impossible to secure [a] complete concert of action."[10]

In his postwar reminiscences, Huguenin expressed great confidence in his men's morale and abilities, recalling that he personally stepped forward on occasion to inspire the troops further. When he learned that shelling had cancelled religious services at Sumter since 1863, he invited Rev. Peter F. Stevens, a Citadel professor and superintendent when Huguenin was a cadet there, to deliver a Sunday service. Huguenin recalled that Stevens arrived early one Sunday morning under heavy fire and began preaching. "Never in the whole of my life," the commander attested, had he heard such a sermon. The circumstances might have further inspired him, but he didn't doubt "the occasion lent force to his thoughts and fire to his language. . . . It was truly a very impressive occasion." After being escorted around the fort "as much as the heavy fire" permitted, Reverend Stevens returned that night to Sullivan's Island.[11]

An otherwise ordinary event—incoming mortar fire, on the calm, hot night of July 28—presented another opportunity to boost morale. As Huguenin worked in his office to the sound of heavy shelling, his feathered companion "Game Rooster

10 Huguenin Journal, 1:37, 2:3-8, 12-13.

11 Ibid., 2:10-12.

Dick" began vocalizing, and like most roosters, had little concern for the hour. Seizing the opportunity, Huguenin, bird under his arm, ascended to the southeast angle, the closest point to Morris Island. While he and other officers watched, the bird "commenced to crow most vigorously [and] the enemy could hear . . . Sumter's Gamecock" amidst the crash and boom of mortar fire.

Captain Johnson, inspecting repairs at the southwest angle, had intended to join Huguenin, but at 3:45 a.m. a mortar shell fragment struck him in the head, inflicting a serious wound. Huguenin, hearing the engineer had been killed, rushed to the hospital only to learn that Johnson's wound wasn't "necessarily mortal," though he was unconscious. The commander ordered that Johnson be taken to the city, where he endured a protracted period of recovery. He was promoted to major in October and didn't return to duty at Sumter. Following Charleston's evacuation in February 1865, Johnson served with the Army of Tennessee until its surrender two months later.[12]

Like other Fort Sumter commanders, artillery fire injured Huguenin twice. Shortly after taking command, he was knocked down by "a shower of brickbats from the parapet" and sustained a "few bruises." That August, as he was crossing the parade ground, the lookout warned of an incoming shell and Huguenin took cover. After it exploded, he resumed his journey, intending to cross the open ground before the next round. But near the center, rather than run, Huguenin froze at the lookout's next warning. He saw the shell hit the gorge bombproof and hurtle into the air. The last thing he remembered was its explosion. He awoke on the surgeon's table with his left arm "apparently paralyzed" by a fragment that had "scraped" from the left shoulder to the elbow. His badly bruised arm hung useless in a sling "for many days." He also became deaf in his left ear.

Coincidentally, before Johnson was wounded, Huguenin had asked him to recommend someone to assume the fort's engineer duties if Johnson became unable to do so. Johnson said no one was better qualified than Lt. Edwin J. White, who had previously served at Sumter with Johnson and had commanded the engineer operations in his absence. On the night of July 30, 1864, White began his duties as the fort's chief engineer until its evacuation the following February.

White's first suggestion addressed the fundamental issue of securing the nightly supply delivery under the fort's cover before daylight. When boats arrived, cargo was stacked onto the wharf's limited space then carried singly through the sally port's narrow opening and "long narrow passageways," which had just enough

---

12 Huguenin Journal, Pt. 2:17-18; Compiled Service Records of Confederate Soldiers Who Served in Organizations Raised Directly by the Confederate Congress, Engineers, NA/RG 109. On January 9, 1861, Stevens had commanded the cadets firing on the *Star of the West*. He resigned as colonel of Holcombe's Legion in October 1862 to become an Episcopal priest.

room for two men to pass each other. Bulky items like timbers were hoisted over the parapet and into the fort. White improved this inefficient and dangerous system. Using 20-foot-long, 12x12-inch timbers, he constructed a 5 ½-foot-high, 62-foot-long tunnel running from the sally port through the adjoining northwest angle casemate to the parade ground. There a newly built tramway crossed the parade ground from the sallyport to the right face.[13]

*   *   *

One ongoing issue drove the siege in an alarming new direction that summer. The relentless Federal shelling of Charleston had not only damaged private property, but it obviously endangered the lives of women and children. To prompt a halt to the shelling, on June 1 Maj. Gen. Samuel Jones sent a request to Richmond for 50 Union prisoners, including Brig. Gen. Truman Seymour, captured at the battle of the Wilderness, and other "officers of high rank." As a captain in 1861 Seymour had led Company H, 1st U.S. Artillery during Sumter's bombardment. In 1863, as a brigadier general, he commanded the troops that made the July 18 assault on Battery Wagner and was wounded during the battle. Jones proposed confining the officers to civilian areas of Charleston "under enemy fire." His request was approved on June 13, and he informed General Foster that five generals, including Seymour, and 45 field officers had arrived in the city "for safekeeping." He would provide them "commodious quarters" in areas where "non-combatants," mostly women and children, had been exposed "day and night to the fire of your guns."

Foster's reply questioned Jones's "sense of humanity" in allowing women and children to remain in areas shelled "for many months." He referenced the August 1863 communications between Gillmore and Beauregard when the Swamp Angel had fired on Charleston and protested exposing "defenseless prisoners of war . . . to constant bombardment," which he considered "an indefensible act of cruelty . . . designed only" to halt the Federal bombing.

His objective and duty, Foster continued, was to destroy the "means of continuing the war" in Charleston: arsenals, a military supply depot, and munitions manufacturing, as well as the construction of additional ironclads. Foster added that he had forwarded Jones's message to Washington and requested 50 Confederate "prisoners of like grades" to be placed "in positions exposed to the fire of your guns."

In late June, 50 captured Southern officers arrived on Hilton Head Island. On July 1, the Union generals in Charleston wrote Foster requesting a prisoner exchange. Though the practice had been halted a year earlier by the Federal

13 Huguenin Journal, 2:20, 21-22; Johnson, *Defense of Charleston Harbor*, 231.

government, Foster nevertheless inquired of Washington. Lincoln allowed the exchange, which took place outside Sumter on August 3 during a truce. The released Confederate officers cheered as they passed the fortifications. The garrisons, standing on the parapets, echoed the sentiment. The U.S. officers cheered upon seeing Fort Putnam's colors; as their boat pulled away, a band on board played "Home, Sweet Home."[14]

Though this imaginative attempt to halt Federal artillery fire into Charleston failed, it had significant consequences. From June 14 to August 3, renewed shelling from 30- and 100-pounder Parrotts rained on the city for 34 days; over 1,500 shells fell, with 1,100 of them being termed "Good Shots." The others were described as either "Falling Short," "Premature Explosion," or "Tripped." On the day of the prisoner exchange, both Charleston and Fort Sumter were shelled before and after it occurred. General Schimmelfennig reported suspending fire as the "rebel steamer [came] out of the harbor" and resumed after its return. Most of the 30-pounder Parrott shells lobbed at Charleston were "Good Shots." The fort took 265 rounds from 30-,100-, and 200-pounder Parrotts, 12- and 24-pounder rifled James guns, and 10-inch mortars.[15]

In July, Charlestonians witnessed the arrival of more prisoners, spawned by Sherman's Atlanta campaign. Six hundred captives out of more than 2,300 U.S. officers were temporarily relocated to Charleston from Macon, Georgia. Foster learned of their arrival and believed Jones had deliberately placed officers under fire in the city once again. He sent a note to the Confederate commander, who denied asking for the officers and stated that they were bound for another location. On August 4 Foster informed Washington that an exchange could be made easily. In a follow-up message he averred that shelling the city wouldn't injure the Union officers because he knew "their exact position" and could avoid them easily.

Jones continued holding the prisoners in Charleston, prompting Foster to immediately request that 600 Confederate officers be sent to him. He also demanded that Jones remove any prisoners of war under fire. Jones explained that he was trying to relocate officers who would leave as soon as arrangements were made. He further offered to exchange them "rank for rank," but Foster spurned this proposal and stated flatly that he would put the Confederate officers "under your fire, as an act of retaliation." On August 7, when the Rebels (known as the "Immortal 600") arrived, they were placed in an open 1½-acre stockade between

14 *OR* 35/2:132, 134-135, 162-163, 205; *OR* Series 2/7:185; "Exchange of Prisoners," *Charleston Mercury*, Aug. 2, 1864; "The Exchange of Prisoners," *Charleston Courier*, Aug. 4, 1864.

15 Records of the Adjutant Generals Office, 1780s-1917, Quincy A. Gillmore File, Report of the Bombardment of Charleston, NA/RG 94.

Forts Strong and Putnam. Jones questioned Richmond if it were "proper to retaliate by placing Yankee officers in Sumter or other batteries." His suggestion came to nothing.[16]

The two sides exchanged artillery fire throughout September; on Morris Island, the penned prisoners and their guards endured shells from the Confederate batteries on James Island. Some landed within the compound without exploding. Occasionally a shell from Fort Shaw exploded prematurely, sending fragments into the stockade.

The prisoner situation, already bad, worsened noticeably when Atlanta and its environs fell to Sherman's army on September 2. The Confederacy immediately relocated thousands of Northern prisoners held in Georgia. On September 23 Jones informed Samuel Cooper that Charleston now housed 8,000 prisoners, "including 1,800 commissioned officers." He was struggling to arrange their transfer in the midst of a yellow fever epidemic. All the Federals had been transferred by October, and the Confederate officers on Morris Island left the stockade and were sent to Fort Pulaski, ending the ordeal.[17]

*　　*　　*

The Department of South Carolina, Georgia, and Florida underwent changes in the fall of 1864. Lieutenant General William J. Hardee, a former corps commander in the Army of Tennessee, replaced Samuel Jones as commander of the department in October. Jones was assigned command of "District of South Carolina," which comprised most of the state. Hardee arrived in Charleston on October 5 and assumed command. On the last day of the month, just over 15,000 troops were reported as "aggregate present" in the department, while the "effective total present" was nearly 12,500 soldiers. More than 4,700 served in South Carolina, including "detachments" from the 32nd Georgia and the 1st South Carolina acting as Fort Sumter's garrison. By comparison, the Federal Department of the South reported nearly 17,800 "present and absent" with more than 14,000 "present"; the greatest number, almost 5,500, were engaged with the siege operations against Charleston. The total number of Union and Confederate naval personnel, sailors, and marines is unknown. In Atlanta, Sherman had some 60,000 Union soldiers who were about to begin their "March to the Sea."[18]

*　　*　　*

16 *OR* 35/1:23 and 35/2:247; *OR* Series 2/7:567, 625, 763, 783, 819.

17 *OR* Series 2/7:866, 1016, 1058, 1073.

18 *OR* 35/2:320, 635, 637, 643.

In August, the "third major bombardment" began as the shelling of the city continued. Union gunners firing on Fort Sumter had depleted their powder and were compelled to borrow 100 barrels from the Navy. Two weeks later, the Navy provided another "450 barrels" and "1,000 30-pounder shells." Despite these shortages, the Federals directed 5,000 shots at the fort from a 6-pounder James rifle, a 300-pounder Parrott, a 10-inch Columbiad, and 10- and 13-inch mortars. More than 4,200 of these struck Sumter.

A new threat now menaced the fort. In mid-summer Gen. Foster reported that he would attempt to "explode large torpedoes" against the fort and its boom, and on the night of August 28 he initiated this plan. A pontoon boat loaded with a ton of black powder was "floated down into the left flank," but the Federals misjudged the current and the "torpedo" exploded about 50 yards from the wall, causing no apparent damage.

Huguenin reported that at 9:15 p.m. a "torpedo" floated from the direction of Fort Johnson and "exploded near our wharf." The *Courier* noted that upon first hearing it, people thought the explosion had been detonation of 200-pounder Parrott shell fired into the city. The paper reported the sighting of three barges about 200 yards from the fort's "West face" (left flank), whereupon Capt. John F. Lewis and a detachment of Company I, 32nd Georgia mounted the parapet and opened fire. After two shots, the barges exploded about 30 feet from the wall, near the wharf. The explosion was so powerful that "some of the officers on the southwest angle were knocked down."

Huguenin's postwar recollections provided more detail about this event. A sentry on the southwest angle parapet raised the alarm when he observed something floating, rang the bell, and fired his musket. The garrison reported to their positions, and Huguenin made his way to the southeast angle. After a few minutes, he assumed it was a false alarm, but Lewis reported seeing either a large boat or several small ones lashed together. Huguenin believed this to be a feint and that the right flank or southeast angle would be attacked. He ordered the officer back to his post to open fire with mountain howitzers. Immediately after Lewis departed, the "torpedo" exploded "just off" the wall. From the southeast angle, it appeared that the entire left flank had blown up. Hastening to the area, Huguenin found the wall intact and the soldiers "liberally splattered with mud."

The Federals made a second attempt against the boom on September 1. "The enemy again attempted to blow up the fort with a torpedo," Huguenin reported. But the attack didn't succeed: the explosives detonated "about 300 yards off the east angle." According to the Union report, the device consisted of "six torpedoes, made of barrels set in frames," each packed with "100 pounds of powder." It was "set afloat with the flood-tide" and "probably exploded too early," they surmised, and perhaps damaged only "two lengths or links" of the boom.[19]

The new threat heightened the level of vigilance within the fort, but some defenders didn't get the message. Two nights later at about 4:00 a.m., Huguenin checked Company I, 32nd Georgia's location in the southwest angle's second tier. A third of the troops were "not dressed and armed" as "distinctly prescribed." They were thus ill prepared to man the parapet in time to meet an assault. Captain Lewis, the company commander, was absent, but Huguenin had the senior officer, Lt. A. S. Brooks, arrested. Those adjudged to be flouting orders were ordered to report to him after daylight "for such punishment" as was deemed "proper."

Brooks was sent to the city under arrest, and each of the soldiers was ordered to "carry a 32-pound ball in a bag on his shoulder for two hours" as punishment. Shortly after this punishment started though, several others from Company I began removing the bags from their shoulders. Huguenin responded to the "disturbance, seized the ring-leader," and "jerked him into the office," where he ordered Lt. William G. Ogier to place a pistol to his head with orders to "blow his brains out upon the slightest movement." Then the captain with a few officers arrested two or three more men. Sympathetic members of Company I rushed "to get their guns and release their companions," but Huguenin ordered the "iron doors . . . to other parts of the fort closed and locked" to prevent their joining "the rest of garrison who might have sympathized with them." The 12-pounder mountain howitzer at the sally port was turned to face the malcontents. Trained artillerymen, members of Companies A and H of the 1st South Carolina Regulars, manned the gun, while the remaining soldiers stood by with muskets. Huguenin stood a few feet in front of the field piece when about 40 of the Georgians descended the stairs to the left flank first-tier. The captain instructed the gun's commander that if he stepped out of the passage to open fire and continue firing until it was clear.

At this critical moment, quartermaster/commissary officer Capt. George W. Lamar "rushed to the foot of the stairway" and appealed to his fellow Georgians to remember who they were, the cause for which they had enlisted, the circumstances they were in, and that they served at a "post of honor." Beyond that, they were in the wrong and the commander's orders must be obeyed. He then pointed to the howitzer and infantry and warned that if they entered the passage, none of them would leave alive. The mutineers grudgingly retired to their quarters. Afterward, Huguenin and a guard went to the quarters of Companies B and H at the other

---

19 *OR* 35/1:15, 69, 70, 72, 75, 238, 240; Report of the Bombardment of Fort Sumter; "Siege of Charleston," *Charleston Courier*, Aug. 29, 1864; Huguenin Journal, 2:33-34.

side of the fort and found them "much excited" by the rumors, but their officers "faithful to me and their duty."

Huguenin disarmed Company I and wired that they be relieved, but headquarters transferred all three companies that night. Captain John A. Phillips with five other officers and 190 men from the 32nd arrived at the fort to replace their fellow Georgians. Huguenin recalled that the arrested soldiers were placed in irons and taken to Charleston that night; three were court martialed and shot; the others were pardoned at his request. He considered the entire event a "mutiny," and it was, perhaps, the greatest threat during his command; he wrote that Company I went on to serve again at Fort Sumter without incident.[20]

* * *

According to Huguenin, on September 4, coincident with the firing of Sumter's sunset gun, the third major bombardment ended. Captain Johnson counted 14,666 rounds fired in the 60-day bombardment and 59 documented casualties (30 soldiers and 29 laborers): 10 killed or mortally wounded, 48 wounded, and one injured.

Foster reported to General Halleck on September 6 that "a want of ammunition" had "forced" an almost complete cessation of firing on Sumter. Not only had his requisitions not been entirely filled, he complained, but he had been ordered to send ammunition to Fort Monroe, Virginia (perhaps to support Grant's siege of Petersburg). Captain Johnson would have disputed Foster's statement. He reported that same day that the fort's eighth (and last) "minor bombardment" had begun. It ended nearly two weeks later on September 18, with 573 rounds having been fired and seven more men wounded. [21]

Despite a lack of ammunition, Brig. Gen. Rufus Saxton, Alexander Schimmelfennig's replacement as commander of Morris Island's Northern District, reported to Foster on September 8 that every day he "passed considerable time . . . experimenting with the fire" on Charleston. Like his predecessors, Saxton thought he had devised a workable plan to put the city at his mercy. A "sufficient number" of 30-, 100-, and 200-pounder Parrotts, "well sighted, with good iron carriages" capable of a 40-degree elevation, with 53-second "time-fuses, or good percussion shells, with plenty of grease for the projectiles," all under "careful superintendence of the firing," would accomplish the goal. He recommended that 30- and 100-pounder Parrotts placed in "our most advanced works," each

---

20 Huguenin Journal, 2:23-30.

21 Fort Sumter Casualty List, FOSU Research Files; *OR* 35/2:273; Johnson, *Defense of Charleston Harbor*, xix, 236.

with 600–700 rounds, along with the "naval battery" when it became operational, should all open fire on Charleston. With the "navy induced to sail in, the city would be completely destroyed or surrendered to our arms." Saxton's meticulous suggestions were not adopted.

The issue of Ft. Putnam's Parrott's failing while firing on Charleston returned in September. Beginning on the 4th and ending on the 17th, four 100-pdrs. failed —two using an 11 lb. charge. In October Battery Chatfield had five to burst. On the 4th, though, a 200-pdr. blew out its breech at the reinforce "squarely just in front of [the] vent." The shell continued 4 ½ miles to Charleston. Eight days later a 100-pdr. burst. As part of his experimental fire on the city, Saxton had ordered 11 lb. charges (a pound more than the regulation) to be used. It proved to be "too great [and] much of the powder was blown out of the gun." The next day another failed on its 31st round using an 11 lb. charge; the shell exploded in the bore demonstrating "conclusively that 11 lbs. [of] Powder could not be burned" in 100pdrs. A 200-pdr. burst firing its 227th round, although it's shell continued to the city. On October 17 still another 100-pdr. failed firing its 705th round, the barrel to the rear of the trunnions "blown into an immeasurable number of pieces." Nevertheless, the shell was "thrown about 4000 yards." None of the burst guns at Putnam or Chatfield resulted in casualties.[22]

No longer under heavy fire from Morris Island, Fort Sumter's officers spent the long nights playing "chess, cards, and various games" to help them stay awake while on duty. Those off duty generally slept or just talked. Reading was "out of the question." The only "good lights" at night were in the hospital and adjutant's office. Huguenin read official reports and newspapers, while the men had other reading material available—a small but appreciated luxury.

On October 11, during the final minor bombardment, Pvt. Arthur Grimball wrote his father that he had been up all that night due to a false alarm and was going to spend 10 days in Charleston, where he would "take a good bath, for down here that luxury is unheard of." Huguenin reported that on October 17 the fort responded to the Union batteries in the only way left to them: with small arms. In his report a couple of days later Foster noted that "sharpshooters with telescopic rifles" so greatly annoyed the working parties at Fort Putnam that the gunners could accomplish "little work . . . in the daytime in the front batteries on Morris Island." Firing on Sumter had "almost entirely ceased," he continued, and "the rebels are now taking advantage of the quiet" to make repairs. Indeed, the lull allowed the garrison to accomplish a great deal, especially by strengthening the weak right flank, where they constructed a "heavy crib-work" filled with sand

22 OR 35/2:265, 276; Gillmore, *Bombardment of Charleston*; OR 35/2:265, 276.

on the wall's interior. A "splendid bomb-proof" built against the cribwork and running the length of the right flank could accommodate 200 soldiers. Huguenin relocated his private quarters to a room next to the southeast angle. From there he could quickly use a "special stairway" to the angle's parapet.

From September 18 through the end of the month, Sumter experienced only "desultory" fire, except for six days of "brisk" shooting of about 200 rounds. From the end of October to the end of November, the Morris Island guns fired 715 rounds. On November 12 fragments from a 30-pounder shell killed Lt. John W. Trussell and Pvt. H. Sawyer of the 32nd Georgia and mortally wounded Pvt. Daniel McDougal of the 1st South Carolina Artillery. These three soldiers may have been the last to lose their lives at Fort Sumter. [23]

Shelling from the Union batteries fell off precipitously after that. On November 20, Brig. Gen. Johnathan P. Hatch, commander of the Department of the South's Northern District, informed Foster that he thought the "battering of Sumter . . . an idle waste of material," and Washington seemed to agree. Halleck informed Foster three days later that General Grant had directed no further "expenditure of ammunition upon Charleston and Fort Sumter" except to halt the establishment of new batteries in the fort. The "throwing of an occasional shell into Charleston, if circumstances should require," on the other hand, was approved.[24]

*　　*　　*

Shelling continued almost daily in Charleston through the autumn of 1864, but the Federals' waning stores of powder and ammunition greatly reduced its intensity. Nevertheless, for more than a year local newspapers reported on the bombardment of the city and its consequences. From September to December, the *Courier* noted around 4,450 shells fired into Charleston, but did not reveal how many reached the city, exploded prematurely, or failed to detonate. The paper also reported 31 civilian casualties of all ages and both races and genders. Three military casualties also occurred: the explosion of a 200-pounder Parrott shell killed three members of the 32nd Georgia.[25]

Shells falling on the lower part of the city caused "considerable social distress." Abandoned homes and businesses provided easy targets for thieves. While walking

---

23 Huguenin Journal, 2:35, 38; *OR* 35/1:23, 242; Arthur Grimball to Father, Sep. 11, 1864; Johnson, *Defense of Charleston Harbor*, xix; Fort Sumter Casualty List.

24 *OR* 44:506, 535, 666.

25 "Siege of Charleston," *Charleston Courier*, Oct. 27, 1864. Lieutenants Lewis P. Mays and John Darden and Sgt. Joseph H. Shannon were killed; Lt. David E. Willis was wounded. With respect to the civilian casualties, no obituaries or 1860 census data have been located in reported incidents in which names were given.

Right flank bomb-proof (with chimneys), 1865. *LOC*

up Meeting Street, Moses, one of ex-Gov. Robert F. W. Alston's slaves, told Arthur Grimball that "some persons" were in the family house on Lamboll Street. Grimball looked inside and witnessed it being robbed by a man and woman. He yelled at the man, who jumped out a window. Grimball lost sight of him in the ensuing chase but caught the woman, who "begged and cried . . . for God[']s sake to let her go." After "using towards her a great deal of language more expressive than polite," he released her. Grimball then went inside and found most of the furniture missing. An oil painting and bureau were gone, and "if Grand pa's Picture was there that is also gone." While the chairs and sofa were still there the mohair seats had been removed. In his father's room, the bureau's "looking glass" and tin bathtub were gone.

He then moved a number of pieces of furniture to the front of the house and planned to move the rest in time. He left to complete some family business and returned with a policeman. As they entered, they saw a boy carrying two chairs down the stairs. The youth was arrested and to Grimball's consternation, found hiding "behind the drawing room door . . . [was] the very same woman I had left off about an hour before." After she was arrested, he "got out of the boy where the man was," went there, arrested him, and all were taken to the "Guard house." The next day Grimball appeared at the "Mayor's Court" where the three miscreants were "all sent to the house of Correction." He wrote that he planned to visit the mayor in an attempt to recover some of the stolen items and to see the robbers "dealt with as severely as I possibly can."[26]

Despite more than a year of siege warfare, almost continual shelling, and a yellow fever outbreak, daily life in Charleston continued. Newspapers reported local events and advertised merchandise for sale. Merchants still offered a variety of goods; their ads for imported items—ladies' and gentlemen's fabric, shoes, gaiters, gloves, and the like—testified to blockade runners' effectiveness. The list continued: "Groceries and Dry Goods"—tea, coffee, "crushed mustard," flour, sugar, and other items such as tobacco, "Segars," Irish whiskey, Scotch, and other liquors; "Fruit and Oriental Trees," "Imported English Garden Seeds," and Irish and sweet potatoes. As Christmas approached, papers advertised numerous books and local seasonal items including oysters, apples, and even "Fat Turkeys."

Notices of monthly meetings—for fire companies and Masonic chapters among others—appeared as usual. Grand social events were advertised in the last two months of 1864. Three "Deutches" balls sponsored by the city's German community, a "Pleasure Ball" at the Charleston and Savannah Railroad Depot, and a "Grand Concert" in the "Hall in the Citadel" were trumpeted. Official military orders as well as state and national government notices also ran in the papers.[27]

* * *

December was a quiet month for all. Morris Island gunners fired upon the city on six days and at Sumter on only two. The *Courier* reported 145 rounds directed at the city from December 1-5, and five on December 20. Major Johnson documented only seven rounds fired at the fort on one day but didn't mention the 26 rounds fired on December 5.[28]

Sherman's capture of Atlanta and subsequent March to the Sea culminated with the capture of Savannah on December 21. In the meantime, Northern and

---

26 Arthur Grimball to Father, Oct. 26, 1864.

27 From the *Charleston Courier*: "Deutsches Ball" (Dec. 6 and 21, 1864 and Jan. 20, 1865), "Pleasure Ball" (Dec. 7, 1864), and "Grand Concert" (Dec. 21, 1864).

28 Johnson, *Defense of Charleston Harbor*, xix; *Charleston Courier*, "Siege of Charleston," Dec. 2, 3, 5, 6, and 21, 1864.

Southern authorities agreed to exchange those prisoners who were sick, lame, or in need of medical attention beyond the limited capabilities of the prison camps. The exchanges began in November on the Savannah River between Savannah and Fort Pulaski, but as Sherman neared the city, the exchange operation moved to Charleston. A cease fire between the opposing forces in and around Charleston Harbor ran from December 4-17, during which thousands of prisoners were exchanged near Fort Sumter. No work could be performed on either side's fortifications, the two sides agreed, but Union operations against the blockade would continue.

The only violation of the truce occurred on December 5 when Capt. Huguenin, believing it had expired, ordered his sharpshooters to fire on Morris Island. The Union guns retaliated, targeting Sumter and the James Island defenses. An hour later a boat with a white flag approached Morris Island with a communication from Huguenin and met a Federal picket boat. He had learned that the truce was still in effect and apologized for targeting them. Colonel E. N. Hallowell, Morris Island's commander, accepted the apology and his guns fell silent. This was the last known combat action from Fort Sumter. No other incidents occurred, and the prisoner exchange continued. The truce lapsed at 10:00 a.m. on December 17. Though Gen. Schimmelfennig indicated he was ready to resume the bombardment of points around the harbor, his guns stayed quiet, save for two incidents of firing on the city reported by the *Courier*: five shells on the morning of December 20 and more around midnight ten days later.[29]

*　　*　　*

The misery of approaching winter quickly diluted any relief the garrison felt at the cessation of shelling. "[W]e suffered much from the cold," Huguenin recalled. Sumter relied on vessels to provide it with everything. In the absence of fresh bread, soldiers ate the hardtack stored with the reserve rations. Units rotating into and out of the garrison for short terms weren't issued vegetables, unlike the officers of the "permanent garrison" who regularly received a generous amount. The commander dispatched his boat weekly to Sullivan's Island to pick up clean clothes, and it brought back oysters, a welcome supplement to the garrison's rations. His "friends in the country" sent him "boxed . . . country produce" as well. Overall, Huguenin recalled that "we lived very comfortably."

29 *OR* 44:648, 739; "Siege of Charleston," *Charleston Courier*, Dec. 21 and 31, 1864.

Moreover, the Confederates closed out 1864 on a high note. On New Year's Eve, a picket boat from the CSS *Indian Chief* captured two "Yankee barges" and their crews near Sumter.[30]

*   *   *

On December 18, 1864, Halleck congratulated Sherman on his campaign's success to that point. "Should you capture Charleston, I hope that by some accident the place may be destroyed, and if a little salt should be sown upon its site it may prevent the growth of future crops of nullification and secession." After capturing Savannah three days later, Sherman began planning his campaign into the Carolinas. He did not contemplate destroying Charleston, however. The city wasn't his objective; on January19, Sherman informed the Department of the South's commander, Maj. Gen. John G. Foster, of his plans. He deemed trying "to enter Charleston Harbor by its direct channel or to carry it by storm or James Island as too hazardous to warrant the attempt," and asked Foster to conduct "demonstrations" there as "diversions" to his operations into South Carolina's interior. He would "keep up the delusion of an attack on Charleston," he told Halleck, while Foster continued his "demonstration" on the city.

Dahlgren had met with Sherman and Foster two weeks earlier and requested from Secretary Welles "reinforcements for aggressive cooperation." After meeting with his senior commanders off Charleston Harbor on January 15, the South Atlantic Blockading Squadron commander decided to move against Sullivan's Island. Dahlgren therefore ordered obstructions near Sumter to be examined and that the monitors USS *Patapsco* and USS *Lehigh* remove torpedoes. That night Lt. Cmdr. Stephen P. Quackenbush, the *Patapsco*'s commander, reported that on his third sweep "nearly in a line between Sumter to Moultrie . . . we struck and exploded a large torpedo, or torpedoes" near a buoy. The monitor sank about 800 yards from the fort, with only 2 feet of its smokestack remaining above water. Quackenbush and 48 officers and men escaped, but 62 others lost their lives. These men may have been the last to die during the siege of Charleston.[31]

During the first week of January 1865, heavy artillery continued to target Fort Sumter. The *Daily Courier* reported on January 4 that between 9:00 a.m. and 10:00 p.m. guns on Morris Island directed 55 rounds at the fort and a "few at Sullivan's Island," followed the next night by more heavy fire. At 3:00 a.m. on January 7, nine mortar shells arced toward Sumter and the next day's paper reported that a few shots were fired, the last directed at the battered fort. By Maj. John Johnson's

---

30 Huguenin Journal, 2:2-35, 38, and 3:3-6; "Siege of Charleston," *Charleston Courier*, Jan. 3, 1865.

31 *OR* 44:741, 47/2:97, 136; *ORN* 16:131, 172, 171-176.

count, however, 64 rounds were fired at Sumter in January. Also, on the night of January 19, the steamer *Randolph* "went ashore" near the fort. Morris Island guns opened fire and continued the next day, destroying the vessel. On January 26, they fired once on Charleston, the only time that month. Johnson wrote that Sumter wasn't shelled in February. As for Charleston, the newspaper recorded two shells on February 6, eight on February 10, 15 on the thirteenth, and an even dozen on the following day, the last shots from Morris Island.[32]

*   *   *

Early in February, now-Lt. Col. John C. Pemberton returned to Charleston. He had been appointed inspector general of the Confederate armies' artillery and ordnance the previous month and was now reviewing the Department of South Carolina, Georgia, and Florida's "mounted artillery." After completing his inspection on February 10, he went to Fort Sumter after dark on the 11th and spent that night and the following day there. Huguenin recalled that in the absence of hostile fire he "had an opportunity to show [Pemberton] the exact condition of the fort and explain all our preparations to meet an assault. He expressed himself . . . very much pleased and was astonished at our strength . . . under such disadvantages."[33]

As February progressed, Sherman's move toward Columbia revealed to the Confederates that the capture of Charleston was not his goal. On February 14, Beauregard wired General Hardee in Charleston that holding the city was "now reduced to only a question of a few days." Charleston's fall would not jeopardize the state's safety, "but the loss of the garrison would greatly contribute to that end." The next day, Beauregard ordered Hardee to begin withdrawing immediately. Hardee started the evacuation but fell ill, and Maj. Gen. Lafayette McLaws assumed command, briefly delaying the full implementation of the plan until February 17 and the early morning hours of February 18.[34]

Confederate defenders pulled out of their numerous positions in and around the city and began moving to the state's interior. That night, a new second national

32 "Siege of Charleston" column, *Charleston Courier*, Jan. 6, 9, 21, and 26, Feb. 7, 11, and 15, 1865; Johnson, *Defense of Charleston Harbor*, xix, xx.

33 Huguenin Journal, 3:3-5. Pemberton had led the department from March until September 1862, when he was replaced by Beauregard. He then commanded the Department of Mississippi and East Louisiana, where on July 4, 1863, he surrendered Vicksburg to U.S. Grant. His surrender of the Confederacy's last major point on the Mississippi River (the smaller garrison of Port Hudson, Louisiana capitulated on July 9), combined with his Philadelphia nativity fostered the belief among many in the South that he harbored traitorous tendencies. In April 1864, he resigned his lieutenant general's commission and requested to serve as a lieutenant colonel of artillery, which was granted.

34 *OR* 47/2:1180, 1194, 1205.

flag was delivered to Fort Sumter to be raised on the following morning to show the Federals that nothing out of the ordinary was happening. But the enemy had broken the C.S. signal code the previous year. A curt February 17 message ordered the burning of "all the papers" before the detail left the fort. The Federals knew an evacuation was imminent but were unaware that most of the Confederate defenders had left Charleston during the night of February 17-18.

Huguenin recalled nothing of note until the evacuation order. He had then to "bow to the inevitable" despite his conviction that the "fort was stronger & in better condition to resist a bombardment or an assault than ever before," and that the garrison was committed to the "idea that Sumter should never be captured." His men "could have fought the fort to the last extremity."

Upon receiving orders, he began quiet preparations but kept the information to himself. On the night of February 16, the "negro laborers," "sick and wounded," and "spare baggage" were sent to Charleston. He also sent off "the two flags which had flown over the fort during the great sixty-day bombardment." Huguenin's "servant Frank" delivered the flags and the captain's personal effects to his aide's wife at Sumter Court House.[35]

On the morning of February 17 the new second national flag was raised over Sumter, and Huguenin informed the garrison that they had been "ordered to evacuate the fort" that night. The sunset gun was fired as usual, and "all the preparations for an assault" were made. About 9:00 or 10:00 p.m., however, two small steamers arrived and the entire garrison except the guard detail boarded the boats. Huguenin, his adjutant, and chief engineer Lt. E. J. White relieved the guard and "ordered them to embark." Near midnight the commander reported that the enemy did "not fire a single shot at us" though they fired "heavily on Sullivan's Island." Major Johnson recorded that the men of Fort Sumter's last garrison were from two companies of the 1st South Carolina and three of the 32nd Georgia.

Huguenin ordered that "no public property of any description [would be] destroyed except some whiskey," which he prudently emptied into the water to keep his men from finding it and creating "a disturbance." Although he burned his "library of valuable military works," he sewed his "official records . . . in a pair of my drawers and carried them along with us." After visiting "every portion of the fort, with a heavy heart" he went down to the wharf. "[N]o one was left behind. . . . I felt as if every tie held dear to me was about to be severed. The pride and glory of Sumter was there and now in the gloom of darkness we were to abandon her, for whom every one of us would have shed the last drop of his blood. Oh! the irony of fate to give up that heroic spot without one last struggle in its defense."

35 Dennison, *Shot and Shell*, 295; Huguenin Journal, 3:6-7.

At the wharf Huguenin asked the lieutenant in charge of the boats if all had boarded and then helped him cast off the lines. Huguenin "was the last Confederate to leave the grand old Sumter." Johnson likewise recalled the departure: "Fort Sumter loomed grandly before their lingering eyes for a few minutes . . . then the dark night enveloped it and they saw it no more."[36]

---

36 Huguenin Journal, Pt. 3:7-8; Johnson, *Defense of Charleston Harbor*, 259.

Chapter 12

It Don't Look Much Like a Fort Inside

February–April 1865

*B*y dawn on February 18, 1865, Confederate forces had evacuated Charleston and its defenses, but for the previous week, the fates and fortunes of several blockade runners hung in the balance. On February 12 the *Chicora* successfully slipped out of the harbor through the corridor of U.S. warships, but two days later, the outbound *Celt* ran aground off Fort Moultrie. Four days later, the *Syren*, the war's most successful blockade runner, ran the gauntlet into Charleston Harbor. It had navigated the journey more than 30 times, but her crew, knowing they could no longer escape, fired the ship in the Ashley River on February 18. Union forces "captured" it, put out the blaze, and repaired the vessel. Attempting to lure ships into the harbor, the Federals maintained the Confederate signal lights on Sullivan's Island. About 9:00 p.m. on February 18, the *Deer* fell prey to the ruse and ran aground near Sullivan's Island trying to enter the harbor and was also "captured." In a desperate move, the *G. T. Watson* cast off from a burning dock on the night of February 17, slipped through the fleet, and docked in Nassau, Bahamas, three days later, carrying cargo and news of Charleston's fate.[1]

In the early morning hours of February 18, about an hour past midnight, men of the 3rd Rhode Island Heavy Artillery on Morris Island observed the Ashley River bridge ablaze and flames in the city. Burning debris from exploding powder magazines on Confederate ironclads had torched wharves and shoreline structures on the Cooper River. An hour later, "a most brilliant and exciting scene" confronted

---

1 Stephen R. Wise, *Lifeline of the Confederacy: Blockade Running During the Civil War* (Columbia, SC, 1988), 210-211.

them: a ship in the mouth of the Cooper had been set afire. Flames "mounted the rigging, and through the darkness [blazed into] the sky," illuminating the harbor "with all its grand surroundings, and the proud, doomed city, in the background."

On Sullivan's Island, Battery Bee's magazine exploded about 6:00 a.m., and the Rhode Islanders said it appeared as if the island's "whole upper portion . . . had lifted up into the air. The force of the explosion . . . shook Fort Strong and the whole of Morris Island." Union gunners ceased firing around 3:00 a.m. and soon after, torpedo-wary monitors cautiously made their way into the harbor's entrance. The USS *Canonicus* approached Fort Moultrie and fired perhaps the last two rounds of the siege. There was no response.[2]

As the *Canonicus* advanced, two row boats oared away from Morris Island— one with members of the 52nd Pennsylvania headed to Fort Sumter, and the other to Moultrie. When the Pennsylvanians landed at Sumter around 9:00 a.m., Maj. John Hennessy hoisted their regimental flag over the works. Cheers erupted from both Morris Island and Union vessels. After 15 minutes or so inside what was left of Sumter, eyes turned toward the ultimate prize: Charleston.

Units from both the U.S. Army and Navy raced to dock there first. Major John A. Hennessy's boat stopped only long enough at Fort Ripley to again raise their colors; his boat landed first in the city at about 10:00 a.m. Shortly afterward officers met a city alderman with a white flag bearing a note from Mayor Charles MacBeth that the Confederate military had evacuated Charleston. MacBeth himself had "remained to enforce the law and preserve order until you take such steps as you may think best." About this time two companies of the 52nd landed, 30 soldiers from the 3rd Rhode Island, and some from the 127th New York. By around 11:00 a.m., the 52nd's regimental flag was raised a third time at the Customs House at Broad and East Bay streets; it was the first U.S. banner to fly over the city in more than four years. Union command headquarters was established shortly afterward at The Citadel. Then the arsenal was secured, and every available man was impressed to fight the nearly 20 fires burning in the city. At around 5:00 p.m., the first full Union regiment arrived in Charleston: the 21st U.S. Colored Infantry.[3]

*   *   *

Just over a week before the evacuation, on February 9, Gen. Gillmore had assumed command of the Department of the South from General Foster. The War Department issued General Orders No. 24 on February 21, directing that

---

2 Denison, *Shot and Shell*, 296; *ORN* 16:258.

3 Smith B. Mott, *The Campaigns of The Fifty-Second Regiment Pennsylvania Volunteer Infantry* (Philadelphia, 1911), 169-172; *OR* 47/1:1018-1020; *OR* 53/61.

Maj. John Hennessey and the 52nd Pennsylvania Vol. Inf. Regt. flag, first U.S. colors flown over Ft. Sumter since April 14, 1861. *Pennsylvania Capitol Preservation Committee & The Campaigns of The Fifty-Second Regiment Pennsylvania Volunteer Infantry*

a national salute (one shot for each state) be fired at noon on February 22 at West Point and every fort, arsenal, and army headquarters to honor the restoration of the "flag of the Union" over Sumter. Three days earlier, Gillmore had invited Brevet Maj. Gen. Robert Anderson to "[c]ome down if you can, & hoist the old flag over [the fort] . . . If you come we will do the thing with éclat."

President Lincoln determined to make re-raising the flag a formal ceremony on the fourth anniversary of the fort's surrender. On March 27, Stanton issued General Orders No. 50, which stated that at noon April 14, Anderson would "raise and plant . . . the same U.S. flag which floated over the battlements . . . during the rebel assault, and which was lowered and saluted . . . when the works were evacuated," culminating in a 100-gun salute from Sumter and a "national salute from every fort and rebel battery" that had fired on the fort. The order further called on the Rev. Henry Ward Beecher to "deliver a public address" and Rear Adm. John A. Dahlgren's command at Charleston "to participate in the ceremonies." Stanton ordered Sherman to conduct "suitable ceremonies," but since the latter was then engaged in operations against Confederate forces in North Carolina, Gillmore was tapped to "make proper arrangements for carrying out the President's orders."

On April 5, Sherman wrote Anderson of his happiness that raising the 1861 flag fell "to the lot of one so pure and noble to represent our country in a drama so solemn, so majestic, and so just. It looks as a retribution decreed by Heaven itself." Furthermore, he continued, "you may think of me as standing by your side." He recalled his time in Charleston in 1846 when as a lieutenant he and Anderson had served together at Fort Moultrie; he signed the letter "Your lieutenant."[4]

When the appointed day came, Dahlgren ordered six warships and others that could "be spared" to take positions near the fort. When the flag was "hoisted . . . each vessel will man yards [horizonal bars on the mast] or rigging [and] give three cheers." Each ship would fire a 100-gun salute "beginning with the senior ship's first gun." Lieutenant Commander E. P. Williams, the only officer present who had participated in the 1863 assault on Sumter, was given the honor of commanding the sailors and marines in the fort at the ceremony. Before noon on April 14, as many as 3,000 soldiers, sailors, marines, and civilians assembled at Fort Sumter.[5]

William A. Spicer, who had sailed on the steamer *Oceanus* from New York to attend the ceremony, described the event. While on a light draft transport on the way to the fort from Charleston, he observed the "gay and glorious appearance" of the harbor. "The war vessels beautifully decorated with flags and streamers and ensigns . . . stretched from mast to mast and made a splendid show. Monitors, gun boats, blockade-runners &c were all represented." Spicer and his fellow passengers were the first civilian guests to arrive and noted that Robert Smalls's *Planter* was moored at the dock crowded with African American passengers, none of whom had been invited to the ceremony. After climbing a long flight of steps to the top of the wall and another to the interior, Spicer noticed "wide plank seats to accommodate several thousand people" set up on the parade ground; he "hurried ahead and got a good one." The "old Fort" was "very battered and crumbled" and some walls looked "like great heaps of sand and broken stone." Parts of the left flank facing Charleston, however, were "quite regular" though "it don't look much like a Fort inside . . . with the walls thickened by sandbags placed one over the other."

4 *OR* 47/2:512, 3:34, 41, 51-52, 107-108.

5 *ORN* 16:315-316.

Festooned ships of the US fleet at the fort, April 14, 1865. *LOC*

A noon salute announced Gillmore and Anderson's arrival. Gillmore and one of Anderson's daughters flanked the April 1861 commander as he descended the stairs. Also in attendance were Maj. Gens. Abner Doubleday and Samuel W. Crawford, Col. Norman J. Hall, and the Rev. Matthias Harris. Doubleday had commanded Company E, 1st U.S. Artillery at the fort in 1861, as well as the cannon that had fired the first shot in defense of the Union. Crawford, once Sumter's assistant surgeon, was now a brevet major general commanding an infantry division in the Army of the Potomac. After Appomattox he hastily made his way to Charleston. Hall, a lieutenant in the 1st U.S. Artillery at Sumter in April 1861, had risen to the rank of colonel commanding a brigade in the Army of the Potomac. Reverend Harris had offered the prayer at the fort on December 27, 1860, when the flag was first raised.[6]

His ships were "not to flag or fire" until the banner unfurled over Sumter, Dahlgren recorded, but upon receiving news of Appomattox, he had his ships guns fire in celebration of that first. Arriving at the fort later that morning with "Fox and ladies and a crowd of naval officers," Dahlgren noted that the reception was tremendous, with "large detachments of marines and infantry" on the wharf and wall.[7]

Spicer described the festivities in detail. The sailors formed "rows" from the base of the stairs to the decorated speakers' stand. Around 1:00 p.m. the program began. After about 20 minutes Anderson and Peter Hart moved from the platform

6 Diary transcript, William A. Spicer Papers, 1865-1885, FOSU Research Files, 3-5. Other notable guests included Assistant Secretary of the Navy Gustavus V. Fox; John G. Nicolay, one of Lincoln's secretaries; and Peter Hart, who had served with Anderson in the Mexican War and at Fort Sumter in 1861.

7 *ORN* 16:373.

Ft. Sumter's Left Flank Wall with the steps used to enter the fort for the April 15, 1865 ceremony. *LOC*

to the nearby flagpole, which had been placed exactly as it was in 1861. Reverently removing the "old flag" from the fort's mail bag, they and three sailors attached it to "the halyards, and all helped hoist it a little way." Then the general "seized the lines alone and sent the old . . . torn and shattered flag . . . back to its old place . . . amid the most deafening cheers."

The flag, now fully hoisted, was visible from all but one "Rebel Battery" that had fired upon it. A national salute thundered from Sullivan's Island, Cummings Point on Morris Island, and Fort Johnson. Only the mortar battery in Mount Pleasant that had fired against it in 1861 remained silent. One hundred salutes responded from Fort Sumter and all the warships around the fort fired as ordered. "It was a glorious sight, and one which no one will ever forget."

Beecher started to speak as the noise died down, and Spicer, now upon the gorge's rampart for a "good view of the harbor," began collecting "a few relics." He returned as the ceremony ended, heard the "rousing cheers" for "Pres. Lincoln, the

Maj. Gen. Anderson raising the flag, April 14, 1865. *LOC*

Soldiers & Sailors &c," and watched the crowd disperse and make its way to the dock. Greatly delayed in crossing the *Planter* to his vessel—it had become grounded at the wharf at low tide—he now had the opportunity to shake Anderson's hand and request an autograph. He then walked across the *Planter*'s deck, boarded his ship, and "left old Fort Sumpter [sic] with the Stars & Stripes waving over it."[8]

*   *   *

Spicer and others on the *Oceanus* continued celebrating and prepared for the evening's grand military ball. At the Charleston Hotel the group received an invitation to a dinner hosted by Gen. Gillmore. During the drinks afterward, he observed that Anderson presented the best among the many toasts to President Lincoln and gave an excellent speech, which happened, he noted, "just about [the] time . . . the President was assassinated." Three days later on April 17, the travelers' steamer arrived at Fort Monroe, Virginia. There Anderson wired

8 Spicer Diary, 5-9. At this time there is no known description of the re-raising of the flag that states if it was the garrison or storm flag. A blurred photo taken on April 14, 1865, shows the flag being raised. Based on this it appears to be the storm flag.

Rev. H. W. Beecher, standing, in front of Gen. Anderson, with a cane and seated on the platform's floor. *LOC*

Secretary Stanton stating that his mission had been completed.[9]

Spicer's journal also provided an unvarnished description of occupied Charleston. He reported that after leaving the dinner, he and his companions made for the ball in a carriage "through the desolate city. . . . [W]e saw nothing till we got to our destination but ruins on either hand." The ride took them along Broad Street, a large section of which had been destroyed in the December 1861 fire, then arrived at a fine house that had been deserted when the city was evacuated. He described the house as "3 stories high, with fine piazzas, extending the whole length." "[F]ine mirrors . . . paintings [and] vases &c" remained but most of the furniture had been taken.

Although scheduled to depart on April 15, the *Oceanus*'s passengers agreed to stay another day to see more of the city. At their first stop they witnessed William Lloyd Garrison and other abolitionists addressing "thousands" of former slaves. They then attended a meeting at "Zion Church and another in Citadel [Marion] Square" led by the Reverend Beecher. The walls of St. Michael's Church were "torn through" and damaged, but the steeple, "the favorite target for our soldiers" during the shelling, "got off unharmed." From its top they had "a splendid view of the City and harbor." The church's interior was nothing but "a heap of rubbish, and our people were carrying away, anything they could lay their hands on, even to the cherubs over the Altar." Stealing a book for himself, Spicer then visited the *Daily Courier*'s office and secured 20 copies of the latest issue with the "account of the Fort Sumpter Celebration."

9 Ibid., 4; *OR* 47/3:242; Jensen, *Fort Sumter Flags*, 213-225, 230-231. Anderson kept the garrison and storm flags from the 1861 surrender until his death in 1871, and Mrs. Anderson did so until her death in 1905. On March 16, 1905, Sophie C. Anderson, one of their daughters, wrote President Theodore Roosevelt that their mother's will specified that "the dear old Sumter flags be given back to the Country their proper custodian." The president accepted them, and Secretary of War William Howard Taft acknowledged their receipt with "grateful thanks." Both were placed in a glass case in the secretary's reception room. In 1954 the Department of Defense transferred them to the National Park Service, which placed them on exhibit at Fort Sumter and Fort Moultrie National Historical Park.

"[V]ery politely treated" in Charleston, he and his party "enjoyed the freedom of the City." They "rode about on impressed horses at our pleasure and were allowed to take away as relics . . . anything we could lay our hands on, and pick as many flowers as we pleased." Practically everyone they encountered was either U.S. military, "contrabands without number, or poor whites." Older citizens or higher classes had mostly fled their splendid residences. What few "'sesech' remaining haven't troubled us any, and since have taken the oath of allegiance in order to keep their property." They also visited the arsenal, the city jail, and Magnolia Cemetery, and saw "squads of contrabands" drilling in U.S. uniforms before returning to the ship.[10]

The *Oceanus* began its return voyage on April 16. The catastrophic fire of December 1861 had destroyed hundreds of homes and businesses, and the 1863-65 bombardment left almost everything below Calhoun Street desolated. On September 4, 1865, a reporter described a "city of ruins, of desolation, of vacant houses, of widowed women, of rotting wharves, of deserted warehouses, of weed-wild gardens, of miles of grass-grown streets." It would take decades for Charleston to recover.[11]

*   *   *

Like the city, Fort Sumter had survived the war, though it was almost unrecognizable. Until July 1863, its five walls towered just over 50 feet above the harbor's waters. They had been the chief target of Federal heavy guns during a 587-day siege. More than 46,000 smoothbore and rifled solid shot and shell, totaling approximately 7 million pounds, had been fired at the 2 ½-acre target, and by 1865 it had been reduced to an "earthen and masonry ruin." Exterior sections of only three walls were recognizable. Inside, the officers' quarters, left and right flank barracks, four of the five stair towers, and large sections of several interior walls had been pounded to rubble. Of Sumter's 135 gun emplacements, all 53 on the third-tier had been destroyed; of the 82 casemates, only 23 first-tier and half a dozen second-tier were intact and usable.

During the 1863-65 shelling, at least 339 soldiers and civilians serving at the fort, both white and enslaved, were killed or wounded. Fifty-one soldiers, six "negro laborers," and one white civilian Confederate engineer corps employee were either killed or mortally wounded. Another 185 soldiers, 65 enslaved laborers, and a civilian employee were wounded. Thirty soldiers were listed as injured. In 1861

10 Spicer Diary, 3-4.

11 Sydney Andrews, *The South Since The War: As Shown by Fourteen Weeks of Travel and Observation in Georgia and the Carolinas* (Boston, 1866), 1.

the U.S. garrison suffered one soldier killed and another mortally wounded. Seven soldiers and one U.S. Corps of Engineers civilian employee were wounded April 12-14, 1861. The four killed and 19 wounded in the September 9, 1863 U.S. Navy and Marine amphibious assault must also be included in this tally. Combining both Union and Confederate losses, at least 372 men became casualties of war at Fort Sumter from April 1861 to February 1865.[12]

12 "Fort Sumter Casualty List."

Chapter 13

Adapting to Conditions of Modern Defense

1865–1888

General Gillmore ordered Fort Sumter inspected shortly after Union forces occupied the city and harbor defenses. Only exterior areas of the right and left faces and the left flank were visible. The right flank and gorge exteriors appeared to have been demolished. Relentless fire had reduced both walls to sloping piles of brick rubble, stone, earth, and sand to the water's edge, and solid shot and shell fragments littered the slopes. Cannons that had fallen or been bombarded off the barbette lay strewn about the slope as well.

Consequently, the gorge and right flank, the left face, and the left flank interiors had been exposed to continuous shelling. The left face, adjoining left shoulder angle, and stair tower had suffered the brunt of "reverse fire" from Morris Island. Some of this fire and naval artillery had destroyed the left flank enlisted men's barracks and barbette gun emplacements. The four second-tier casemates next to the left shoulder angle had also been reduced to rubble. The other four to the left remained serviceable. Only the original left gorge angle stair tower had survived. It remained nearly its original height, though wood had replaced the granite steps. Only ladders, temporary stairs, or graded ramps allowed access to the rampart at other points. From the left shoulder angle, the second casemate on the first-tier left face had been converted into the fort's principal magazine. The East Battery's smaller service magazine in the right face and two small reserve magazines, one at the gorge bombproof and the other where the small arms magazine had exploded in December 1863, remained intact. The parade ground had been hollowed out about 2 ½ feet below its original 5-foot level; timbers,

The fort's right flank littered with rubble, debris, US artillery rounds & fragments, and a damaged 10-in. Columbiad, with fraises on the parapet and upright iron girders at the water's edge, 1865. *LOC*

planks, artillery rounds, damaged cannon barrels and carriages, and other debris littered the area. What appeared to be a wooden storage building stood at the left gorge angle, and only one of the two hot shot furnaces remained, probably the one near the right shoulder angle.[1]

Only nine serviceable guns remained in Fort Sumter. The left flank's West Battery mounted only the rifled and banded 32-pounder "sunset gun." Two

---

1 Johnson, *Defense of Charleston Harbor*, 273; Barnes, "Fort Sumter: February 17, 1865," *Fort Sumter Historic Structure Reports*.

10-inch Columbiads and a 7-inch rifle in the East Battery and five 12-pounder mountain howitzers on the parapet remained in place.

Gillmore commanded the Department of the South until November 17, 1865; in December he resigned his commission as major general of volunteers but continued in the service as a major in the Corps of Engineers. Conscious of Sumter's strategic location, Gillmore submitted plans near the end of 1865 to restore it to a functioning fortification. When no action was taken, he submitted another in August 1868. He aimed to mount 28 15-inch smoothbores or 12-inch rifled guns in casemates, and one 20-inch or two 15-inch guns "en barbette" and locate them on each face and flank, and at each gorge and shoulder angle. The barbette guns would be mounted as a pair on either side of the salient. If only one were to be used, it would be on the salient.

To accomplish this, Gillmore proposed that the fort's original structural plan be modified, with the gorge undergoing the biggest change. He planned to restore the original sally port but recess 160 feet of the center wall about 12 ½ feet with loopholes for small arms. Store rooms, guard rooms, and casemated quarters for a company of artillery would be constructed on its interior. He estimated the cost at over $546,500. The Board of Engineers for Fortifications reluctantly rejected Gillmore's proposal, citing both "great cost to the public" and the war debt.[2]

The following year Congress appropriated funds for Fort Sumter but provided only enough for the Army to maintain a minimal level of on-site supervision. This duty was commonly assigned to a few men in ungarrisoned fortifications. At Sumter an ordnance sergeant, designated fort keeper, and two soldiers resided on-site. Their primary duties were to maintain the guns and magazines and to provide security. Beginning in 1866, a lighthouse keeper joined the other men to maintain a navigational light on the right face next to the right shoulder angle. James Kearney, who performed that duty between 1866 and 1873, had been an ordnance sergeant assigned as Sumter's "light-keeper" through the April 1861 bombardment. Discharged after 25 years of service in 1864, he later joined the Lighthouse Service. Kearney is the only known soldier to have served at Fort Sumter before, during, and after the Civil War.[3]

In 1868 Gillmore observed that Sumter maintained "the same general appearance [as] at the close of the war." Storms, rains, waves, and high tides, however, had exposed more of the gorge and right flank walls. An August

2 Gillmore, *Supplemental Report*, 16; Babington, "Fort Sumter: 1876," *Fort Sumter Historic Structure Reports*, 3-8; Cullum, *Biographical Register*, Gillmore, 2:368-369.

3 Registers of Enlistments in the United States Army, 1798-1914, 1864-1865, A-K, James Kearney, NA/RG 94.

Ruins of Ft. Sumter's left flank (left) and gorge (right), 1865. *LOC*

inspection revealed that the gorge, from the top of the original sally port door to the left gorge angle, remained intact and "appeared to be in good condition," but the half down to the right gorge angle (the area closest to Morris Island's guns) had suffered major damage. On the left flank, four second-tier casemates near the left gorge angle had survived, but their embrasures had been bricked up, with narrow vertical openings left for small arms fire. The third-tier barbette had been destroyed as well as the other second-tier gunrooms down to about the mid-level of the embrasures. What survived of this section's wall had been reinforced with gabions. The first-tier casemates were in fair condition, but the inspection report expressed concern that several cracks in the exterior wall could affect their stability. The left face parapet down to the second-tier's floor had been destroyed. (Major John Johnson's memoir described it as having the appearance of "a range of rocky mountains.") The first-tier's arches and the support piers facing the parade ground had been sorely damaged; the Confederates had bricked up the embrasures, filling the casemates with sand and debris through which they had run a tunnel connecting the left flank and right face. The salient angle, where the left and right faces met, retained its original height. Most of the right face exterior had been reduced to about 35 feet and evidenced effects of persistent shelling. A section about the width of two casemates survived up to the third-tier, where it joined the right flank angle. All of the right flank wall to the right gorge angle appeared to have been destroyed. Five guns remained: two 10-inch Columbiads and three rifled and banded 42- pounders.

In January 1870, five years after Gillmore's first funding request, the Board of Engineers approved a temporary plan to address Sumter's reconstruction, but it didn't incorporate any of the general's recommendations except the placement of barbette guns. Instead, the plan called for nine 15-inch smoothbores and four

Front range light above the "East Battery" right face cribwork. To the left is the right shoulder angle and beginning of right flank eroded by storms, rains, and high tides, 1866. *LOC*

"corresponding rifles" to be placed "en barbette" at each of the fort's five angles, and two more at each face and flank; the gorge was to remain unarmed. The walls' height would be lowered from 26 feet to 13 feet, and the exterior of both face and left flank walls would be reconstructed with common concrete. The right flank and gorge walls would be rough masonry, using the original scarp's ruins. Quarters for an artillery company were to be built on the gorge interior.[4]

4 Babington, "Fort Sumter: 1876," 8-11.

Over a period of seven budget years (July 1, 1870-June 30, 1877), nearly $188,000 was appropriated for the fort's reconstruction. But progress was slow. Before any work could be done, laborers first had to clear rubble and debris, wooden bombproofs, sandbags, gabions, brick debris, and other materials from the old Confederate defenses, discarding or salvaging "great amounts of old timbers, iron, and brass." The left flank's second-tier casemates were torn down, and work began on its barbette. In 1871 less than $2,500 had been allocated for "contingencies, and preservation and repair" since most of those funds had been designated to clear 14 nearby ironclads and wooden vessels sunk during the war. The next year, however, Congress approved sufficient funding, and over the next five years the project went on, albeit with constant revisions.

Workmen cleared the right half of the gorge to its foundation and built a new exterior brick wall, and the other half was repaired. Most of the gorge was reduced to a height of 13 feet, while the left gorge angle rose to 22 feet. The interior areas of the gorge were found to be littered with broken casemates; laborers removed the debris to create space for mounting four 13-inch seacoast mortars by June 1874. Later, the mortars were dismounted in favor of Gatling guns (which were never installed); the sally port was "fenced up" and later "bricked up into an embrasure." At the left gorge angle and left flank, the two first-tier and the adjoining flank's eight casemates were repaired, their roofs were asphalted and topped with sand and brick, and retaining walls were raised in the rear of the gunrooms. After removing the surviving second-tier casemates workers demolished the ruins of the others and lowered the wall to an overall height of 22 feet. Both it and the gorge wall were capped with granite. Upon its completion, three gun platforms were built on the left flank's barbette.

Plans called for bricking up the C.S. sally port, converting it into an embrasure, and opening a new one in the fourth casemate from the postern (which still serves as the fort's main entrance). The gunrooms on either side were altered for possible use as guard rooms, and an earth-covered tunnel connected the sally port to the parade ground. From this tunnel two more passageways, each covered with more than 8 feet of earth, branched to the right face. Rainwater draining off the left face casemate roofs filled two new 5,000-gallon cisterns on either side of this gallery, as well as the original cistern below the newly repaired and strengthened sally port's floor.

On the left gorge angle's exterior, workers removed the Confederate cribwork that protected it from Federal gunfire from Morris Island, reduced the wall height to 22 feet, and incorporated the serviceable sections of the timbered wharf on the left flank's exterior into a new wharf and quay. Two years of continuous bombardment had rendered the interiors of the left shoulder angle and left face all but destroyed.

Workers removed the rubble and debris from the barbette and second-tier down to the top of their first-tier and lowered the wall to 20 feet. The left face first-tier casemates were uncovered, and while the one next to the salient angle was in good condition, the other eight were not. All the ruins, debris, sand fill, and gallery were removed, except for sound portions of the casemate support piers. By June 1873, work on the left face was complete, and two 15-inch smoothbore Rodmans were mounted on the center section of the barbette.

The salient angle retained its original height and an inspection revealed that its first-tier casemate was serviceable. Both the angle and right face walls were lowered to the top of their first-tiers, 24 feet in height. Only three of the nine right face casemates remaining were in "fairly good condition." All the gunrooms were cleared of sand and debris, the arches were repaired, and retaining walls were built in the rear of the gunrooms. By June 1874 nine 100-pounder Parrotts had been mounted in the right face casemates, plus one in the salient angle casemate and one in the adjoining left face casemate. Crews built two casemate magazines at the right face and the salient. A 75,000-gallon cistern, the largest at Sumter, was located below the salient.

Some exterior portions of the wall, about two casemates wide, stood at their original height at the adjoining right shoulder angle before reconstruction began in 1874. The two surviving second-tier casemates were converted into "a small timbered gallery leading to a room with loopholes for muskets to fire on the parade." In places, the adjoining right flank rose only 20 feet above high tide and its exterior, a mass of rubble, sloped down toward the water. Atop the 12-foot-high wall's interior stood the quarters that had been built in 1864. Two tiers of gabions sat atop the 10-foot-wide structure and once they were removed along with rubble and ruins of the right flank barracks and casemates, the right flank was rebuilt with concrete, its exterior faced with brick, and two 200-pounder Parrotts mounted on the barbette.

On September 28, 1874, a destructive hurricane interrupted the reconstruction project and seriously damaged the fort. Storm-driven tides and wind forced torrents of water through the right face embrasures and sally port and waves washed over the right flank and scoured away part of its parapet. Water rose to a depth of 8 feet on the parade ground, and fire broke out when bags of lime and cement in a wooden building reacted with standing water. Though that building was destroyed, the workers' quarters and kitchen, as well as the fort keeper's quarters and office, were saved. The storm caused an estimated $3,000 worth of damage.

Though plagued by insufficient funding again in 1877, Gillmore, now a lieutenant colonel, submitted yet another plan to update the fort "when funds shall be available." He reported on June 30 that although an April storm had slightly damaged Sumter, it was in good overall condition. Six guns were mounted "en barbette"—four 200-pounder Parrotts and two 15-inch Rodmans. Eleven 100-pounder Parrotts occupied the right face first-tier casemates, but four 13-inch seacoast mortars, the Confederates' two 10-inch Columbiads, and three rifled and banded 42-pounders were not mentioned. (A November 1873 inspection had reported the Confederate guns mounted in casemates "in very bad condition and scarcely serviceable.")[5]

Work continued into the 1880s amid the familiar refrain of limited funds and frequent storm damage. The absence of a fort keeper to maintain the guns hastened Sumter's deterioration. A light keeper maintained the lighthouse/range light, which was funded by the Treasury Department's Lighthouse Board. Funding for a fort keeper and quarters was restored to no good end. Neglect and exposure to the elements irreparably damaged the fort's guns, which either rusted solidly or were rendered unusable by their rotting platforms. A December 1884 report stated that none of the barbette guns could be fired safely. Two years later, the rusted 100-pounder Parrotts mounted in the first-tier were likewise found to be useless, and no longer able to be traversed.[6]

*   *   *

Another hurricane struck Charleston on August 25, 1885, severely damaging the city and Fort Sumter; hence most of the funds for the 1886 budget year were designated for repairs. The storm "washed away a great part" of the right face "exterior slope and coping" and while it was repaired, constant waves crashing against this wall would oblige additional repairs to the slopes. The storm also broke up the wharf's planks, "tore away the sallyport gate," and "set afloat everything movable in the fort, [with] the water standing five feet deep in the center of the parade." The 100-pounders were rusted and useless. The wharf planks were later "spiked down" and large amounts of sand in the casemates and debris on the parade ground were removed. No funds were requested for the subsequent budget year.[7]

A year later yet another catastrophic natural disaster occurred. On August 31, 1886, a major earthquake estimated at 7.0 magnitude, its epicenter some 30 miles inland, shook Charleston for about 60 seconds. Aftershocks continued

5 Babington, "Fort Sumter: 1876," 12-41; "Fort Sumter Range Lighthouse," South Carolina Lighthouses, Fort Sumter Range, Charleston, SC, www.lighthousefriends.com/light.asp?ID=1770, accessed April 3, 2023.

6 Comstock, "Fort Sumter: 1899," 3-4.

7 *Annual Report of the Chief of Engineers, United States Army, to the Secretary of War for The Year 1886, Part I* (Washington, D.C., 1887), 1126; *Annual Report of the Chief of Engineers, United States Army, to the Secretary of War for The Year 1886, Part I* (Washington, D.C., 1886), 34-35.

almost daily for several weeks. The scope of the damage was immense. According to the U.S. Geological Survey's annual report, there was scarcely "a brick or stone building which was not more or less cracked" in the city. Sixty people lost their lives, and the damage was estimated at over $4 million.

Sumter fared better than did Charleston. Lighthouse Keeper Kenneth Maher reported the first tremor, which lasted for 43 long seconds, at 9:50 p.m., followed by four minor aftershocks. During the first eight days of September, eight "rumbling or growling" aftershocks, each of three to five seconds in length occurred; a couple were large enough to shake houses. Maher observed that before the earthquake occurred, the chickens were "very uneasy, cackling &c, and dogs were very restless, acting unusual . . . crouching and hiding." During the earthquake a chimney was knocked down, and the "chimney on [the] lamp in the lens of the light-house was thrown out . . . and broken on the floor. Other articles on the lower floor . . . were thrown about in every direction."[8]

*   *   *

A report dated December 31, 1886, addressed the ongoing deterioration at Sumter, in spite of the work already completed. It stated that although the "masonry is generally in fair order, the earth slopes are badly defaced by rain storms," the right face parapet's exterior slope and those of the left flank "south of the sally port" showed "signs of giving way," and large quantities of sand had drifted onto the parade ground. The 1870 two-story frame building on the parade ground used as "laborers quarters and lately by the Ordnance Sergeant" had been repaired, but the chimney top had been toppled in the earthquake. The surviving left gorge angle stair tower and the remnants of the other four had been removed. The 1874 hurricane had severely damaged and washed away part of the wharf, which had not been repaired. The 1881 gale blew it "entirely . . . away." A dozen years later a new wharf replaced it, and a report recommended that it be extended to reach deep water once operations resumed.

The "masonry work of the nineteen . . . casemates" remained "in fair condition," but the 100-pounder Parrotts' embrasure shutters were damaged. Salt water "dashing through" onto the gunroom floors had rusted their iron traverse rails and the guns could not be moved. The two 15-inch Rodmans on the left flank stood in "serviceable order" and the four 200-pounder Parrotts, two on the right

8 J. W. Powell, *Ninth Annual Report of the United States Geological Survey to the Secretary of the Interior, 1887-'88* (Washington, D.C., 1889), 248, 323; "Fort Sumter Range"; Otto W. Nuttlie, G. A. Bollinger, and Robert B. Herrmann, *The 1886 Charleston, South Carolina, Earthquake—A 1986 Perspective*, U.S. Geological Survey Circular 985 (Washington, D.C., 1988), 12, 44; *Year Book—1887 City of Charleston, So. Ca.* (Charleston, 1887), 35.

face and two on the right flank, were in position, but no notation was made of their condition. The four 13-inch mortars and six Confederate guns—two "old" 10-inch Columbiads and four rifled and banded 42-pounders—were described as "On Hand Not Mounted."

Gillmore, still eager to see Sumter restored after 17 years of sporadic and insufficient funding, wrote optimistically in 1887 that the reconstruction started in 1870 to transform the structure for "modern defense" was "now well advanced." He envisioned the completed work to include: seven new permanent gun platforms, "most of the earthwork on the gorge face," and the "arrangement of a room for torpedo defense." He also recommended ten 15-inch Rodmans mounted "en barbette," and nineteen 8- or 10-inch Rodmans or "corresponding rifles" placed in casemates. None of these recommendations were implemented.

Gillmore observed that the fort's masonry and casemates were "generally in fair order," but the various natural disasters had "badly defaced" some of the earthen slopes and one area showed "signs of giving away." The problem of large amounts of wind-driven sand accumulating on the parade ground continued. Though the barbette service magazines were in fair condition, the principal magazine's concrete had been disfigured and patches had fallen out. The cracks that had been observed for years in several casemate archways in the sally port's concrete gallery, and in the passage leading to the parade ground from the northwest face barbette, appeared to have widened since the earthquake. Gillmore considered the three left flank stone platforms for the 15-inch Rodman to be "in serviceable condition." The five 15-inch wooden platforms and the two for "smaller calibres" on the "three channel fronts," on the other hand, were decayed. Many of the 15-inch gun platform timbers, stored in casemates since 1874, had rotted, but their iron components remained serviceable. The fort's armament had not changed since 1874.

Only one of the fort's five cisterns provided potable water. The "generally brackish" water in the original cistern under the sally port rose and fell with the tide, but once repaired, the container could hold 3,700 gallons. The two cisterns on either side of the gallery joining the sally port were likewise cracked, and the largest cistern, near the salient angle, held a "large quantity of sand and brackish water." Only the parade ground cistern remained intact; it held 3,500 gallons of fresh water. The condition of a sixth cistern, a 675-gallon tank under the lighthouse keeper's quarters, was not noted in the report.

Despite mounting problems, Gillmore doggedly remained faithful to his project. Promoted to colonel in 1883, he had not only provided oversight of Sumter's reconstruction, but was also responsible for improving rivers and harbors in the southeast, including Charleston Harbor's ship channels. Four natural channels converged near Fort Sumter: the Main Channel, the deepest, paralleled

Morris and Folly Islands. North of that were the shallower Swash, North, and Beach/Maffitt Channels and additional narrow access/exit points. Confederate blockade runners had preferred to use the North and Beach Channel.

To provide a direct, accessible shipping lane, Gillmore opted to widen and deepen the Swash Channel. Work began in 1882 with the construction of two jetties designed to direct the harbor's strong tidal outflow through the new channel, thus preventing it from filling with silt. One jetty off Sullivan's Island anchored its north side, and the other anchored the south side off Morris Island; each was roughly 3 miles long and built primarily of stone. Angling toward each other until 2,900 feet apart, they then ran parallel for another 6,000 feet. Completed in 1895, they still serve Charleston Harbor, assuring its place as one of the East Coast's most active shipping ports. Gillmore didn't live to see his greatest contribution to Charleston's postwar recovery; the 63-year-old colonel died April 11, 1888, and was buried at the West Point Chapel Cemetery. Lieutenant Fredrick V. Abbot, who had served as Gillmore's assistant since 1884, assumed engineering duties in Charleston Harbor upon the colonel's death. The 1879 West Point graduate, promoted to captain, oversaw multiple projects in the harbor until 1897.[9]

* * *

Amid ongoing repairs, the *Charleston News and Courier* noted a unique event on August 9, 1889: the "mustering in of the Major Robert Anderson Post [of the] Grand Army of the Republic." This post was the first "organized in the Cradle of Secession by white veterans." National, regional, and local G.A.R. officers and comrades (members), as well as a number of "Ex-Confederates" and ladies, attended the ceremony. Nineteen officers and comrades were sworn in as members of the post in the public ceremony, and afterward the veterans and guests experienced firsthand the consequences of inadequate funding that made Sumter "dangerous to life and limb." Two of them "received painful injuries" while descending the poorly maintained rampart steps when leaving the fort.[10]

Veterans made the pilgrimage to Charleston during the post-war years. In April 1890 former members of the 127th New York toured where they had served during the siege but were disappointed to find most of the war's landmarks and earthworks gone. Fort Sumter's only occupants were the lighthouse keeper, his family, and an artillery sergeant who provided them with a "soldier's welcome" and in return, received a "fever preventative" (their remaining liquor). "Aside from

9 Babington, "Fort Sumter: 1876," 41-44; Gillmore, 2:370; Cullum, *Biographical Register*, 3:308, 4:306, and 5:283-284.

10 "In Sumter's Battered Walls," *Charleston News and Courier*, Aug. 10, 1889. The G.A.R. was a Union veterans organization founded in 1866.

repairs to walls and the removal of rubbish that was the chief feature of the place when the old flag was raised in 1865," noted one veteran, "little had been done to give it the appearance of a fortress and as we walked around its walls the wonder was that it had so long and successfully withstood attacks and capture."[11]

From May 10–13, 1899, the National United Confederate Veterans Reunion was held in Charleston, and Fort Sumter welcomed its greatest number of visitors since the flag re-raising on April 14, 1865. Excursions to the fort were offered on all four days to veterans, family members, friends, dignitaries, and politicians. Some included a stop at Fort Johnson, and passing the "site of Battery Wagner" and Fort Moultrie.

The *News and Courier* devoted nearly its entire 28-page May 10 edition to the event. Advertisements offered various souvenirs including a "handsome Gilt Badge, engraved with a picture of Fort Sumter, surmounted with Confederate flags, enamelled with colors" for 25 cents, and a "Pocket Match Box, made of Nickel, covered with White Celluloid. On one side a handsome engraving of Fort Sumter, on the reverse two Confederate Flags, crossed, all enamelled in colors" for 35 cents each.

The paper detailed a recreation of Fort Sumter's bombardment held on Charleston's Colonial Lake the night of May 10. An enormous crowd of nearly 10,000 watched as a "navy representing the Confederate States ripped the life out" of a replica of the fort placed on the lake, the "brief but fierce engagement" produced a "fine spectacle." Ten small boats, each flying a Confederate flag, stormed the fort, which fell "after a hard struggle." During the battle, huge fireballs struck its side then "sputtered into the water" while "giant torpedoes" from the stronghold exploded beneath the lake's surface, sending up large plumes of water. Several ships burned, demonstrating that the "fort was not taken without loss of fighting craft." Neighborhoods near the lake were "brilliantly illuminated" as "streaks of fire and colored light shot through the heavens." At the end of the reenactment, the 15 men "manipulating the battle" from inside the fort had to "get out in a jiffy" as it was consumed by flames. The reporter waxed rhapsodic, pronouncing it to be "the best free show of the kind ever seen in Charleston."[12]

11 Franklin McGrath, *The History of the 127th New York Volunteers "Monitors," in the War for the Preservation of the Union—September 8th, 1862, June 30th, 1865* (n.p., 1898), 173-174.

12 *Charleston News and Courier*: "Re-Union United Confederate Veterans" (May 10-13) and "Stormed Fort Sumter" (May 11, 1899).

Chapter 14

A Disgrace to the Country

1898–1948

*B*y 1880 the U.S. Army numbered just over 28,000 soldiers, most of whom served on the western frontier. The Navy's condition was similar. In 1881 it comprised 140 vessels, but only 52 were operational. Of these, 17 were iron-hulled ships and 14 were Civil War monitors. The fleet had no rifled breechloading cannons; most were short range muzzle-loading smoothbores, inferior to current advancements in weaponry. In 1885 President Grover Cleveland appointed a board headed by Secretary of War William C. Endicott to propose a plan for new coastal defenses. Ultimately, it recommended 27 locations, including Charleston, for new concrete fortifications, artillery, and "submarine mines." This became known as the "Endicott System."

As was its wont, Congress approved only limited funds to upgrade coastal defenses. Corps of Engineers commander Brig. Gen. Thomas L. Casey's 1889 annual report reflected frustration and dismay. "The permanent defenses of this country remain in the same inefficient condition . . . since the close of the civil war," and the nation was "absolutely helpless against the attack of any third-rate power possessing modern iron-clad vessels armed with heavy rifled cannon." Congress finally allocated funds for Fort Sumter in 1890 and 1891; this money was used to enclose the second left flank casemate from the left shoulder angle in thick concrete, converting it into a mining casemate. Inside, electrical batteries powered a cable gallery that ran under the exterior wall and connected to mines in the shipping channel. The work, completed in 1893, cost $13,100. Still, the fort's condition was deplorable, prompting Lt. Col. Henry L. Abbott to refer to it as "a disgrace to the country" in a letter to Gen. Casey. "It is the most prominent object to be seen by foreign vessels entering the port and . . . it proclaims at once the utterly defenseless condition of the port." Two years passed before another comprehensive harbor defense plan emerged. These defenses were expanded into the twentieth century, creating the Fort Moultrie Military Reservation (FMMR) on Sullivan's Island, which, including Fort Sumter, eventually encompassed over 300 acres.[1]

*   *   *

On August 27-28, 1893, yet another destructive hurricane hit the Charleston area. A storm surge of more than 16 feet and wind gusts topping 115 mph caused major damage and loss of life. Waves battered Sumter's 17-foot right flank wall and the 7- to 12-foot earthen fill on top of it, toppling its two 200-pounder Parrotts and washing away 70,000 cubic yards of soil. The *News and Courier* reported the effects of the hurricane for several days, including an article entitled "The Siege of Fort Sumter," highlighting Lighthouse Keeper Thomas H. Britt's account of the storm. As it worsened, Britt raised the distress flag, and he and seven others (most likely his family) took refuge in a magazine. The family lost everything but the clothes they were wearing as the storm tore their home from the gorge esplanade. The hurricane's fury, Britt said, overturned "two eight-inch Parrott rifles . . . and buried [them] in the sand. I never want to go through such a thing again." They hid in the magazine for 36 hours and were "all glad to be among the living" afterward.

A new dwelling was promptly built for Britt and his family, and a navigational (front range) light and fog bell were installed. From 1856 to 1915, except during the Civil War, a lighthouse keeper was stationed at Sumter. Thomas Britt performed this duty for 26 years, from 1889 to around 1921, the longest tenure in the fort's history. The light, fog-bell tower, and residence were relocated to the left shoulder angle during the Spanish-American War and Battery Huger's construction. A new light keeper wasn't assigned to Sumter until 1930.[2]

1 *Report of the Secretary of War* (Washington, D.C., 1880), 1:v; Leonard Alexander Swann, Jr., *John Roach, Maritime Entrepreneur: The Years as Navy Contractor, 1862-1886* (Annapolis, MD, 1965), 153; *Annual Report of the Chief of Engineers, United States Army, to the Secretary of War for The Year 1889* (Washington, D.C., 1889), 1-4; Comstock, "Fort Sumter: 1899," *Fort Sumter Historic Structure Reports*, 28; Charles W. Snell, "Battery Isaac Huger (1891-1941), Historic Structure Report, Historical Data Section, Fort Sumter National Monument, South Carolina (Draft)," Oct. 19, 1977, (Denver Service Center, Historic Preservation Division, National Park Service, Department of the Interior), 10-13; Karl Philip Sondermann, "Remembering the Legacy of Coastal Defense: How an Understanding of the Development of Fort Moultrie Military Reservation, Sullivan's Island, South Carolina, Can Facilitate its Future Preservation," MS thesis, The Graduate Schools of Clemson University and College of Charleston, 2013, 29-30, FOSU Research File.

2 "The Siege of Fort Sumter," *Charleston News and Courier*, Aug. 30, 1893; Comstock, "Fort Sumter: 1899," 5; https://history.uscg.mil/Browse-by-Topic/Assets/Land/Lighthouses-Light-Stations/Article/1926753/fort-sumter-range-lights, accessed April 2, 2023; United States Lighthouse Society, https://uslhs.org/education/glossaries-facts-trivia/lighthouse-glossary-terms, accessed April 2, 2023.

In 1895, amid the possibility of war between the United States and Spain over the issue of Cuba's desire for independence, Congress began increasing its allocations for coastal defense. That year, the majority of $75,000 appropriated for the FMMR was earmarked to build Battery Capron, mounting sixteen 12-inch rifled mortars, on Sullivan's Island. Fort Sumter received funds to repair the hurricane-damaged right flank and gorge angle walls and increase their height to 28 feet. A 455-foot-deep well was dug in the parade ground, and in March 1896, a wharf with a bridge 84 feet long and 12 feet wide was completed. Located at the right shoulder angle, it became the fort's main entrance, replacing the one on the left flank. Further plans involved constructing a three-gun "lift battery." In 1897, Maj. Ernest H. Ruffner, a Kentuckian who had graduated first in his 1867 class at West Point, replaced Lt. Col. Abbott. Among his other duties, he improved Charleston's fortifications and served until January 1, 1900.

After the explosion and sinking of the USS *Maine* in Havana's harbor on February 15, 1898, Congress authorized the construction of the coastal defenses recommended by the Endicott Board on March 9. In Charleston, Major Ruffner, South Carolina's coast defenses engineer, received two telegrams from the Corps of Engineers commander, one in mid-March and the other on April 25, the same day the United States declared war on Spain, directing construction of a battery for two 12-inch guns inside the fort instead of the three-gun "lift battery." During the ensuing Spanish-American War only two modern artillery batteries on Sullivan's Island defended Charleston Harbor. Batteries Capron and Jasper, mounting four 10-inch disappearing rifled, breechloading guns, were completed during the war. Two Civil War-era 15-inch Rodmans were mounted in Fort Moultrie.

Throughout the war, Sumter's "marine mining casemate" served as operational headquarters for the 38 "torpedoes" laid in Charleston Harbor. They were detonated in place after the war except for one, "badly cracked and leaking," that was relocated to deep water. The "mining casemate" was abandoned in 1899, and a new one was built at Fort Moultrie later that year.[3]

* * *

The United States Lighthouse Society defines "Range Lights" as follows: "The two lights associated to form a range, which often, but not necessarily, indicates a channel centerline. The front range light is the lower of the two, and nearer to the mariner using the range. The rear range light is higher and further from the mariner. When the ship is in the proper channel, the lights will be in alignment."

3 Sondermann, "Remembering," 31-33, 37-38; Comstock, "Fort Sumter: 1899," 5-7, 29; Cullum, *Biographical Register*, 5:134; *Annual Report of the Chief of Engineers, United States Army, to the Secretary of War for The Year 1899* (Washington, D.C., 1899), 862-865.

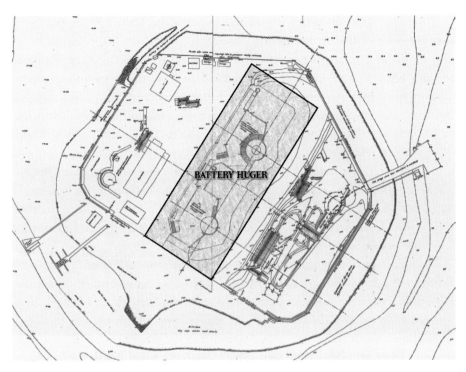

Battery Huger's orientation inside Ft. Sumter *AC*

Work on the "Endicott System" continued nationwide; construction of Charleston's defenses lasted until 1906. The harbor counted nine batteries, one at Fort Sumter and eight on Sullivan's Island. Sumter's unnamed fortification bisected the parade ground and used about 11,000 cubic yards of Rosendale concrete, forming a massive (22 feet high and up to 90 feet wide) structure. The south end of it destroyed 90 feet of the gorge's brick wall and every remnant of the original sally port. Occupying about a third of the fort's interior and facing the new shipping channel, it ran 270 feet from there north across the parade ground nearly to the salient angle.

A grillage of heavy steel I-beams embedded in 5 feet of the foundation's concrete crossed at right angles. The beams positioned closer together under the gun emplacements supported the additional weight. The gun in the south emplacement (toward the gorge) was mounted on a fixed barbette carriage, while the one in the north emplacement (toward the salient angle) operated on a disappearing carriage positioned below the parapet to shield it and the crew from incoming fire. Once loaded, raised, and fired, the recoil returned the gun to its protected position. The fixed gun and its nearly 52-ton carriage weighed 110 tons. The other gun, its

Firing Gun No. 1 (fixed gun) Battery Huger, pre-World War II. *FOSU*

103-ton disappearing carriage, and an 81-ton counterweight totaled about 242 tons. The 36 ½-foot barrels alone weighed 57 ½ tons, and both fired a 975-pound shell or 1,070-pound solid shot and ranged almost 10 ½ miles with a muzzle velocity of over 2,000 feet per second.

The top of the battery sloped to the front, directing rainwater for collection into three cisterns capable of storing 25,000 gallons. The lower level included ammunition storage, a powder magazine, and a guard room. Behind the lower level ran an open passageway. Adjoining it, a retaining wall rose to the level of the gun loading platforms. Fill (earth, dredge, sand, debris, and marsh mud) was piled to the top of this wall and continued across the parade ground to the top of the gorge, left flank, and left face. A covered passageway from the battery crossed the parade ground to the 1870s gallery, which in turn led to the left flank sally port. Laborers removed most of the 1870s magazines, other galleries, and earlier elements. The continued dumping of fill in front of the battery up to a depth of 30 feet covered the salient angle, right face, and right flank. Finished in June 1899 at a cost of $98,800, the unnamed battery was transferred to the artillery.[4]

4 Comstock, "Fort Sumter: 1899," 5-12, n26, 86; Snell, "Battery Huger," 21, 22.

Official reports referenced the obsolete and rusted Civil War-era guns positioned at multiple locations within the brick fort. A notation in an 1897 report observed that 18 inches of sand were in the right face gunrooms, and a second report in 1899 recommended that since the guns and carriages were useless, their embrasures should be sealed and the casemates "closed and partially filled with earth." The 1900 armament report stated that only the two new 12-inch guns were mounted. The 100-pounder Parrotts had been buried, two 200-pounder Parrotts lay in sight on the ground, and the 1893 storm had buried two more. It is likely that the rifled and banded guns, four 42-pounders, and two 24-pounders sat on the parade ground while two 10-inch Columbiads and two 15-inch Rodmans were left unmounted on the left face. The 13-inch mortars either stood on the parade ground or were stored in a casemate. In 1901 the Rodmans and Parrotts were buried in the fort's earthwork. The two 10-inch guns, donated to the city of Charleston in 1899, were moved in 1900 and mounted in The Battery (White Point Garden), where they still stand. On January 1, 1900, Capt. James C. Sanford, West Point class of 1884, assumed engineering duties from Major Ruffner. Sandford was "in charge [of] the Charleston, S.C. Engineer District" until 1903.[5]

*   *   *

By 1901, several wooden buildings had been constructed behind the battery. The ordnance sergeant's quarters and a 50-man barracks stood near the gorge, and the left shoulder angle contained the lighthouse keeper's quarters with a small cistern underneath, the lighthouse, a bell tower, and an oil house. The next year, demolition of the old "wooden structures in front of the guns" and most of the "old masonry . . . projecting above grade" continued. The right flank was cut down and a coping placed on top to allow for the depression of the 12-inch guns. Sometime after 1903 about half of the fill behind the battery as well as the sergeants' quarters and enlisted men's barracks were removed. The interior of the gorge, left flank, and left face remained covered while the "hole in front of the battery" where the two 100-pounder Parrots had fallen after the 1893 hurricane was nearly full. Earthen fill still covered the gorge, left flank, and left face; the new parade ground measured about 5 feet higher than the original level.[6]

5 Comstock, "Fort Sumter: 1899," 22-25; Ryan, "Historic Guns," 79; Cullum, *Biographical Register*, 5:353. The previously unreported two 24-pounders were probably uncovered at the fort during work done prior to 1900.

6 Ryan, "Historic Guns," 79; *Annual Report of the Chief of Engineers, United States Army, to the Secretary of War for The Year 1902* (Washington, D.C., 1902), 25-26; Fort Sumter National Monument Historic Structures Report, Part 1—Development History "Chronology of Fort Sumter Development & Use," 17.

Sergeant (left) and Enlisted Barracks (right), c. 1901. *FOSU*

*   *   *

Fort Sumter entered the new century with a flourish. On April 8, 1902, President Theodore Roosevelt, in Charleston for an event, toured the harbor and stopped at the fort. As part of the visit, "artillerymen worked the big guns and [Roosevelt made] a complete tour of the magazines, store houses, machine rooms, etc." While on the fort's ramparts, a brisk wind blew the president's hat off. Private Fred Stent rescued it and kept it out of the water; Roosevelt thanked Stent and gave him a "hearty handshake for his enterprise and daring."

Two years later, the unnamed concrete fortification received its official designation: Battery Isaac Huger. During the Revolutionary War, Isaac Huger rose from lieutenant colonel in the state militia to brevet major general in the Continental Army. His selection honored South Carolina's role in the Revolution and its continuing importance in the defense of the U.S. coast.[7]

Another major hurricane punctuated the city's second decade in the new millennium on August 28, 1911. Though it created severe problems for Charleston, Sumter itself escaped nearly unscathed. Just outside the fort the storm exposed

7 William Gaines, "A History of the Modern Defenses of Charleston, South Carolina, Part I, 1894-1939," *The Coast Defense Study Group Journal* (August 1998),72; "A Trip to Fort Sumter," *Charleston News and Courier*, April 9, 1902; Edgar, *South Carolina Encyclopedia*, 464-465. Huger is pronounced HU-JEE.

two 42-pounders, one rifled and banded and the other a banded smoothbore, probably dumped and forgotten during Huger's construction. They were recovered in 1912. The War Department donated the smoothbore to the G.A.R. post in Kingwood, West Virginia, where it stands today in front of the Preston County Court House. The other, a rifled and banded gun, was donated to the R. E. Lee Camp Confederate Soldiers' Home in Richmond, Virginia, and is still mounted in front of its chapel.[8]

* * *

Moving toward modernization, the Army abolished the old artillery regimental system and entirely reorganized it in 1901. It designated 126 companies as heavy (coastal) artillery and 30 as field (light) artillery. In 1903 the 3rd and 16th Companies, Coast Artillery (CA) were stationed at Fort Moultrie, while the 36th served at Battery Huger. Two years later, Roosevelt requested that Secretary of War William Howard Taft review the Endicott Board's report to evaluate the effectiveness of U.S. coastal defense. The report of the National Coast Defense Board (the "Taft Board") found the Endicott defenses and the CA units adequate but recommended updating the guns, materiel, and equipment. In 1907, the heavy companies were reorganized into the Coast Artillery Corps (CAC), which expanded to 170 companies and organized the field companies into regiments.[9]

The quiet U.S. political and military climate from 1905 to the outbreak of World War I reduced Fort Sumter's role in defending Charleston, even though its battery housed the heaviest and longest-range guns. Throughout the decade, various CAC company detachments garrisoned the military reservation on Sullivan's Island and were stationed at Fort Sumter. From January 1905 to January 1914, the number of soldiers assigned to Sumter ranged from one non-commissioned officer (NCO) up to 12 enlisted men and an NCO. It is not known if any personnel were stationed there from January 1914 to September 1917. In 1916, as an additional defensive measure, a 60-inch search light was positioned about 75 feet off the center of the gorge.

In 1916, Congress passed the National Defense Act, which reorganized the Army yet again. The CAC increased in size, had its units re-designated, and the FMMR's garrison grew from three to four companies, newly designated the Coastal Defenses of Charleston (CDC). When the U.S. entered World War I in 1917, five South Carolina National Guard Coastal Artillery companies were

8 Comstock, "Fort Sumter: 1899," 25, n83; Ryan, "Historic Guns," 80-82.

9 Stokeley, *Fort Moultrie*, 63; Gaines, "Modern Defenses" I, 74; Sondermann, "Remembering," 41, 44-45.

activated and joined the garrison. The post's harbor defense mission expanded to include training for as many as 3,000 troops at the reservation. Sumter's population reflected the growing number of soldiers at the FMMR. In September a "small caretaking garrison" was installed before its activation, and later that year a company of 114 soldiers was stationed there. Forty-five soldiers lived in a parade ground barracks behind Huger, while the rest of the garrison lived in Sumter's casemates and sallyport. A second housing structure was completed in 1918. One served as a temporary officers' quarters with a mess kitchen and the enlisted men's mess. The other was used as the enlisted barracks and included showers and a latrine. From June-September 1918, the 8th Company CDC garrisoned the fort though neither it nor the FMMR saw military action during the war.[10]

The November 1918 armistice ended not only the war in Europe but also the FMMR's training mission. Only a caretaker detachment of two CAC companies comprised the FMMR garrison by 1921. The next year a third company was reactivated, and two battalions of the 8th U.S. Infantry were transferred to the reservation. Whether soldiers were stationed at Fort Sumter during this time isn't known, but the fort certainly changed. Sometime before February 1921, a new "Quarter Master's Wharf" was built off the center of the left face wall to replace the 1893 dock. The Army demolished the officers' quarters in 1925 and three years later began tearing down most of the enlisted barracks, save for the 30-foot section containing the latrine and showers. The Civilian Conservation Corps (CCC) constructed a new brick latrine in 1933.[11]

After only seven years of postwar quiet, the FMMR resumed its earlier war mission of training National Guard and Reserve units. In 1926 Georgia and North and South Carolina units began two weeks' annual training at the post, and as many as 300 men trained on the various batteries, including Huger's 12-inch guns. A year later, the FMMR's mission expanded to include training members of the Senior Reserve Officer Training Corps (ROTC), who were assigned there for six weeks. A civilian-military training camp supervised by 8th Infantry officers provided month-long instruction in military life for up to 600 Georgia and Carolina men between the ages of 17 and 29, evaluating them for possible commission as Army Reserve second lieutenants upon course completion. A CCC facility operated at the reservation to provide instruction and employment for thousands of young men. Organized into companies, they went on to work in South Carolina state

10 Snell, "Battery Huger," 43; Sondermann, "Remembering," 102-103, 108-109; Fort Sumter National Monument Historic Structures Report, Pt. 1—Development History, "Chronology of Fort Sumter Development and Use," 17, 18; Gaines, "Modern Defenses" I, 71, 80, 81; "Garrison of Fort Sumter, South Carolina, 1905-1914," 1-5, FOSU Research Files.

11 Snell, "Battery Huger," 49-51.

---

parks, national parks, and national forests building roads, trails, and structures. By 1933, the FMMR had evolved into an important, active, and self-contained Army post with officers' quarters, enlisted barracks, and housing for NCOs with families. A movie theater, library, band pavilion, and gymnasium provided spare time diversion for civilians and military personnel living on the island. Other buildings, including a chapel, a fire station, stables, a post exchange, and a hospital, lent a sense of permanence to the post.

Colonel George C. Marshall arrived in June 1936 as commander of the 8th Infantry but transferred only months later after his promotion to general. Despite its importance, the FMMR operated with reduced funding during the Great Depression, though some improvements were made in the 1930s at Battery Huger. Both 12-inch guns, out of level since 1926, were corrected and the battery commander's station was rebuilt. The entire project was completed in January 1932. Over time small quantities of water seeped into the magazines, power plants, and plotting rooms of FMMR's batteries, including Huger. To eliminate perpetual dampness in these areas, they were swabbed with coal tar. Remaining areas of the batteries were painted to provide a "uniform appearance." Reducing glare off the bare concrete was an added benefit.[12]

* * *

In 1931-32, three monuments were placed at Sumter. Two were dedicated on April 11, 1931: the first, the Confederate Defenders Monument, was located in the exterior wall to the left of the sally port. Donated by the Charleston Chapter of the United Daughters of the Confederacy, it read: "In reverential memory of the Confederate garrison of Fort Sumter who during 4 years of continuous siege and constant assaults from April 1861 to February 1865, defended this harbor without knowing defeat or sustaining surrender." The second monument was the Anderson Flagpole. The 1919 will of Eliza Anderson Lawton, one of Robert Anderson's daughters, provided $25,000 for the placement of a statue of her father at the fort. Eleven years later Congress acted on her request, but rather than commission a statue, it approved an 80-foot flagpole monument on the left face wall near the dock. "In honor of Major Robert Anderson and the 128 men of his command," read the inscription, "who for 34 hours April 12-13, 1861, withstood

12 Gaines, "Modern Defenses," I, 85; "Chronological Time Frame-Fort Sumter Construction and Preservation," 12, FOSU Research File; Snell, "Battery Huger," 48-49. From 1939 through World War II, Marshall served as Army chief of staff under Franklin D. Roosevelt and then as Harry S. Truman's secretary of state and secretary of defense. He is best known for developing and implementing the "Marshall Plan" to rebuild postwar western Europe, for which he was awarded the Nobel Peace Prize in 1953.

United Daughters of the Confederacy Monument dedication, April 11, 1931. *FOSU*

the destructive bombardment of Sumter and withdrew with the honors of war. The War of Secession began here."

A third monument, solely honoring the 1861 U.S. garrison, was situated atop the gorge and dedicated on August 30, 1932. The bronze tablet mounted on the side of an 8-foot-tall granite monument reads: "In memory of the Garrison Defending Fort Sumter during the bombardment April 12-14, 1861." It also lists the garrison's members. Between December 1958 and May 1959, both Union monuments were relocated: the Anderson Flagpole to the top level of the fort in the center front of Battery Huger, and the 1861 U.S. garrison monument to the parade ground near the gorge.[13]

* * *

Into the twentieth century Fort Sumter continued to attract visitors, but the very first commercial excursion took place the day after Anderson's surrender. At least one boat operator offered a $1 harbor ride that included passing "sufficiently near" the fort to see its exterior. Ten days later another vessel offered a trip to the fort—the first documented commercial excursion for visitors to Sumter. How

13 From the *Charleston News and Courier*: "They Merit the Memorial," "Memorials to Confederate and Federal Defenders to Be Dedicated," "Confederate and Federal Memorials Are Dedicated," "Sumter Tablet Unveiling Today, and "Union Troops At Sumter Honored," Apr. 10 and 11, and Aug. 30 and 31, 1932, Robert Anderson File, FOSU Research Files.

Maj. Gen. Robert Anderson Flag Pole dedication, April 11, 1931. *FOSU*

many visited the site during the war is unknown, nor is the number who sailed on their own to Sumter after the war. Notable visits include the 1889 trip by Union veterans and guests who founded the Anderson GAR Post, a visit by 127th New York veterans in 1890, the 1899 United Confederate Veterans Reunion, and President Theodore Roosevelt and guests' stop in 1902. An idea of the numbers can be inferred from an 1881 fort keeper's report that expressed a need to extend the wharf for the safe landing of Sumter's many visitors. "[T]he interest that now attaches to it will endure forever," predicted the prescient observer. Notably, a 1933 Army report commented that the recently constructed brick latrine "primarily" served "the hundreds of visitors . . . now coming to view the old fort."

Not until 1926, though, did a daily harbor tour include a stop at Fort Sumter. It operated for only a year. In 1930, Fort Sumter Navigation Tours, Inc. began offering a two-hour harbor tour for a dollar that operated only in the spring. The company hired William R. Greer, the last known Confederate veteran living in Charleston who had served in Sumter, as its tour guide. His former unit, Company B, 25th South Carolina, was posted there in 1863-64. Greer died in 1932, and Capt. S. E. Baitary, the tour boat owner who had been privy to the old vet's stories, began providing the tours.

In the spring of 1931, Gray Line Tours, Inc., which had also begun daily tours to the fort, increased their frequency to three a day. In 1937 the company added a speedboat and started offering year-round tours. The significant bump in visitation

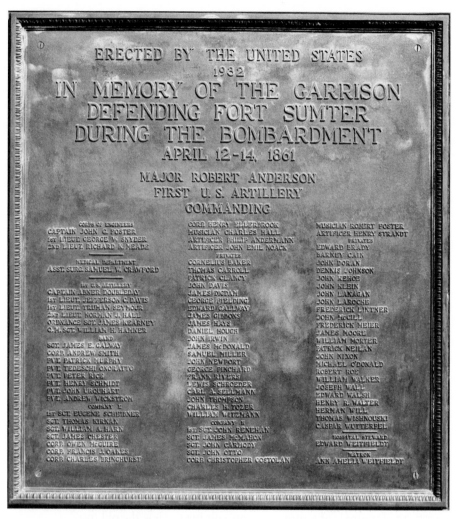

ERECTED BY THE UNITED STATES
1932
IN MEMORY OF THE GARRISON
DEFENDING FORT SUMTER
DURING THE BOMBARDMENT
APRIL 12-14, 1861
MAJOR ROBERT ANDERSON
FIRST U. S. ARTILLERY
COMMANDING

CORPS OF ENGINEERS
CAPTAIN JOHN G. FOSTER
1st LIEUT. GEORGE W. SNYDER
2nd LIEUT. RICHARD K. MEADE

MEDICAL DEPARTMENT
ASST. SURG. SAMUEL W. CRAWFORD

1st U. S. ARTILLERY
CAPTAIN ABNER DOUBLEDAY
1st LIEUT. JEFFERSON C. DAVIS
1st LIEUT. TRUMAN SEYMOUR
2nd LIEUT. NORMAN J. HALL
ORDNANCE SGT. JAMES KEARNEY
Q.M. SGT. WILLIAM H. HAMNER

BAND
SGT. JAMES E. GALWAY
CORP. ANDREW SMITH
PVT. PATRICK MURPHY
PVT. TEDESCHI ONORATTO
PVT. PETER RICE
PVT. HENRY SCHMIDT
PVT. JOHN URQUHART
PVT. ANDREW WICKSTROM

COMPANY E
1st SGT. EUGENE SCHEIBNER
SGT. THOMAS KIRNAN
SGT. WILLIAM A. HARN
SGT. JAMES CHESTER
CORP. OWEN McGUIRE
CORP. FRANCIS J. OAKES
CORP. CHARLES BRINGHURST

CORP. HENRY ELLERBROOK
MUSICIAN CHARLES HALL
ARTIFICER PHILIP ANDERMANN
ARTIFICER JOHN EMIL NOACK

PRIVATES
CORNELIUS BAKER
THOMAS CARROLL
PATRICK CLANCY
JOHN DAVIS
JAMES DIGDAM
GEORGE FIELDING
EDWARD GALLWAY
JAMES GIBBONS
JAMES HAYS
DANIEL HOUGH
JOHN IRWIN
JAMES McDONALD
SAMUEL MILLER
JOHN NEWPORT
GEORGE PINCHARD
FRANK RIVERS
LEWIS SCHROEDER
CARL A. SELLMANN
JOHN THOMPSON
CHARLES H. TOZER
WILLIAM WITZMANN

COMPANY E
1st SGT. JOHN RENEHAN
SGT. JAMES McMAHON
SGT. JOHN CARMODY
SGT. JOHN OTTO
CORP. CHRISTOPHER COSTOLAN

MUSICIAN ROBERT FOSTER
ARTIFICER HENRY STRANDT

PRIVATES
EDWARD BRADY
BARNEY CAIN
JOHN DORAN
DENNIS JOHNSON
JOHN KEHOE
JOHN KLEIN
JOHN LANAGAN
JOHN LAROCHE
FREDERICK LINTNER
JOHN McGILL
FREDERICK MEIER
JAMES MOORE
WILLIAM MORTER
PATRICK NEILAN
JOHN NIXON
MICHAEL O'DONALD
ROBERT ROE
WILLIAM WALKER
JOSEPH WALL
EDWARD WALSH
HENRY R. WALTER
HERNAN WILL
THOMAS WISHNOUSKI
CASPAR WUTTERPEL

HOSPITAL STEWARD
EDWARD WEITFIELDT

MATRON
ANN AMELIA WEITFIELDT

U.S. 1861 Garrison Monument, dedicated Aug. 30, 1932. *Historical American Building Survey*

necessitated the purchase of a larger boat, carrying 25 to 30 passengers, in 1940. The two companies competed for tourist dollars until 1940, when Baitary ceased his operation. Gray Line continued until the summer of 1942, when World War II-related activity at Sumter forced a halt to the tours. Gray Line's March 3–June 29, 1934, visitation records count 972 visitors to the fort. That number increased almost tenfold to 9,463 by 1941. Between early 1934 and late summer 1942, Fort Sumter welcomed a grand total of 30,920 visitors. By 1935, to welcome visitors to the fort two of the four 13-in. seacoast mortars had been mounted on either side of the sally port. In 1969 one was transferred to Petersburg National Battlefield and the other was moved to "Cannon Row" between Ft. Moultrie and Battery Jasper. The status of the other two mortars is unknown.[14]

* * *

On August 11-12, 1940, another hurricane struck the area. The *News and Courier* quoted Pvt. George Kimrey's phone report. One of five people who had stayed at the fort, Kimrey said 20-foot waves destroyed 40 feet of the dock, damaged the searchlight trestle, and some rocks at the base of the walls "were washed a short distance away." "Fort Sumter, the most exposed part of Charleston, suffered small damage," but salt spray "got over everything, even into the 12-inch guns which had to be cleaned thoroughly because rust started to form almost before the storm was over." But the grass was green now, and a "loosely placed" pile of cannon balls had not been disturbed by rushing water around it. Kimrey wondered if the waves would flood the fort, but as the winds subsided, he pronounced it "one of the safest places to be." Henry Gullette, his wife, and two children, who also lived there, rode out the storm. Gullette, the "coast guard radio operator . . . kept his regular schedule without a break." The sum of $7,845 was allocated to repair the damages.[15]

In September 1940, Congress enacted the first peacetime conscription law in the nation's history. It doubled the size of the Army and reactivated numerous units. Battery K, 13th CA reinforced Battery D at the FMMR, and the 70th CA Regiment replaced the transferred 8th U.S. Infantry. National Guard units were also called into active service; among these were the 2nd and 3rd Battalions of the 252nd North Carolina CA, which were ordered to the FMMR. When they arrived, they garrisoned in tents, since units from other coast artillery outfits (the 13th and 70th CA) were already there. Units of the 252nd and 70th had been transferred by April 1941. The 263rd South Carolina CA was federalized and ordered to the FMMR. This unit manned and monitored Charleston's harbor defenses for the rest of the war, including newly installed searchlights and an anti-submarine net laid across the channel.

Before the United States was drawn into World War II, naval leaders understood the need for "adequate joint provisions for defense of harbors" better than Congress. A system was necessary to guard against "air, submarine, and surface action by enemy or neutral craft . . . threatening our harbors or by the shipping

14 From the *Charleston Courier*: "Carolina" and "Excursion," Apr. 15, 1861; Rock L. Comstock, "Short History, Fort Sumter," Project No. 14, Fort Sumter National Monument, Research Report, June 1956, 9-13 36, Appendix C, 55; Ryan, "Historic Guns," 23.

15 "Four on Fort Sumter Get Closeup View of Hurricane," *Charleston News and Courier*, Aug. 16, 1940; Snell, "Battery Huger," 51-52.

using them." Both the Army and Navy moved to secure harbor entrances; the Army with Harbor Defense Command Posts (HDCPs) and the Navy with Harbor Entrance Control Posts (HECPs). At Fort Moultrie a World War I era, two-story frame building served as the HDCP/HECP for most of World War II.[16]

After Pearl Harbor, Battery D, 13th CA and six batteries of the 263rd CA manned the FMMR's defenses, including the 263rd's Battery F at Battery Huger. These units were on 24-hour alert from early December 1941 to October 1942. Huger was among those most vigilantly maintained because "in all probability, the coastal frontier would be subject to minor attack." Five months into the war, most of Battery D's personnel had been shipped out; the remainder transferred to the 263rd, graduating from tents into barracks. After the arrival of recruits undergoing basic training, the regiment's strength doubled.

By 1942 three rows of tents on the parade ground served as the garrison's quarters. Before the end of the war the tents had been replaced by wooden buildings on the left flank, left gorge angle, and gorge. These included the commander's office, officers' quarters, a post exchange/supply room, two enlisted barracks, and a latrine. The pre-war lighthouse keeper's residence served as quarters for three Navy signalmen. Also, a second 60-inch search light was positioned on the salient angle.[17]

By the summer of 1942, the probability of an enemy naval surface attack had greatly subsided, and comprehensive training (including gas attack alerts and drills, gun drills and firing, inspections, and schools for officers and NCOs) became the priority. Although the probability of a surface attack was remote, German U-boats were another matter entirely. Well known to the U.S. military, these submarines operated in waters near the shoreline. Indeed, between mid-January to July 1942 more than 360 merchant ships were sunk in these coastal American waters.

Charleston's first experience with U-boats occurred on May 9, 1942, when the Coast Guard cutter *Icarus* sank *U-352* off Cape Lookout, North Carolina. *Icarus* retrieved 33 survivors, including two wounded, one of whom died while en route to Charleston. The next day the *Icarus* briefly landed at Fort Moultrie before continuing to the Charleston Navy Yard, where the prisoners were turned over to the Navy. The dead German crew member was buried in the Beaufort National

16 Edwin C. Bearss, "Fort Moultrie, 1776-1947" (n.d.), 180-184. Admiral Karl Doenitz reported to Hitler that people on the beach and "sometimes entire coastal cities" witnessed the blaze of the tankers these submarines destroyed.

17 Photos of Fort Sumter (circa 1942 and 1945), FOSU Research File. World War II-era photographs illustrate some of the activity at Fort Sumter. One image, circa1942, reveals the rows of tents, and a later photo shows several buildings on the left flank wall's fill. The mess hall was located off the center of the left flank wall, and two enlisted barracks angled off the left gorge, not far from the latrine located near the center of the gorge. All buildings inside and outside the fort were wooden. The second photo also depicts the newly installed 60-inch search light.

Garrison buildings c.1945. *FOSU*

Cemetery. *Icarus* was the second U.S. warship to sink a U-boat during the war, and the first to take German prisoners.

The next incident happened just off Charleston Harbor in late July. A U-boat successfully laid 12 mines in the harbor's channel. Although sighted several times, the enemy sub avoided detection by air and sea patrols, departing as stealthily as it came. The harbor closed until the mines were detonated at sea. Six weeks later, another submarine, *U-455*, approached the channel entrance in the pre-dawn hours of September 18, 1942. Its captain reported that the sea was calm and the night clear. From about 7 miles away, 3 miles beyond Fort Sumter, he could see the lights of Charleston and the headlights of vehicles crossing the Grace/Cooper River bridge. Seeing a tanker leaving the harbor, the captain took advantage of the lowered submarine netting, entered the outer harbor, and laid several mines. *U-455* suspended the operation when a jetty obstructed its way. After spending the next day on the bottom, the submarine laid a dozen mines that night and left the area undetected. For five days, normal harbor operations continued, but on September 24 a minesweeper located and denotated one of the mines, and the harbor was once again closed. The ensuing search for mines continued until October 1, when the port reopened. None of the submarine's mines sank or damaged a ship.[18]

---

18 Bearss, "Fort Moultrie," 193-197; William H. Thiesen, "The Long Blue Line: Cutter *Icarus* and the Sinking of *U-352*," Nov. 23, 2017, https://www.history.uscg.mil/Research/THE-LONG-BLUE-LINE, accessed Apr. 11, 2023.

By 1940 the War Department deemed most of the FMMR's Endicott batteries, including Battery Huger, obsolete and declared that they would be abandoned after new emplacements were constructed. Not until the war turned in the allies' favor, however, did it authorize the immediate abandonment of most of the batteries. During the winter of 1942-43, all the guns except for those in the three Sullivan's Island batteries, including Battery Huger's 12-inch pieces, were dismounted and scrapped. The others were transferred to U.S. allies.

In 1943, Huger received four 90-millimeter guns; two were mounted in front of the battery and two were on mobile carriages. Battery Jasper on Sullivan's Island mounted two others, and these two batteries worked cooperatively to protect the channel's submarine net. World War II-era photos also reveal the 90-millimeter guns and two .30-caliber machine guns at the fort, one on the left face beside Sumter's wharf and another in front of Battery Huger next to the gorge. These guns, the channel's submarine netting, other batteries on Sullivan's Island, and surface and air patrols protected Charleston and its harbor until the end of the war. Not one of these guns ever fired against the enemy.[19]

*   *   *

Fixed brick coastal defenses had been proven obsolete by 1862, and the late nineteenth- and early twentieth-century concrete batteries that replaced them couldn't withstand the weaponry of World War II, which clearly demonstrated the superiority of long-range naval guns and aircraft in modern war. Fort Sumter's once strategic location in the mouth of Charleston Harbor had become irrelevant.

In 1947 the FMMR, including Fort Sumter, was closed and placed under the jurisdiction of the War Assets Administration. In light of the fort's national historic significance, on April 28, 1948, President Harry Truman signed an act "to establish the Fort Sumter National Monument in the State of South Carolina." Three months later, the U.S. Army Corps of Engineers officially transferred Fort Sumter to the National Park Service. In 1947, Fort Moultrie, Battery Jasper, and an incomplete World War II battery on Sullivan's Island were transferred to the state of South Carolina. On September 7, 1960, the state in turn transferred them to the national monument. The national monument was renamed Fort Sumter Fort Moultrie National Historical Park in 2019.

The significance of Fort Sumter in United States history, specifically during the Civil War period, has drawn millions of people to it from around the world. As of 2022, annual visitors to the old brick fort number more than 300,000.[20]

---

19 Sondermann, "Remembering," 190, 198; Bearss, "Fort Moultrie," 199.

20 Comstock, "Short History," Appendix A, 51; Stokeley, *Fort Moultrie*, 72.

Bibliography

Government Publications

Powell, J. W., Dir., *Ninth Annual Report of the United States Geological Survey to the Secretary of the Interior 1887-'88*. Washington, D.C.: Government Printing Office, 1889.

Stokeley, Jim, *Fort Moultrie, Constant Defender*. Washington, D.C.: Handbook 136, Division of Publications, National Park Service, U. S. Department of the Interior, 1985.

No Author, *American State Papers: Documents Legislative and Executive of the Congress of the United States, Military Affairs*, vol. 5, Twenty-third Congress, Second Session, No. 591, "The Construction of Fort Sumter, Charleston Harbor, South Carolina," 463-472.

———. *Fort Sumter National Monument, Historic Structures Assessment Report*, August 5, 1992.

———. *The Echo*, Fort Sumter Fort Moultrie National Historical Park, July 11, 2020.

The War of the Rebellion: A Compilation of the Official Records of the Union and Confederate Armies, 128 vols. Washington, D.C.: Government Printing Office, 1880-1901.

Official Records of the Union and Confederate Navies in the War of the Rebellion, 30 vols. Washington, D.C.: Government Printing Office, 1894-1922.

Government Documents Unpublished

Fort Sumter Fort Moultrie National Historical Park: Bearss, Edwin C. "Fort Moultrie 1776-1947," No date.

Comstock Jr., Rock L., *Organizations At Fort Sumter, 1861-1865*. Fort Sumter National Monument, Project No. 12, 1954.

———. *Short History, Fort Sumter*. Project No. 14, Fort Sumter National Monument, Research Report, June 1956.

Jensen, Leslie D., Contract Historian. "The Fort Sumter Flags, A Study in Documentation And Authentication, The Historical Report, U.S. Department of the Interior, National Park Service, Harpers Ferry Center," WV, March 1982.

Champneys, Captain John Tunno. "Fort Sumter Letter Book September 12, 1863-October 28, 1863." Original "1861-1863 letterbook," J. T. Champneys Papers, Accession #992, Special Collections Dept., University of Virginia Library, Charlottesville, VA. Typed transcript Fort Sumter Fort Moultrie National Historical Park Research Files, April 2005.

Cadwallader Jones Papers. Southern Historical Collection, Manuscripts Department, Wilson Library, The University of North Carolina, Chapel Hill, NC. Copied Lt. Iredell Jones 1863 letters. Typed transcript, Fort Sumter Fort Moultrie National Historical Park Research Files, Sept. 2004.

Hatcher, III, Richard W. "Fort Sumter Casualty Lists." Fort Sumter National Monument, 2014.

Honour, Theodore A. "Letters Written to my Wife During the years of the war Between The United States of America And The Confederate States from Eighteen hundred and Sixty One to Eighteen hundred and Sixty five." Fort Sumter Fort Moultrie National Historical Park Research Files, typed transcript, no date.

Huguenin, Thomas Abram. "A Sketch of the Life of Thomas Abram Huguenin, written at the request of my family." Parts 1, 2, and 3. Typed transcript, Fort Sumter Fort Moultrie National Historical Park Research Files, no date.

Marvel, William. "The First to Fall: The Brief and Bitter Life of Daniel Hough." No date, Fort Sumter Fort Moultrie National Historical Park Research Files.

McCabe Family Papers, 1863-1972, Mss1M1233a, William G. McCabe August 17-October 23, 1863 diary, Virginia Historical Society, Richmond, VA. Typed transcript, Fort Sumter Fort Moultrie National Historical Park Research Files, 2012.

William A. Spicer Diary, William A. Spicer Papers, 1865-1885. Manuscript Department of the William A. Perkins Library, Duke University. Typed transcript Fort Sumter Fort Moultrie National Historical Park Research Files, March 2004.

Ryan, Mike. "The Historic Guns of Forts Sumter and Moultrie," May 1997.

Snell, Charles W. "Battery Isaac Huger (1891-1941), Historic Structure Report, Historical Data Section Fort Sumter National Monument, South Carolina (Draft)," Denver Service Center, Historic Preservation Division, National Park Service, United States Department of the Interior, Denver, Colorado. Oct. 19, 1977.

Theodore Cline Talbot Papers, Manuscript Division, Library of Congress. Copied letters 1860-1862 letters. Typed transcript Fort Sumter Fort Moultrie National Historical Park Research Files, Aug. 2000.

Fort Sumter Fort Moultrie National Historical Park Research Files

    Anderson, Gen. Robert
    Calhoun, Col. William R.
    Elliott, Gen. Stephen
    Hall, 2nd Lt. Norman Johnathan
    Huguenin, Col. Thomas
    Meade, Jr., Maj. Richard Kidder
    Mitchel, Cpt. John C.
    Ripley, Gen. Roswell S.
    Rhett, Col. Alfred M.
    Skillen, Sgt. James
    Snyder, Lt. George Washington
    Talbot, Lt. Theodore
    Yates, Lt. Col. Joseph A.

"GARRISON OF FORT SUMTER, SOUTH CAROLINA, 1905-1914." Fort Sumter National Monument File No. 611, Monument Development 1949-1953.

Fort Sumter Historical Structure Reports, 1829-1899.

    Babington, John, Historian Fort Sumter National Monument, "Fort Sumter: 1876," March 1, 1954.

    Comstock, Jr., Rock L., Historian Fort Sumter National Monument, "Fort Sumter: 1899," June 8, 1954.

Pemberton, Jr., Heath L., "Fort Sumter: Chronological Construction History With Architectural Detail", September, 1959.

Frank Barnes, Historian Fort Sumter National Monument, "Fort Sumter: December 26, 1860"; "Fort Sumter: April 12, 1861"; "Fort Sumter: April 7, 1863"; and "Fort Sumter: February 17, 1865", February 21, 1950.

No author, "Chronological Time Frame-Fort Sumter Construction and Preservation," No Date.

———. "Fort Sumter Letter Book. Official correspondence of the U.S. Army Corps of Engineers Assigned to Charleston Harbor and other regional duties July 27, 1854-April 9, 1861." Original: Charleston Museum collections Charleston, SC. Transcribed by Fort Sumter National Monument Staff, 2002.

———. Fort Sumter National Monument Historic Structures Report, Part 1-Development History, "Chronology of Fort Sumter Development and Use," No date, and Part III. "Chronological History of Fort Sumter," August 5, 1992.

Manuscript Collections

National Archives, Washington, D.C.

Record Group 29

Census of the United States, 1860, South Carolina, Charleston County.

Record Group 94: Records of the Adjutant Generals Office, 1780s-1917

Letters Received by the Office of the Adjutant General Main Series, 1805-1889, 1822-1860, 1861-1870

Gillmore, Quincy A. File, Box 2, Jan-Mar 1865, Report of the Bombardment of Fort Sumter, January 1st, 1864 to January 1st 1865, and Report of the Bombardment of Charleston, January 1st, 1864 to January 1st 1865.

Hall, Norman J., 1863 File.

Talbot, Theodore J., 1847-1862 Files.

Registers of Enlistments in the United States Army, 1798-1914, 1864-1865, A-K, page 557.

Record Group 109: Complied Service Records

Confederate, Miscellaneous.

Confederate, South Carolina.

Confederate Generals and Staff Officers, and Nonregimental Enlisted Men.

Confederate States Army Casualties: List and Narrative Reports, 1861-1865, List and Reports of Casualties In Individual States, South Carolina, Fort Sumter.

War Department of Confederate Records, Department of South Carolina, Georgia and Florida, Telegrams Sent 1863-64.

Confederate Soldiers Who Served in Organizations Raised Directly by the Confederate Government.

Record Group 217: Records of Military Contracts and Leases, 1811-1870.

New-York Historical Society Museum & Library, New York, NY

Guide to the Alexander Robert Chisolm Papers 1861-1908, MS 670-5, Biographical/Historical note.

South Carolina Historical Society, Charleston, SC:

Gerard-Honour family papers, 1839-1968, Theodore A. Honour letters, 1862-1865, Manuscript 0391.02.02.

Samuel Wagg Ferguson memoir, 1900. Ferguson, Samuel Wragg, 1834-1917, Manuscript 0114.00.

Southern Historical Collection, Manuscripts Department, Wilson Library, The University of North Carolina, Chapel Hill, NC:

Grimball Family Papers, 1683-1930. Copied 1862-1864 letters. Typed transcript Fort Sumter Fort Moultrie National Historical Park Research Files, April 2010.

Stephen D. Lee Papers, 1784-1929, Collection No. 02440. "Civil War Journal of Colonel Stephen D. Lee", 1945 typed transcript.

Newspapers

The Charleston Daily Courier, 1860-65

Charleston Mercury, 1860-65

Charleston News and Courier, 1931, 1932, 1940

Charleston Evening Post, 1901

The Daily Dispatch, Richmond, VA, April 16, 1861

Primary Sources

Published

Andrews, Sydney. *The South Since The War: as shown by fourteen weeks of travel and observation in Georgia and the Carolinas*. Boston: Ticknor and Fields, 1866.

Barnard, George N. Text on the verso of stereoview No. 30, "Interior view of Fort Sumter," Charleston, SC, University of South Carolina Digital Collections, Accession No. 15241.75.

Chepesiuk, Ron & John Thompson. "Eye Witness to Fort Sumter: The Letters of Private John Thompson." *The South Carolina Historical Magazine*, vol. 85, no. 4, (Oct. 1984), 271-279.

French, J. Clement. *The Trip of the Steamer Oceanus to Fort Sumter and Charleston, S.C.* Brooklyn, "The Union" Steam Printing House, 1865.

Crawford, Samuel Wylie, Bvt. Maj. Gen. *The Genesis of The Civil War: The Story of Sumter, 1860-61*. New York: Charles L. Webster & Company, 1887, reprint Digital Scanning, Inc., 1999.

Cullum, George W. Bvt. Maj. Gen. *Biographical Register of the Officers and Graduates of the U.S. Military Academy At West Point, N. Y. From Its Establishment In 1802 to 1890 With the Early History of the United States Military Academy*. vols. 1, 2, 3 & 4. New York and Cambridge, MA: Houghton, Mifflin and Company, The Riverside Press, 1891.

Denison, Frederick. *Shot and Shell: The Third Rhode Island Heavy Artillery Regiment In The Rebellion, 1861-1865*. Providence, RI: J. A. and R. A. Reid, 1879.

Doubleday, Abner. *Reminiscences of Forts Sumter and Moultrie in 1860-'61*. Charleston, SC: The Nautical & Aviation Publishing Company of America, 1998 reprint, originally published: New York: Harper & Bros., 1876.

Dowdey, Clifford, ed. *The Wartime Papers of R. E. Lee*. Virginia Civil War Commission. Boston, MA and Toronto, Canada: Little, Brown and Company, Boston & Toronto, 1961.

Fletcher, Miss A. *Within Fort Sumter; or, A View of Major Anderson's Garrison Family For One Hundred And Ten Days, By One of the Company*. New York: N. Tibbals & Company, 1861.

Freemantle, Lieut. Col. Arthur F. *Three Months In The Southern States: April-June 1863*. New York: Published by Joh Bradburn, 1864.

Gillmore, Q.A. *Engineer and Artillery Operations Against the Defenses of Charleston Harbor in 1863.* New York, NY: D. Van Norstrand, 1865. General Gillmore's Report, 84-88, Appendix A, Supplement Report, 148-157, Plates XI to XXXIII.

————. *Professional Papers, Corps of Engineers U.S.A., No. 16.-Supplement. Supplementary Report To Engineer and Artillery Operations Against The Defences of Charleston Harbor In 1863.* New York, NY: D. Van Nostrand, 1868.

Haskin, Brevet Captain William L., complier. *The History of the First Regiment of Artillery From Its Organization in 1821, To January 1st, 1876.* Portland, ME: B. Thurston and Company, 1879.

Hayes, John D., ed. *Samuel Francis Du Pont A Selection From His Civil War Letters*, vols. 1-3. Ithaca, NY: Published for The Eleutherian Mills Historical Library, Cornell University Press, 1969.

Hunter, Alvah F. & Symonds, Craig L. eds. *A Year on a Monitor and the Destruction of Fort Sumter.* Columbia, SC: University of South Carolina Press, first paperback edition, 1991.

Johnson, John. *The Defense of Charleston Harbor, including Fort Sumter And The Adjacent Islands. 1863-1865.* Freeport, NY: Books For Libraries Press, Freeport, NY, reprint 1970, first published 1889.

Johnson, Robert Underwood & Buel, Clarence Clough, eds. *Battles and Leaders of the Civil War*, vols 1 & 4. New York, NY and London: Thomas Yoseloff, 1956, reprint, The Century Co., 1887-1888.

Lebby, Robert. "The First Shot on Sumter." *South Carolina Historical and Genealogical Magazine,* vol. 12 (July 1911).

Marszalek, John F., ed. *The Diary of Miss Emma Holmes 1861-1866.* Baton Rouge, LA and London: Louisiana State University Press, 1994 edition, new material added.

McGrath, Franklin. "Material Collected and Arranged." *The History of the 127th New York Volunteers "Monitors" in the War for the Preservation of the Union-September 8th, 1862, June 30th, 1865.* Privately Published. No Date.

Mott, Smith B. *The Campaigns of The Fifty-Second Regiment Pennsylvania Volunteer Infantry.* Philadelphia, PA: J. B. Lippincott Company, 1911.

Powe, James Harrington & Lynch, Harriet Powe, ed. *Reminiscences & Sketches of Confederate Times By One Who Lived Through Them.* Columbia, SC: The R. L. Bryan Company, 1909.

Pryor, Mrs. Roger A. *Reminiscences Of Peace And War.* New York, NY: The Macmillan Company, 1904.

Ripley, Warren, ed. *Siege Train The Journal of a Confederate Artilleryman in the Defense of Charleston.* Columbia, SC: Published for the Charleston Library Society by the University of South Carolina Press, 1986.

Roland, Lawrence S. & Hoffius, Stephen G., eds. *The Civil War in South Carolina*, Parker, F. L. "The Battle of Fort Sumter As Seen From Morris Island," F. L. Parker, vol. 62, no. 2, April 1961, 65-71 and Horres, C. R. "An Affair of Honor at Fort Sumter.", vol. 102, no. 1, Jan. 2001, 6-26, *Selections From The South Carolina Historical Magazine.* Charleston, SC: Home House Press, Charleston, SC, 2011.

Scarborough, William Kauffman, ed. *The Diary of Edmund Ruffin*, 3 vols. Baton Rouge, LA: Louisiana State University Press, 1976.

Scott, Colonel H. L. *Military Dictionary: Comprising Technical Definitions; Information On Raising and Keeping Troops; Actual Service, Including Makeshift And Improved Material; And Law, Government, Regulation, And Administration Relating To Land Forces.* Fort Yuma, AZ: Fort Yuma Press, reprint 1984, D. Van Norstrand, New York, NY and Trubner & Co., London, 1864.

Sherman, General William T. *Memoirs of General William T. Sherman.* NY: D. Appleton and Company 1875, 2 vols.

Spicer, William A. *The Flag Replaced On Sumter. A Personal Narrative*. Providence, RI: The Providence Press Company, 1885.

Taylor, Frances Wallace, Matthews, Catherine Taylor & Power, J. Tracy, eds. *The Leverett Letters: Correspondence of a South Carolina Family, 1851-1868*. Columbia, SC: University of South Carolina Press, 2000.

Vizetelly, Frank. "Charleston Under Fire." *Cornhill Magazine*, vol. 10, July to December, 1864, 99-110. London: Smith, Elder, & Co., 1864.

Welles, Gideon. *Diary of Gideon Welles Secretary of the Navy Under Lincoln and Johnson*, vols. 1-3. Boston, MA and New York, NY: Houghton Mifflin Company, 1911.

Woodward, C. Vann, ed. *Mary Chesnut's Civil War*. New Haven, CT and London: Yale University Press, 1981.

No Author. *Report of the Secretary of War*, vol. 1. Washington: Government Printing Office, 1880.

————. *Third Annual Reunion of the Association of the Graduates of the United States Military Academy, at West Point, New York, June 14, 1872*. New York: Crocker and Company, 1872.

————. *Sixth Annual Reunion of the Association of the Graduates of the United States Military Academy, at West Point, New York, June 14, 1872*. New York: A. S. Barnes & CO., 1875.

————. *Twenty-Third Annual Reunion of the Association of the Graduates of the United States Military Academy, at West Point, New York, June 9, 1892*. Saginaw, MI: Seeman & Peters, 1892.

————. *Twenty-Fourth Annual Reunion of the Association of the Graduates of the United States Military Academy, at West Point, New York, June 9, 1893*. Saginaw, MI: Seeman & Peters, 1893.

————. *Twenty-Eighth Annual Reunion of the Association of the Graduates of the United States Military Academy, at West Point, New York, June 10th, 1898*. (Saginaw, MI: Seeman & Peters, 1897).

Secondary Sources

Books

Ballard, Michael B. *Pemberton A Biography*. Jackson, MS & London: University Press of Mississippi, 1991.

Barratt, Peter. *Farragut's Captain: Percival Drayton 1861-1865*. Annapolis, MD: Naval Institute Press, 2019.

Bennett, Chet. *Resolute Rebel, General Roswell S. Ripley, Charleston's Gallant Defender*. Columbia, SC: The University of South Carolina Press, 2017.

Brennan, Patrick. *Secessionville Assault on Charleston*. Campbell, CA: Savas Publishing Company, 1996.

Burton, E. Milby. *The Siege of Charleston 1861-1865*. Columbia, SC: University of South Carolina Press, 1970.

Browning, Jr., Robert M. *Success Is All That Was Expected The South Atlantic Blockading Squadron during the Civil War*. Washington, D.C.: Brassey's Inc., 2002.

Cauthen, Charles Edward. *South Carolina Goes To War 1860-1865*. Columbia, SC: University of South Carolina Press, 2005 reprint.

Chaffin, Tom. *The H. L. Hunley, The Secret Hope of the Confederacy*. New York, NY, Hill and Wang, 2008.

Coker, Michael D. *The Battle of Port Royal*. Charleston, SC: The History Press, 2009.

Coker III, P. C. *Charleston's Maritime Heritage, 1670-1865 an illustrated history.* Charleston, SC: CokerCraft Press, 1987.

De La Cova, Antonio Rafael. *Cuban Confederate Colonel, The Life of Ambrosio José Gonzales.* Columbia, SC: The University of South Carolina Press, 2003.

Edgar, Walter, ed. *The South Carolina Encyclopedia.* Columbia, SC: The University of South Carolina, 2006.

Field, Ron. *1st South Carolina Artillery (Calhoun's/Rhett's).* Gloucestershire, Great Britain: Lower Swell, 1999.

Gordon, Armistead Churchill. *Memories and Memorials of William Gordon McCabe,* vols. 1-2. Richmond, VA: Old Dominion Press, Inc., 1925.

Henderson, Lillian, Rigdon, John. *Roster of the Confederate Soldiers of Georgia,* vol. 8. Powder Point, GA: Eastern Digital Resources, 2007.

Hughes, Nathaniel Cheairs, Jr. & Whitney, Gordon D. *Jefferson Davis in Blue The Life of Sherman's Relentless Warrior.* Baton Rouge, LA: Louisiana State University Press, 2002.

Klein, Maury. *Days of Defiance Sumter, Secession, and the Coming of the Civil War.* New York, NY: Alfred A. Knopf, 1997.

Lewis, Elizabeth Wittenmyer. *Queen of the Confederacy, The Innocent Deceits of Lucy Holcombe Pickens.* Denton, TX: University of North Texas Press, 2002.

Lineberry, Cate. *BE FREE OR DIE, The Amazing Story of Robert Smalls' Escape From Slavery To Union Hero.* New York: Picador St. Martin's Press, 2017.

Reed, Rowena. *Combined Operations in the Civil War.* Annapolis, MD: Naval Institute Press, 1978.

Roberts, William H. *USS New Ironsides In The Civil War.* Annapolis, MD: Naval Institute Press, 1999.

Swann, Jr., Leonard Alexander. *John Roach, Maritime Entrepreneur: the Years as Navy Contractor 1862-1886.* Annapolis, MD: Naval Institute Press, 1965.

Swanberg, W. A. *First Blood The Story of Fort Sumter.* New York, NY: Charles Scribner's Sons, 1957.

Wates, Wylma A. *A Flag Worthy of Your State and People: The History of the South Carolina State Flag.* Columbia, SC: South Carolina Department of Archives and History, 2nd edition, 1996.

Waugh, John C. *Surviving The Confederacy, Rebellion, Ruin, and Recovery: Roger and Sara Pryor During the Civil War.* New York, NY: Harcourt, Inc., 2002.

———. *Class of 1846, From West Point to Appomattox: Stonewall Jackson, George McClellan and Their Brothers.* New York, NY: Warner Books, 1994.

Williams, T. Harry. *P. G. T. Beauregard Napoleon in Gray.* Baton Rouge, LA: Louisiana State University Press, 1954.

Wise, Stephen R. *Gate of Hell Campaign for Charleston Harbor, 1863.* Columbia, SC: University of South Carolina Press, 1994.

———. *Lifeline of the Confederacy, Blockade Running During the Civil War.* Columbia, SC: University of South Carolina Press, 1988.

Periodical Articles

Ferguson, Gen. Samuel W. "With Albert Sidney Johnston's Expedition To Utah, 1857," Collections of the Kansas State Historical Society, 1911-1912, Vol. XII, 1912, 303-312.

Gaines, William. "A History of the Modern Defenses of Charleston, South Carolina Part I 1894-1939." *The Coast Defense Study Group Journal,* Volume 12, Issue 3, August 1998, 55-90.

————. "A History of the Modern Defenses of Charleston, South Carolina Part II, The Harbor Defenses of Charleston in World War II." *The Coast Defense Study Group Journal*, Volume 12, Issue 4, November 1998, 35-59.

Holsworth, Jerry W. "Friends to the Death," *Civil War Times*, vol. 45, no. 7, 38-45.

Johnson, Mark. "Emory Upton's Twenty-Six: Desertion and Divided Loyalties of US Army Soldiers, 1860-1861," *Journal of Military History*, vol. 81, no. 3, July 2017, 657-666.

Online Sites

Losson, Christopher T. "Samuel Wragg Ferguson (1834-1917) Confederate General," Ted Ownby & James G. Thomas, *Mississippi Encyclopedia* (University of Mississippi, Center For The Study of Southern Culture, 2017), http://mississippiencyclopedia.org/entries/samuel-wragg-ferguson, accessed April 24, 2021.

Nuttlie, Otto W., Bollinger, G. A., & Herrmann, Robert B., T*he 1886 Charleston, South Carolina, Earthquake - A 1986 Perspective*, U.S. GEOLOGICAL SURVEY CIRCULAR 985. United States Government Printing Office, 2nd printing 1988. https://pubs.er.usgs.gov. Accessed March 25, 2021.

Thiesen, William H. "The Long Blue Line: Cutter Icarus and the sinking of U-352," Coast Guard Compass, The official blog of the U.S. Coast Guard, November 23, 2017, https://coastguard.dodlive.mil. Accessed June 16, 2021.

Womack, Ann Talbot Brandon & Womack, Farris W. "James Theodore Talbot 1825-1862," http://freepages.rootsweb.com. Printed copy.

No Author. "Fort Sumter Range Lighthouse," South Carolina Lighthouses, Fort Sumter Range, Charleston, SC, www.lighthousefriends.com/light.asp?ID=1170. Accessed March 21, 2021.

————. "Riggs, Anderson, or Lincoln," Anderson Cottage Archives-President Lincoln's Cottage www.lincolncottage.org. Accessed July 24, 2019.

————. James Theodore Talbot, Special Collections Georgetown University Library, September 10, 2020 email.

————. Battery Huger, http://www.fortwiki.com. Accessed April 8, 2021.

————. New-York Historical Society Museum & Library, Guide to the Alexander Robert Chisolm Papers 1861-1908, MS 670-5, Biographical/Historical note. http://dlib.nyu.edu/findingaids/html/nyhs/chisolm/bioghist. Accessed April 24, 2021

https://usace.contentdm.oclc.org:

No Author, Annual Report of the Chief of Engineers, United States Army, to the Secretary of War for The Year 1886, Part I. Washington: Government Printing Office, 1886.

————. Annual Report of the Chief of Engineers, United States Army, to the Secretary of War for The Year 1889, Part I. Washington: Government Printing Office, 1889.

————. Annual Report of the Chief of Engineers, United States Army, to the Secretary of War for The Year 1899, Part I. Washington: Government Printing Office, 1899.

————. Annual Report of the Chief of Engineers, United States Army, to the Secretary of War for The Year 1902, Part I. Washington: Government Printing Office, 1902.

Dissertations and Theses

Zoebelein, Jennifer Madeline. "Charleston's Forgotten General: Roswell Sabine Ripley," Master of Arts in History thesis, The College of Charleston and The Citadel, April 2008.

Sondermann, Karl Philip. "Remembering the Legacy of Coastal Defense: How an Understanding of the Development of Fort Moultrie Military Reservation, Sullivan's Island, South Carolina, Can

Facilitate its Future Preservation," Master of Science Historic Preservation, the Graduate Schools of Clemson University and College of Charleston, May 2013.

Hattaway, Herman Morell. "Stephen Dill Lee: a Biography," Louisiana State University and Agricultural & Mechanical College, Louisiana State University, LSU Digital Commons, LSU Historical Dissertations and Theses, Graduate School, 1969. https://digitalcommons.lsu.edu.

Index

About the Author

Richard W. Hatcher, III is a native of Richmond, Virginia, and a 1973 graduate of Virginia Commonwealth University with a BA in History. His lifelong love of the subject began during the Civil War Centennial and grew when he later worked as a seasonal employee at Richmond National Battlefield Park. Rick began working permanently with the National Park Service in 1976, and he retired as Historian from Fort Sumter Fort Moultrie National Historical Park in 2015. Rick is the author or coauthor of numerous articles and books including the award-winning *Wilson's Creek, The Second Major Battle of the Civil War and the Men Who Fought It* (2001) and *The First Shot* (2011). He is a regular on the Civil War speaking circuit.